1a 1b 1uno

Teacher's Edition

# ¡En español!

# LECTURAS PARA TODOS

## —with TEST PREPARATION

## McDougal Littell

A DIVISION OF HOUGHTON MIFFLIN COMPANY

Evanston, Illinois • Boston • Dallas

ISBN: 0-618-33489-0

1 2 3 4 5 6 7 8 9 – PBO – 07  06  05  04  03

# What Is *Lecturas para todos?*

**A book that allows students to develop stronger reading skills by encouraging the use of a variety of comprehension and critical-thinking strategies.**

## *Lecturas para todos*, Level 1

### Includes

- *En voces* readings from Levels 1a, 1b, and 1 of *¡En español!*
- Reading support throughout the selections
- A consumable format that allows students to mark up the text
- Vocabulary practice and enrichment
- Comprehension questions and short writing activities
- Additional literature for more reading practice and enrichment
- Academic and informational reading
- Test preparation models, strategies, and practice

## *Lecturas para todos*, Level 2

### Includes

- *En voces* readings from Level 2 of *¡En español!*
- Reading support throughout the selections
- A consumable format that allows students to mark up the text
- Vocabulary practice and enrichment
- Comprehension questions and short writing activities
- Additional literature for more reading practice and enrichment
- Academic and informational reading
- Test preparation models, strategies, and practice

## *Lecturas para todos*, Level 3

### Includes

- *En voces* readings from Level 3 of *¡En español!*
- Reading support throughout the selections
- A consumable format that allows students to mark up the text
- Vocabulary practice and enrichment
- Comprehension questions and short writing activities
- Additional literature for more reading practice and enrichment
- Academic and informational reading
- Test preparation models, strategies, and practice

# The Interactive Reading Process

## Lecturas para todos
**encourages students to write in their books!**

*Lecturas para todos* provides students and teachers with a unique resource that fosters reading comprehension. *Lecturas para todos* encourages students to engage or *interact* with the text. Activities before, during, and after reading a selection prompt students to ask themselves questions; clarify their ideas; and make personal connections—all thinking processes performed by proficient readers.

The following features help students interact with the text:

**PARA LEER**  **Reading Strategy** and **What You Need to Know** give students concrete ways to approach the selection, as well as the background knowledge and context necessary to understand it.

**During Reading**  **A pensar...** This feature appears at the key point of each reading and signals that students need to stop and answer the questions in the margins. These questions allow students to learn and practice a variety of reading skills and strategies, including

- summarizing
- questioning
- predicting
- visualizing
- connecting
- clarifying
- evaluating
- drawing conclusions
- inferring
- stating opinions

- locating main ideas
- making judgments
- analyzing
- identifying cause-and-effect relationships
- understanding an author's purpose
- distinguishing fact from opinion

### A pensar...

1. Cross out the place name that is not a beach in Puerto Rico. **(Clarify)**

   Isla Verde

   San Felipe del Morro

   Luquillo

   Condado

2. What do you think ¡**Buen provecho!** in the last line means? Use context clues to help you. **(Infer)**

**MÁRCALO** ⟩ At specific points in each selection, students are directed to underline, circle, or highlight text that features key vocabulary or grammar concepts. In the *Literatura adicional* section, students focus on one aspect of literary analysis and mark up the text accordingly.

***Palabras clave*** Vocabulary words that are key to understanding the reading are highlighted in bold and definitions are provided at the bottom of the page.

**Reading Tip** Useful, specific reading tips appear at points where language is difficult.

**READER'S SUCCESS STRATEGY** **Reader's Success Strategy** Specifically for struggling readers, these strategies are helpful for all types of learners. The strategies support those students who encode more easily through visuals, those who retain more easily through repetition, and those who just need a little extra help. In every selection, these notes give useful tips for comprehending vocabulary, context, concepts, and more.

**Challenge** These activities help students develop critical-thinking skills and encourage them to apply concepts beyond the printed page. The exercises actively engage students while highlighting the richness of the selections and literature.

***Vocabulario de la lectura*** Words boldfaced and defined in the selection are reviewed, requiring students to use the words contextually. Active vocabulary from the *etapa* appears in blue.

***¿Comprendiste?*** Comprehension activities require students to use their understanding of the selection to extend their reading skills.

***Conexión personal*** These brief writing activities help students connect the reading to their own lives.

**Ongoing Assessment**

In addition to increasing students' involvement in the reading process, ***Lecturas para todos*** offers you, the teacher, a window on students' progress and problems. Students' notes, responses, and other markings could be looked at regularly as part of the ongoing informal assessment process.

**READER'S SUCCESS STRATEGY** When you form mental images as you read, you are visualizing. This can help you understand and enjoy what you are reading. As you read about Puerto Rico, try to imagine how things look, sound, taste, feel, or smell.

**CHALLENGE** Which geographical features of the island of Puerto Rico are mentioned on these two pages? (Analyze)

# Inclusion in the Foreign Language Classroom

## Making Reading More Accessible
### *En voces* and *Literatura adicional*

Spanish educators encounter a unique combination of students because of their objective of adding another language to the student's repertoire. Looking at an individual student's profile, there are those who are still learning how to read and those who read fluently in the same class. There are those who are literate in English but not Spanish; those who are literate in Spanish but not English; those who are not literate but can listen and speak in English and/or Spanish; and those who can listen and speak in Spanish but have an irregular educational history. And there are more languages that have not been mentioned which could fill the page.

*Lecturas para todos* includes more students before, during, and after they read through the enormous range of support and options. Students are reading to learn another language with the kind of accommodations that they need. Every student learns the same information, just not in the same way.

Before students read, they are given the critical background information they need so they are not reading the selection in isolation. These connections and critical background help students with the different cultural backgrounds and make no assumptions about what a student is supposed to already know.

While students read, they interact with what they are reading through point-of-use notes in the margins. Good readers apply certain strategies instinctively when reading. By making these strategies overt, more students can learn to use these strategies and, in turn, learn better reading habits.

Here are some of the features from *Lecturas para todos* that help students while they are reading.
- Reading Tips
- Reader's Success Strategies
- *Márcalo*
- *En voces* Readings on Audio
- *En voces* Reading Summaries on Audio
- *Palabras clave*
- Challenge Activities

*Lecturas para todos* teaches students how to self-monitor, take notes, and apply new reading strategies when they encounter readings in classes, on tests, and in everyday life.

After the selection, the activities concentrate on vocabulary, comprehension, and personal connections. All three types of activities cement students' retention by developing their skills from controlled one-right-answer exercises to personalized open-ended critical thinking activities. This range addresses the broader range of students. Some students are more comfortable beginning with the bigger picture and then citing evidence; others are better at finding the details and then connecting those details to create the bigger picture. Ultimately, students could become comfortable going both from detail to world and from world to detail.

The more vocabulary students build through the rich assortment of readings, the better students are able to think critically and creatively. The use of graphic organizers helps students encode the information in two different ways: linguistically and visually. This helps with retention. Providing students with the opportunity to personalize their thoughts about the selection makes the selection stick. It has been encoded into their brain three ways: through words, through visuals, and through personalization. Therefore, they are much more likely to remember the selection. It has become meaningful to them even if they did not like it. The *Conexión personal* section of the reading gives the student the opportunity to say why.

## Making Strategies More Effective
### Academic and Informational Reading

This section of *Lecturas para todos* shares with students the unique strategies they need with each of these types of reading. Often students are asked to research, yet students do not know how to access different types of readings. This section is a sampling of the different types of tasks that students are asked to perform in school and on standardized tests:

• Analyzing Text Features
• Understanding Visuals
• Recognizing Text Structures
• Reading in the Content Areas
• Reading Beyond the Classroom

This array will develop students' strategies as well as serve as a resource so that when they come across a certain type of reading that they are unfamiliar with, they can see how to get the most out of the reading in the shortest amount of time.

## Making Test Taking More Strategic
### Test Preparation

The final section of *Lecturas para todos* features test preparation for reading, revising, editing, and writing. The section opens with general test-taking strategies.

Each type of test begins with an annotated model that shows students how to analyze the readings, the writing prompts, the direction lines, the questions, and the distractors, as well as work through standardized tests efficiently and effectively. The second step is for the students to practice with the same type of test. The final step is a self-check where students can verify their answers and self-evaluate areas where they may need more practice. This three-step process makes test-taking more transparent for students—demonstrating that it's not just a matter of a lucky guess, but that there are ways to make educated guesses.

This section shows students that once they learn and practice the strategies and avoid the pitfalls, they will be more confident when the *real* test takes place.

## Making Students More Successful

At the end of the year, educators want students to walk out of the classroom knowing more than they did in September. Regardless of the level, students can progress. At right are general strategies for all levels of students. When a student can see his or her individual progress, that is when the student will be motivated to continue studying Spanish.

### Strategies by Student Group

| Strategies for Advanced Group | |
|---|---|
| Advanced students will be placed in accelerated classes in 9th grade and in Sophomore Honors, take the AP Language test (SAT-2) at the end of Junior year, and take the AP Literature test (SAT-2) at the end of Senior year. They will progress rapidly through the basics of the oral language and begin studying literature. | 1. Involve students in a Pen Pal project to develop communication skills with peers in foreign countries. <br> 2. Schedule meetings between Foreign Language and English teachers to develop common rubrics for literary analysis. <br> 3. If taught in a heterogeneous class, substitute more challenging assignments for easier ones. <br> 4. Make sure instruction is sufficiently complex and in-depth. |
| **Strategies for Grade Level Group** | |
| Grade level students are usually college-oriented, have an adequate foreign language reading level, but need lots of visuals for instruction. | 1. Assess what these students already know and adjust the rate of introduction of new material based on frequent assessments during instruction. <br> 2. Provide cumulative review of sound/symbol relationships, vocabulary and grammatical forms taught; use flash cards for class and partner review. <br> 3. Progress through *¡En español!* at the recommended pace and sequence. |
| **Strategies for Students with Learning Difficulties Group** | |
| Learners have the lowest functional vocabulary level, are very visual learners, and need more cumulative review. | 1. Assess what these students already know and adjust rate of introduction of new material based on frequent assessments during instruction. <br> 2. Focus primarily on oral language. <br> 3. Explicitly teach sound/symbol relationships, separating difficult discriminations in introduction. <br> 4. Introduce vocabulary through drawings and personalize vocabulary. <br> 5. Provide daily oral practice through group responding, partner practice, and short presentations. |
| **Strategies for Students Needing Intensive Help (Special Education)** | |
| Intensive needs students are those whose performance is two or more standard deviations below the mean on standardized measures. These students will probably be eligible for special education services. This is a very small percentage of the general population. | 1. Determine reading level in English to guide the introduction of oral language content. <br> 2. Follow the guidelines given for Students with Learning Difficulties. <br> 3. Use a very visual approach and concentrate on oral language. <br> 4. Directly teach sound-symbol relationships and vocabulary by clustering vocabulary words using sound-symbol relationship. <br> 5. Place these students in lower grade level material if at all possible. |

Chart written by Linda Carnine and Doug Carnine

# Reaching All Readers

Spanish teachers may find that the student who struggles to read and write in Spanish is also a struggling reader in English. Improving a student's reading skills in English will also improve his or her success in the second language classroom. Spanish teachers, like all teachers, may find it challenging to accommodate the wide range of reading abilities and interests among their students. For those students who are hooked on reading, the challenge is to provide a steady diet of rich materials. But for many students, reading is a chore that requires enormous effort and yields little success.

Students who are not able to read at grade level often do not succeed in school. While much of the focus of the early grades is on learning to read, the focus shifts in the middle grades to reading to learn. Students who do not have a strong foundation in basic decoding and comprehension skills become struggling readers. Their poor reading ability denies them access to the content of the textbooks; as a result, they fall behind in almost every subject area. Below-level reading ability most often is the result of inadequate decoding skills, poor comprehension, or a combination of both.

Decoding skills provide readers with strategies for determining the pronunciation of the written word. Basic decoding skills involve matching letters and letter combinations with spoken sounds and blending those sounds into words. As students encounter longer—multisyllabic—words, they need to divide these words into manageable chunks or syllables.

Decoding is an enabling skill for comprehension. Comprehension is a process of constructing meaning from text. Readers integrate the information in the text with their prior knowledge to make sense of what they read. Specific comprehension skills and strategies, such as main idea, sequence, and visualizing, can help students recognize the relationships among ideas, figure out text structures, and create pictures of what they read.

## Developing Fluency in All Readers

Reading fluency is the ability to automatically recognize words so that attention can be focused on the meaning of the written material. Fluency involves both decoding and comprehension skills; fluent readers decode text with little or no effort as they construct meaning from that text. Teachers can usually spot readers who struggle with decoding the text. Other readers, however, may be able to say the words and sound as though they are reading, but they have little or no understanding of what they read. These readers often go unnoticed, especially in the content areas.

Fluency is a developmental skill that improves with practice. The more students read, the better readers they become. The reading level at which a student is fluent is called his or her *independent reading level.* However, a student's independent reading level may vary with the type of material he or she is reading. For example, reading a short story is often easier than reading a textbook.

A key part in developing reading fluency is determining a student's independent reading level and then providing a range of materials at that level. Developing Fluent Readers on pages T10–T11 offers diagnostic tools for determining reading levels and tips for improving fluency.

## Helping All Readers Break the Code

There are many reasons that some students struggle with reading. Often poor readers spend most of their mental energy trying to figure out, or decode, the words. With their brains focused on the letters and corresponding sounds, there is little attention left to think about what the words mean. Until readers achieve a basic level of automaticity in word recognition, they are not reading for meaning.

Although most students do have a knowledge

of basic phonics, some students fail to develop strategies for using the letter-sound correspondences. They often have difficulty decoding new words, and multisyllabic words are especially problematic. As students encounter longer words, they need to be able to break these words into parts.

## Establishing a Reading Process

Good readers are strategic in how they approach reading. They consciously or unconsciously do certain things before, during, and after reading. Poor readers, however, often possess few or none of the strategies required for proficient reading. To help struggling readers, establish a routine for reading that involves strategies before, during, and after reading.

- **Before Reading** New ideas presented in reading materials need to be integrated with the reader's **prior knowledge** for understanding to occur. Have students preview the material to see what it is about. Discuss what they already know about the topic and have them **predict** new information they might learn about it. Talk about a **purpose** for reading and have students think about reading strategies they might use with the material.

- **During Reading** Good readers keep track of their understanding as they read. They recognize important or interesting information, know when they don't understand something, and figure out what to do to adjust their understanding. Poor readers are often unaware of these **self-monitoring strategies**. To help these readers become more involved in their reading, suggest that they read with a pencil in hand to jot down notes and questions as they read. If students own the reading materials, they can mark the text as they read. *Lecturas para todos* that accompanies *¡En español!* is ideal for this type of work.

- **After Reading** Provide opportunities for readers to reflect on what they have read. These can involve group or class discussion and writing in journals and logs.

## Creating Independent Readers

As you work to give students the skills they need to read for themselves, you can also incorporate some basic routines into your classroom that will help your students extend their understanding.

- **Read aloud.** People of all ages love a good story. Read aloud to your students and hook them on some authors and genres they might not have tackled themselves. For most material, students' listening comprehension is more advanced than their comprehension of written material. Listening helps them develop the thinking skills needed to understand complex text.

- **Write daily.** Writing is a powerful tool for understanding. Encourage students to use writing to work through problems, explore new ideas, or respond to the literature they read. Encourage students to keep journals and learning logs.

- **Read daily**. Allow time for sustained silent reading. Set aside classroom time for students to read self-selected materials. Students who read become better readers, and students are more likely to choose to read if they can pursue ideas they find interesting.

- **Build a classroom library**. If possible, provide a wide range of reading materials so that students are exposed to diverse topics and genres. Respect students' reading choices. Struggling readers need first to view themselves as readers.

- **Promote discussion**. Set ground rules for discussion so that all opinions are heard. Model good discussion behaviors by asking follow-up questions, expanding on ideas presented, and offering alternate ways of viewing topics.

# Developing Fluent Readers

Good readers are fluent readers. They recognize words automatically, group individual words into meaningful phrases, and apply phonic, morphemic, and contextual clues when confronted with a new word. Fluency is a combination of accuracy (number of words identified correctly) and rate (number of words per minute) of reading. Fluency can be taught directly, and it improves as a consequence of students' reading a lot of materials that are within their instructional range.

## Understanding Reading Levels

Every student reads at a specific level regardless of the grade in which he or she is placed. Reading level in this context is concerned with the relationship between a specific selection or book and a student's ability to read that selection. The following are common terms used to describe these levels:

- **independent level**—The student reads material in which no more than 1 in 20 words is difficult. The material can be read without teacher involvement and is likely to be material students would choose to read on their own.

- **instructional level**—The student reads material in which no more than 2 in 20 words are difficult. The material is most likely found in school and read with teacher involvement.

- **frustration level**—The student reads material in which significantly more than 2 in 20 (or 89%) of the words are difficult. Students will probably get little out of reading the material.

If students read only material that's too easy, growth in skill, vocabulary, and understanding is too slow. If students read only difficult material, they may give up in frustration much too early.

## Providing Reading Materials in the Student's Instructional Range

Most states have testing programs that provide information about each student's reading ability. Once you determine a student's general reading level, you can work with the library media teacher to identify reading materials that will be within the student's instructional level. To develop fluency, students should read materials that contain a high proportion of words that they know already or can easily decode. Work with each student to develop a list of books to read, and have students record their progress on a Reading Log.

## Repeated Oral Readings

Repeated oral readings of passages is a strategy that improves fluency. Oral reading also improves prosody, which is the art of sounding natural when you read, or reading with appropriate intonation, expression, and rhythm.

Beginning readers sound awkward when they read aloud. They pause and halt at the wrong places; they emphasize the wrong syllables; they may read in a monotone. Repeated oral readings can increase fluency and prosody as students 1) identify words faster and faster each time they read; 2) correctly identify a larger percentage of words; 3) segment text into appropriate phrases; 4) change pitch and emphasis to fit the meaning of the text.

To improve fluency and prosody, select passages that are brief, thought provoking, and at the student's current independent level of reading. You may choose narrative or expository text, or have the student choose something he or she enjoys. Performing a play, practicing to give a speech, reading to younger students, and rereading a passage to find evidence in support of an argument are all activities that provide opportunities to reread. For the following exercise, you may choose to pair students together and have them read to each other, or use this as a one-on-one teacher-student or tutor-student activity.

1. Select an excerpt within the student's reading level.

2. Have the student read the passage aloud to a partner. The partner records the number of seconds it takes to read the whole passage, and notes the number of errors. Reverse roles so that each student has a chance to read to the other.

3. Read the passage aloud to the students so that students can hear it read correctly.

4. As homework, or as an in-class assignment, have students practice reading the passage out loud on their own.

5. After practice, have each student read aloud again to his or her partner, who records the time and the number of errors.

6. After repeated practice and readings the student will read the passage fluently, that is, with a moderate rate and near 100% accuracy.

## Repeated Silent Readings

Having students silently read and reread passages that are at their instructional level also improves fluency. As they practice, students will recognize words more quickly each time, will group words into meaningful phrases more quickly, and will increase their reading rate. One nice thing about repeated silent reading is that a student can do it individually. Many students enjoy timing themselves when they read and seeing improvement over time. Have them keep a record on a piece of graph paper.

## Modeling

Students benefit from repeated opportunities to hear Spanish spoken fluently. By listening to live models or CDs, listeners can understand the rhythm of the language and the pitch and pronunciation of particular words and phrases. They can hear when to pause, when to speed up, and what words to emphasize. In addition, you can model or ask an experienced reader to read passages aloud. At most advanced levels, this technique is particularly useful to introduce students to various forms of dialect. As you play the CDs aloud, have students read along silently or chorally, or pause the CDs after each paragraph and have the students try reading the same passage aloud.

## Phrase-Cued Text

Less proficient readers may not know when to pause in text. They may pause in the middle of a phrase, or run through a comma or period. They may not recognize verb phrases, prepositional phases, or even phrases marked by parentheses or brackets as words that "go together." This makes their reading disjointed and choppy, or gives it a monotone quality. Some poems have essentially one phrase per line and can be used to demonstrate to students how to phrase text. Or, you may take a passage and have students rewrite it with one phrase per line, so that they pause at the end of each line. Alternatively, you can show them how a passage should be read by inserting slash marks or blank spaces at appropriate places to pause. Choose passages appropriate to the students' reading level. Have students read and then reread the passage, stopping to pause at each slash mark.

# Reciprocal Teaching

Reciprocal teaching refers to an instructional activity that teaches students concrete, specific, "comprehension-fostering" strategies they will need whenever they approach the reading of a new text. The activity consists of a dialogue between students and teacher, with each taking a turn in the role of the teacher or leader. Classroom use of this activity has been found to improve the reading comprehension of both good and struggling readers.

**Step 1:** Have everyone silently read a short passage (one or several paragraphs) of a new text. Model the following four thinking strategies using only the part of the reading that has been read.

- **Questioning** – Ask the class to think of a question that everyone can answer because everyone has read the same text. Model by generating a question for the class. Call on a student to answer your question. Ask that student to then generate a question for the class and to call on another student to answer her question. Repeat this procedure until you think all students are thoroughly familiar with the facts and details of the passage. (If students do not ask a question beginning with *why*, model one for them to move their thinking from literal to inferential comprehension.)

- **Clarifying** – Model for the class a confusion you need to clarify; for example, a word or a phrase that caused you to pause as you initially read the passage. Think aloud as you discuss your mental engagement with this section, explaining to the class how you figured it out. Ask students if they found any confusing parts when they read the passage. Have a dialogue about the problem-solving methods used by students to make sense of confusing parts.

- **Summarizing** – After students have comprehended the passage as a result of the reciprocal questioning and clarifying strategies, ask them to think of a one-sentence summary for the passage. Ask a volunteer to share his summary statement. Encourage others to revise, if needed, the shared summary by elaborating and embellishing its content. Identify the best summary through a dialogue with class members.

- **Predicting** – Now that students know what the first passage in the reading means, ask them to predict what the author will discuss next.

**Step 2:** Ask everyone to silently read another portion of text. Have a student volunteer repeat step 1, serving as the teacher/leader, over this new portion.

**Step 3:** In groups of four, have students silently read the next portion of text, taking turns role-playing the leader and following the four-step procedure.

**Teacher's Role:** Guide students' practice by monitoring the student dialogue in each group during steps 2 and 3. Remind students of the procedure and give additional modeling of the steps.

Reciprocal Teaching training provides students with explicit ways to interact with new text.

An ongoing review of all of the strategies provides a helpful reminder to students and encourages their pursuit of independent reading.

# Strategies for Reading Copymaster

These comprehension and critical-thinking strategies can help you gain a better understanding of what you read. Whenever you find yourself having difficulty making sense of what you're reading, choose and use the strategy that seems most likely to help.

## Visualize

Visualize characters, events, and setting to help you understand what's happening. When you read nonfiction, pay attention to the images that form in your mind as you read.

## Cause/Effect

Try to figure out what will happen next and how the selection might end. Interpret the facts and infer the effects. Then read on to see how accurate your guesses are.

## Compare/Contrast

Connect personally with what you're reading. Think of similarities and differences between the descriptions in the reading and what you have personally experienced, heard about, or read about.

## Analyze

Question what happens while you read. Searching for reasons behind events and characters' feelings can help you feel closer to what you are reading. Look for patterns, hidden meanings, and details.

## Synthesize

Review your understanding of what you read. You can do this by **summarizing** what you have read, identifying the **main idea**, and **making inferences**—drawing conclusions from the information you are given. Reread passages you don't understand.

## Evaluate

Form opinions about what you read, both as you read and after you've finished. Develop your own ideas about characters and events.

# LECTURAS PARA TODOS

## with TEST PREPARATION

# Teacher's Edition

# 1a 1b 1uno

# ¡En español!

# LECTURAS PARA TODOS

## with TEST PREPARATION

**McDougal Littell**
A DIVISION OF HOUGHTON MIFFLIN COMPANY
Evanston, Illinois • Boston • Dallas

**Cover photo** by Martha Granger/EDGE Productions

**Acknowledgments**

"Cumpleaños," from *Cuadros de familia* by Carmen Lomas Garza. Copyright © 1990 by Carmen Lomas Garza. All rights reserved. Reprinted by permission of Children's Press Books.

"La exclamación" by Octavio Paz, from *The Collected Poems of Octavio Paz: 1957–1987,* edited by Eliot Weinberger. Copyright © Octavio Paz. Reprinted by permission of Maria José Paz.

"En Uxmal" by Octavio Paz, from *The Collected Poems of Octavio Paz: 1957–1987,* edited by Eliot Weinberger. Copyright © Octavio Paz. Reprinted by permission of Maria José Paz.

"Palma sola," from *El libro de los sones* by Nicolás Guillén. Copyright © 1982 Nicolás Guillén. Editorial Letras Cubanas, Instituto Cubano Del Libro, La Habana, Cuba. Reprinted by permission.

Excerpt from *Como agua para chocolate* by Laura Esquivel. Copyright © 1989 by Laura Esquivel. Reprinted by Anchor Books, a division of Random House, Inc.

"Oda al tomate," by Pablo Neruda. Copyright © 1954 by Pablo Neruda and Fundación Pablo Neruda. Reprinted by permission of Agencia Literaria Carmen Balcells, S.A.

**Illustration** and **Photography Credits** appear on page 250.

ISBN: 0-618-33488-2

1 2 3 4 5 6 7 8 9 – PBO – 07 06 05 04 03

# Table of Contents

## En voces *continued*

# Literatura adicional

## Academic and Informational Reading

# Introducing *Lecturas para todos*

***Lecturas para todos*** is a new kind of reading text. As you will see, this book helps you become an active reader. It is a book to mark up, to write in, and to make your own. You can use it in class and take it home.

## Reading Skills Improvement— in Spanish *and* English

You will read selections from your textbook, as well as great literature. In addition, you will learn how to understand the types of texts you read in classes, on tests, and in the real world. You will also study and practice specific strategies for taking standardized tests.

## Help for Reading

Many readings in Spanish are challenging the first time you encounter them. ***Lecturas para todos*** helps you understand these readings. Here's how.

***Para leer*** The page before each reading gives you background information about the reading and a key to understanding the selection.

**Reading Strategy** Reading strategies help you decide how to approach the material.

**What You Need to Know** A preview of every selection tells you what to expect before you begin reading.

**Reading Tips** Useful, specific reading tips appear at points where language is difficult.

***A pensar...*** Point-of-use, critical-thinking questions help you analyze content as you read.

***Márcalo*** This feature invites you to mark up the text by underlining and circling words and phrases right on the page.

>***Gramática*** As you read, this feature highlights key grammar concepts.

>***Vocabulario*** This feature helps you with the new vocabulary as you read the selection.

>***Análisis*** This feature appears in the *Literatura adicional* section and encourages you to focus on one aspect of literary analysis as you read.

**Reader's Success Strategy** These notes give useful and fun tips and strategies for comprehending the selection.

**Challenge** These activities keep you challenged, even after you have grasped the basic concepts of the reading.

## Vocabulary Support

***Palabras clave*** Important new words appear in bold. Their definitions appear in a *Palabras clave* section at the bottom of any page where they occur in the selection. You will practice these words after the selection.

***Vocabulario de la lectura*** Vocabulary activities follow each selection and give you the opportunity to practice the *Palabras clave.* Active vocabulary words from the *etapa* appear in blue.

## Comprehension and Connections

***¿Comprendiste?*** Questions after each selection check your understanding of what you have just read.

***Conexión personal*** These short writing activities ask you to relate the selection to your life and experiences to make what you have read more meaningful.

## Links to ¡En español!

When using McDougal Littell's *¡En español!,* you will find *Lecturas para todos* to be a perfect companion. *Lecturas para todos* lets you mark up the *En voces* selections as you read, helping you understand and remember more.

**Read on to learn more!**

# Academic and Informational Reading

Here is a special collection of real-world examples—in English—to help you read every kind of informational material, from textbooks to technical directions. Why are these sections in English? Because the strategies you learn will help you on tests, in other classes, and in the world outside of school. You will find strategies for the following:

**Analyzing Text Features** This section will help you read many different types of magazine articles and textbooks. You will learn how titles, subtitles, lists, graphics, many different kinds of visuals, and other special features work in magazines and textbooks. After studying this section you will be ready to read even the most complex material.

**Understanding Visuals** Tables, charts, graphs, maps, and diagrams all require special reading skills. As you learn the common elements of various visual texts, you will learn to read these materials with accuracy and skill.

**Recognizing Text Structures** Informational texts can be organized in many different ways. In this section you will study the following structures and learn about special key words that will help you identify the organizational patterns:
• Main Idea and Supporting Details
• Problem and Solution
• Sequence
• Cause and Effect
• Comparison and Contrast
• Persuasion

**Reading in the Content Areas** You will learn special strategies for reading social studies, science, and mathematics texts.

**Reading Beyond the Classroom** In this section you will encounter applications, schedules, technical directions, product information, Web pages, and other readings. Learning to analyze these texts will help you in your everyday life and on some standardized tests.

# Test Preparation Strategies

In this section, you will find strategies and practice to help you succeed on many different kinds of standardized tests. After closely studying a variety of test formats through annotated examples, you will have an opportunity to practice each format on your own. Additional support will help you think through your answers. You will find strategies for the following:

**Successful Test Taking**  This section provides many suggestions for preparing for and taking tests. The information ranges from analyzing test questions to tips for answering multiple-choice and open-ended test questions.

**Reading Tests: Long Selections**  You will learn how to analyze the structure of a lengthy reading and prepare to answer the comprehension questions that follow it.

**Reading Tests: Short Selections**  These selections may be a few paragraphs of text, a poem, a chart or graph, or some other item. You will practice the special range of comprehension skills required for these pieces.

**Functional Reading Tests**  These real-world texts present special challenges. You will learn about the various test formats that use applications, product labels, technical directions, Web pages, and more.

**Revising-and-Editing Tests**  These materials test your understanding of English grammar and usage. You may encounter capitalization and punctuation questions. Sometimes the focus is on usage questions such as verb tenses or pronoun agreement issues. You will become familiar with these formats through the guided practice in this section.

**Writing Tests**  Writing prompts and sample student essays will help you understand how to analyze a prompt and what elements make a successful written response. Scoring rubrics and a prompt for practice will prepare you for the writing tests you will take.

**Point-of-use comprehension support helps you read selections from ¡En español! and develop critical-thinking skills.**

## Reading Strategy

This feature provides reading tips and strategies that help you effectively approach the material.

## What You Need to Know

This section provides a key to help you unlock the selection so that you can understand and enjoy it.

---

### Para leer   *Una encuesta escolar*

#### Reading Strategy

**USE CONTEXT CLUES** You can use the context to guess the meaning of unfamiliar words. Context includes what is written before and after the word. Pictures often contribute to the context too. What do you think the highlighted words mean? Write your answers in the chart below.

• Una encuesta **escolar**

• El papel sale de la impresora con los **resultados** de la encuesta.

| Word | Definition |
|------|------------|
| escolar | |
| resultados | |

#### What You Need to Know

In Mexico, children are required to attend public or private school through grade nine. There are six grades of primary education and three grades of secondary education. The school day for the primary grades is usually from 9 A.M. to 12:30 P.M. and for the secondary grades it is from 7:30 A.M. to 2:30 P.M. Most Mexican students attend public schools, although in the cities many attend private schools. Students who wish to continue their education beyond the secondary level take college preparatory classes for three more years or they attend vocational school, after which they may apply to a university. Both public and private universities in Mexico have highly competitive entrance exams, which applicants must pass in order to gain admission.

24   Lecturas para todos

*¡En español!* Level 1

---

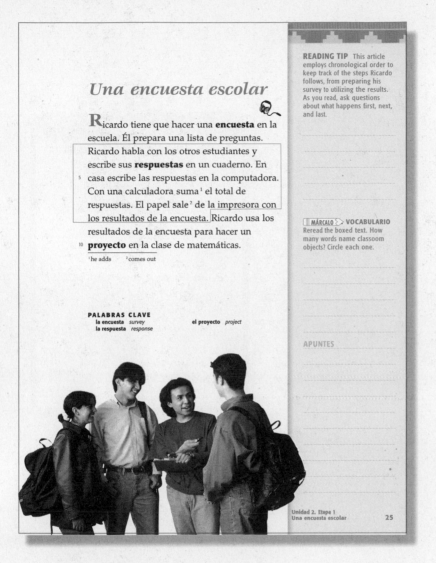

### Una encuesta escolar

**R**icardo tiene que hacer una **encuesta** en la escuela. Él prepara una lista de preguntas. Ricardo habla con los otros estudiantes y escribe sus **respuestas** en un cuaderno. En
5   casa escribe las respuestas en la computadora. Con una calculadora suma[1] el total de respuestas. El papel sale[2] de la impresora con los resultados de la encuesta. Ricardo usa los resultados de la encuesta para hacer un
10  **proyecto** en la clase de matemáticas.

[1] he adds    [2] comes out

**PALABRAS CLAVE**
la encuesta  *survey*          el proyecto  *project*
la respuesta  *response*

**MÁRCALO > VOCABULARIO**
Reread the boxed text. How many words name classoom objects? Circle each one.

APUNTES

**MÁRCALO >**
## VOCABULARIO
This feature helps you with the new vocabulary as you read the selection. Underlining or circling the example makes it easy for you to find and remember.

## PALABRAS CLAVE
Important vocabulary words appear in bold within the reading. Definitions are given at the bottom of the page.

# En voces *continued*

## A pensar...

Point-of-use questions check your understanding and ask you to think critically about the passage.

### A pensar...

1. Reread Ricardo's survey, then take the survey yourself. Fill in the blanks and place checkmarks in the boxes as appropriate. If you have classes not listed on the form, write them in. **(Assess)**

2. In groups, compare your individual responses to the survey. Then prepare the survey results for your group using a format like Ricardo's, as shown on the next page. Were there any questions to which all members of your group had the same response? What did you learn from the results of this survey? **(Tabulate/Summarize)**

**APUNTES**

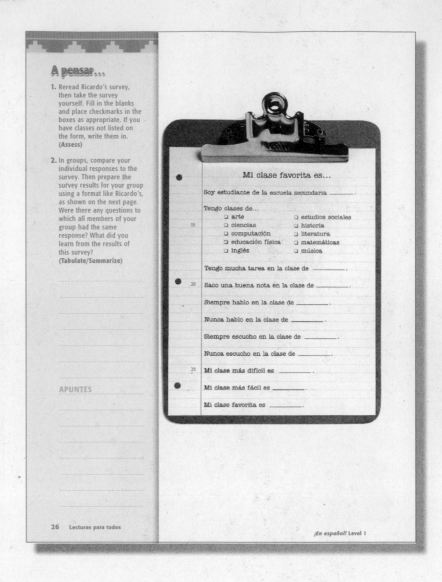

Mi clase favorita es...

Soy estudiante de la escuela secundaria _____.

Tengo clases de...
- ❏ arte
- ❏ ciencias
- ❏ computación
- ❏ educación física
- ❏ inglés
- ❏ estudios sociales
- ❏ historia
- ❏ literatura
- ❏ matemáticas
- ❏ música

Tengo mucha tarea en la clase de _____.

Saco una buena nota en la clase de _____.

Siempre hablo en la clase de _____.

Nunca hablo en la clase de _____.

Siempre escucho en la clase de _____.

Nunca escucho en la clase de _____.

Mi clase más difícil es _____.

Mi clase más fácil es _____.

Mi clase favorita es _____.

**Los resultados**

**Una encuesta a 50 estudiantes**

30  Clase con más tarea: matemáticas
(25 *estudiantes*)

Los estudiantes sacan más buenas notas en la clase de: música
(35 *estudiantes*)

Los estudiantes hablan más en la clase de: literatura
35  (30 *estudiantes*)

Los estudiantes nunca hablan en la clase de: inglés
(25 *estudiantes*)

Los estudiantes escuchan más en la clase de: ciencias
(40 *estudiantes*)

40  Los estudiantes nunca escuchan en la clase de: historia
(20 *estudiantes*)

La clase más difícil es: ciencias
(35 *estudiantes*)

La clase más fácil es: arte
45  (45 *estudiantes*)

La clase favorita es: literatura
(30 *estudiantes*)

**READER'S SUCCESS STRATEGY** Use a chart like the one below to compare and contrast the courses offered at Ricardo's school with the courses offered at your school.

| Ricardo's School |
|---|
| |

| My School |
|---|
| |

**CHALLENGE** Look at the results of Ricardo's survey. Note in the heading how many students he surveyed in all. Then convert the number of students listed in each subcategory to the percentage of all students surveyed. (Calculate)

Modelo: *Clase con más tarea: matemáticas (25 estudiantes: 50%)*

## READER'S SUCCESS STRATEGY

Notes like this one provide ideas to help you read the selection successfully. For example, some notes suggest that you fill in a chart while you read. Others suggest that you mark key words or ideas in the text.

## CHALLENGE

This feature asks you to expand upon what you have learned for enrichment.

# En voces  *continued*

## Vocabulario de la lectura

Vocabulary practice follows each reading, reinforcing the *Palabras clave* that appear throughout the selection. Words that appear in blue are *etapa* vocabulary words in *¡En español!*

---

## Vocabulario de la lectura

### Palabras clave

| | | |
|---|---|---|
| la calculadora *calculator* | **la encuesta** *survey* | **el proyecto** *project* |
| la computadora *computer* | la impresora *printer* | **la respuesta** *response* |
| el cuaderno *notebook* | el papel *paper* | |

**A.** Fill in each blank with the correct form of a **Palabra clave**.

Ricardo prepara una lista de preguntas para su _____ escolar.
                                                    (1)

Primero, escribe las _____ de los otros estudiantes en un
                          (2)

_____. Cuando llega a casa, escribe las respuestas en la
      (3)

_____. Usa una _____ para sumar el total de
      (4)                    (5)

respuestas. El _____ sale de la _____ con los
                     (6)                      (7)

resultados. Ricardo usa los resultados de su encuesta para un _____
                                                                    (8)

que tiene que hacer en la clase de matemáticas.

**B.** Choose two **Palabras clave** and write a sentence with each one.

_____

_____

_____

_____

_____

_____

_____

## ¿Comprendiste?

1. ¿Qué tiene que hacer Ricardo?

_____

2. ¿Qué usa Ricardo para escribir la encuesta?

_____

3. ¿Los estudiantes hablan mucho o poco en la clase de inglés?

_____

4. ¿Es difícil la clase de música o arte en la escuela de Ricardo?

_____

5. ¿Qué clase es la clase favorita de los estudiantes?

_____

## Conexión personal

What is your favorite class? Why do you like it? Write your answers in the web below.

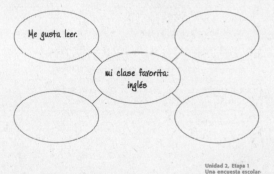

Me gusta leer.

mi clase favorita: inglés

## ¿Comprendiste?
Comprehension questions check your understanding and provide the opportunity to practice new vocabulary words.

## Conexión personal
These short writing activities help you see connections between what happens in the selection and in your own life.

# *Literatura adicional*

Notes in the margins make literature from the Spanish-speaking world accessible and help you read works by famous authors such as García Lorca and Cisneros.

## Reading Strategy
This feature provides reading tips and strategies that help you effectively approach the material.

## What You Need to Know
This section provides a key to help you unlock the selection so that you can understand and enjoy it.

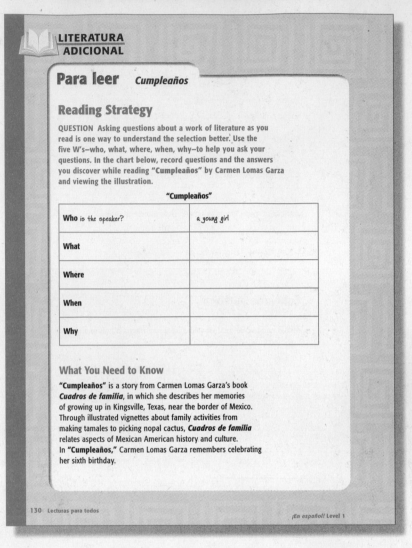

### LITERATURA ADICIONAL

**Para leer**  *Cumpleaños*

#### Reading Strategy

**QUESTION** Asking questions about a work of literature as you read is one way to understand the selection better. Use the five W's–who, what, where, when, why–to help you ask your questions. In the chart below, record questions and the answers you discover while reading "**Cumpleaños**" by Carmen Lomas Garza and viewing the illustration.

**"Cumpleaños"**

| | |
|---|---|
| **Who** is the speaker? | *a young girl* |
| **What** | |
| **Where** | |
| **When** | |
| **Why** | |

#### What You Need to Know

**"Cumpleaños"** is a story from Carmen Lomas Garza's book *Cuadros de familia*, in which she describes her memories of growing up in Kingsville, Texas, near the border of Mexico. Through illustrated vignettes about family activities from making tamales to picking nopal cactus, *Cuadros de familia* relates aspects of Mexican American history and culture. In **"Cumpleaños,"** Carmen Lomas Garza remembers celebrating her sixth birthday.

*Sobre la autora*

Carmen Lomas Garza, artista chicana, nació en Kingsville, Texas, en 1948. Empezó a estudiar arte a la edad de trece años. Sus pinturas, inspiradas en su niñez en el sur de Texas, son escenas típicas de la vida mexicana americana.

~~~~~~~~~~

# Cumpleaños

Ésa soy yo, pegándole[1] a la piñata en la fiesta que me dieron cuando cumplí seis años[2]. Era[3] también el cumpleaños de mi hermano, que cumplía cuatro años. Mi madre nos dio
5 una gran fiesta e invitó a muchos primos, **vecinos** y amigos.

[1] hitting    [2] *cumplí seis años* I turned six    [3] It was

*Cumpleaños de Lala y Tudi by Carmen Lomas Garza, 1989*

**PALABRAS CLAVE**
el (la) vecino(a)    *neighbor*

---

**READING TIP** Review the vocabulary you have learned for family members. Then circle the words in the story that refer to the relatives of the girl who is narrating it.

APUNTES

_____

_____

_____

_____

▌▌▌ MÁRCALO ⟩ **ANÁLISIS**
This story contains vivid descriptions, details that help the reader form a strong mental picture. Underline words or phrases in the story that help you visualize in your mind the activity and excitement of the birthday party.

_____

_____

_____

READER'S
SUCCESS
STRATEGY  As you read, look for depictions of the vocabulary in the illustration. First identify the girl who is telling the story and her father. Then find the following: **la cuerda, el palo, el pañuelo, la piñata.**

Literatura adicional
Cumpleaños                    131

---

*Sobre la autora*
Each literary selection begins with a short author biography that provides cultural context.

▌▌▌ MÁRCALO ⟩ **ANÁLISIS**
This feature encourages you to focus on one aspect of literary analysis as you read.

**READER'S SUCCESS STRATEGY**
Notes like this one provide ideas to help you read the selection successfully. For example, some notes suggest that you fill in a chart while you read. Others suggest that you mark key words or ideas in the text.

# Academic and Informational Reading

**This section helps you read informational material and prepare for other classes and standardized tests.**

## VARIED TYPES OF READINGS

The wide variety of academic and informational selections helps you access different types of readings and develop specific techniques for those reading types.

## Academic and Informational Reading

In this section you'll find strategies to help you read all kinds of informational materials. The examples here range from magazines you read for fun to textbooks to bus schedules. Applying these simple and effective techniques will help you be a successful reader of the many texts you encounter every day.

165

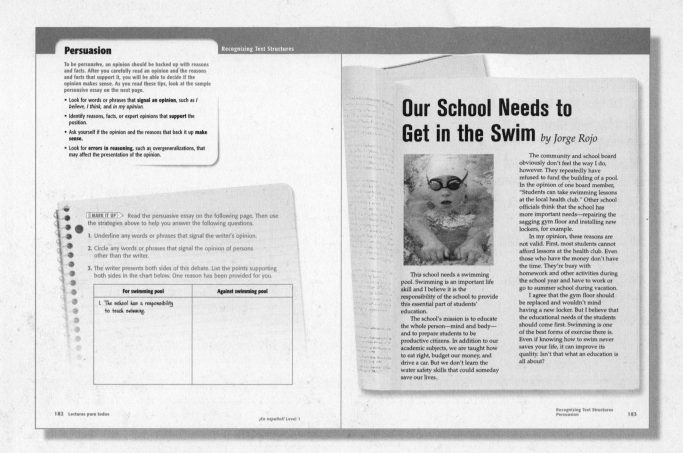

## Persuasion

To be persuasive, an opinion should be backed up with reasons and facts. After you carefully read an opinion and the reasons and facts that support it, you will be able to decide if the opinion makes sense. As you read these tips, look at the sample persuasive essay on the next page.

- Look for words or phrases that **signal an opinion**, such as *I believe*, *I think*, and *in my opinion*.

- Identify reasons, facts, or expert opinions that **support** the position.

- Ask yourself if the opinion and the reasons that back it up **make sense.**

- Look for **errors in reasoning**, such as overgeneralizations, that may affect the presentation of the opinion.

**MARK IT UP** Read the persuasive essay on the following page. Then use the strategies above to help you answer the following questions.

**1.** Underline any words or phrases that signal the writer's opinion.

**2.** Circle any words or phrases that signal the opinion of persons other than the writer.

**3.** The writer presents both sides of this debate. List the points supporting both sides in the chart below. One reason has been provided for you.

| For swimming pool | Against swimming pool |
|---|---|
| I. The school has a responsibility to teach swimming. | |

*¡En español! Level 1*

# Our School Needs to Get in the Swim *by Jorge Rojo*

This school needs a swimming pool. Swimming is an important life skill and I believe it is the responsibility of the school to provide this essential part of students' education.

The school's mission is to educate the whole person—mind and body—and to prepare students to be productive citizens. In addition to our academic subjects, we are taught how to eat right, budget our money, and drive a car. But we don't learn the water safety skills that could someday save our lives.

The community and school board obviously don't feel the way I do, however. They repeatedly have refused to fund the building of a pool. In the opinion of one board member, "Students can take swimming lessons at the local health club." Other school officials think that the school has more important needs—repairing the sagging gym floor and installing new lockers, for example.

In my opinion, these reasons are not valid. First, most students cannot afford lessons at the health club. Even those who have the money don't have the time. They're busy with homework and other activities during the school year and have to work or go to summer school during vacation.

I agree that the gym floor should be replaced and wouldn't mind having a new locker. But I believe that the educational needs of the students should come first. Swimming is one of the best forms of exercise there is. Even if knowing how to swim never saves your life, it can improve its quality. Isn't that what an education is all about?

## SKILL DEVELOPMENT

These activities offer graphic organizers, Mark It Up features, and other reading support to help you comprehend and think critically about the selection.

# Test Preparation for All Learners

*Lecturas para todos* offers models, strategies, and practice to help you for standardized tests.

## TEST PREPARATION STRATEGIES

- Successful test taking
- Reading test model and practice—long selections
- Reading test model and practice—short selections
- Functional reading test model and practice
- Revising-and-editing test model and practice
- Writing test model and practice
- Scoring rubrics

---

APUNTES

### READING STRATEGIES FOR ASSESSMENT

**Find the main idea and supporting details.** Circle the main idea of this article. Then underline the details that support the main idea.

**Use context clues.** To discover what a "pack animal" is, study the words and phrases around it. Which phrase helps define it?

**Notice important details.** Underline the details that explain why alpaca wool is so desirable.

### Reading Test Model
**SHORT SELECTIONS**

**DIRECTIONS** "Warmth from the Andes" is a short informative article. The strategies you have just learned can also help you with this shorter selection. As you read the selection, respond to the notes in the side column.

When you've finished reading, answer the multiple-choice questions. Use the side-column notes to help you understand what each question is asking and why each answer is correct.

### Warmth from the Andes

Southeastern Peru and Western Bolivia make up a geographic region called the *Altiplano*, or High Plateau. This largely desolate mountainous area is home to one of the most economically important animals in South America—the alpaca.

The alpaca is related to the camel and looks somewhat like another well-known South American grazing animal, the llama. Alpacas live at elevations as high as 16,000 feet. At such altitudes, oxygen is scarce. Alpacas are able to survive because their blood contains an unusually high number of red blood corpuscles, the cells that carry oxygen throughout the body.

For several thousand years, the Native Americans of the region have raised alpacas both as pack animals for transporting goods and for their most important resource—wool. Alpaca wool ranges in color from black to tan to white. It is lightweight yet strong and resists moisture. Also, it is exceptionally warm. Alpaca wool is much finer than the

*¡En español!* Level 1

---

## Revising-and-Editing Test Model

**DIRECTIONS** Read the following paragraph carefully. Then answer the multiple-choice questions that follow. After answering the questions, read the material in the side columns to check your answer strategies.

¹Madrid, the capital of Spain. ²It is home to one of that nations cultural treasures—the Prado museum. ³The building was constructed in the late eighteenth century as a museum of natural science. ⁴Then they decided to change it to an art museum in 1819 and it has more than 9,000 works of art. ⁵The museum is located on a street called the Paseo del Prado. ⁶Their are many famous paintings they're, including works by El Greco, Velázquez, and Goya.

**1** Which sentence in the paragraph is actually a fragment, an incomplete thought?

A. sentence 5

B. sentence 3

C. sentence 1

D. sentence 4

**2** In sentence 2, which of the following is the correct possessive form of *nation*?

A. nation's

B. nations's

C. nations'

D. nations

**READING STRATEGIES FOR ASSESSMENT**

Watch for common errors. Highlight or underline errors such as incorrect spelling or punctuation; fragments or run-on sentences; and missing or misplaced information.

**ANSWER STRATEGIES**

Incomplete Sentences A sentence is a group of words with a subject and a verb that expresses a complete thought. If either the subject or the verb is missing, the group of words is an incomplete sentence.

Possessive Nouns In sentence 2, the word *nation* is singular. So, it takes the singular possessive form.

## Writing Test Model

**DIRECTIONS** Many tests ask you to write an essay in response to a writing prompt. A writing prompt is a brief statement that describes a writing situation. Some writing prompts ask you to explain *what, why,* or *how*. Others ask you to convince someone of something.

As you analyze the following writing prompts, read and respond to the notes in the side columns. Then look at the response to each prompt. The notes in the side columns will help you understand why each response is considered strong.

**Prompt A**

Some child-rearing experts believe that young people should be kept busy after school and on the weekends with a variety of structured activities, such as music lessons, sports, dance classes, and so on. Others say that young people today have been "overscheduled" and need more time to themselves—to read, think about the future, and even just to daydream.

Think about your experiences and the way your non-school time is structured. Do you think lots of structure, more personal time, or a combination of the two is most beneficial to young people? Remember to provide solid reasons and examples for the position you take.

**Strong Response**

Today was a typical day for my little brother Jeff. He got up at five o'clock to go to the local ice rink for hockey practice. Then he was off to school. At the end of the school day, Jeff

**APUNTES**

**ANALYZING THE PROMPT**

Identify the focus. What issue will you be writing about? Circle the focus of your essay in the first sentence of the prompt.

Understand what's expected of you. First, circle what the prompt asks you to do. Then identify your audience. What kinds of details will appeal to this audience?

**ANSWER STRATEGIES**

Capture the reader's interest. The writer begins by describing a typical busy day in his younger brother's life.

# Para leer    *Los latinos de Estados Unidos*

## Reading Strategy

**PREVIEW GRAPHICS** Think about how you read English. Do you check photos or other graphics before reading an article? View the graphics that accompany this reading, then predict what this reading is about. After reading, decide whether your prediction was on target or needs adjustment.

**Prediction:** _____

_____

_____

_____

**How close was your prediction?** _____

_____

_____

_____

_____

## What You Need to Know

Every ten years—in years ending in zero—the United States government counts the entire population of the United States. This is known as the U.S. Census. The U.S. Constitution requires that every person in the United States, regardless of age, place of birth, or language is counted in the Census, citizens and noncitizens alike. In addition to counting the total population, the Census also captures information such as language spoken at home, place of birth, and national origin. In recent years, people who were born in a Spanish-speaking country or whose family comes from a Spanish-speaking country have become the largest minority group in the United States.

This reading can also be found on pages 42–43 of the Level 1 Pupil Edition. The audio is on CD 1, Tracks 16–17.

# Los latinos de Estados Unidos 🎧

**E**n **Estados Unidos hay** personas de muchos países de Latinoamérica.

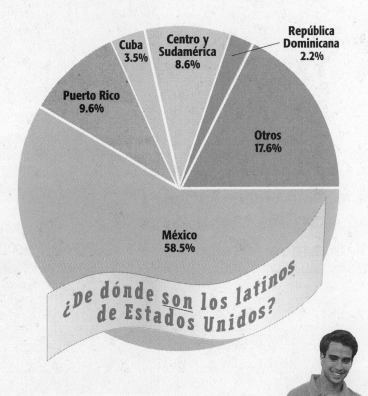

Cuba
3.5%

Centro y Sudamérica
8.6%

República Dominicana
2.2%

Puerto Rico
9.6%

Otros
17.6%

México
58.5%

*¿De dónde son los latinos de Estados Unidos?*

**Francisco:** ¿Qué tal? Me llamo Francisco García Flores. Soy de Puerto Rico, pero vivo en Miami. El hombre de México es mi papá. La mujer es mi mamá.

5

**PALABRAS CLAVE**
**Estados Unidos** *United States*
**hay** *there are*
**Centroamérica** *Central America*
**Sudamérica** *South America*

**República Dominicana**
*Dominican Republic*
**México** *Mexico*

## A pensar...

A pie chart is a circular chart cut into sections like pie pieces. It divides information and shows parts of a whole. Look at the pie chart on the left. What does the chart tell you about where U.S. Latinos are from? From what two countries are the majority of U.S. residents of Latino descent? Write your answer below. **(Analyze)**

The chart tells you that Latinos in the United States come from all parts of the Spanish-speaking world. Mexico and Puerto Rico are the countries of origin for the majority of U.S. Latinos.

**APUNTES**

**Palabras clave**
In Spanish the plural form of compound words is formed by adding an 's' to the first part of the word, as in the case of:

| SINGULAR | PLURAL |
| --- | --- |
| coche cama | coches cama |
| hombre rana | hombres rana |
| palabra clave | palabras clave |

**|||MÁRCALO> GRAMÁTICA**
The verb **ser** is used many
times in this reading. Wherever
you find a form of **ser,**
underline it. Don't forget to
check the caption that goes
with the pie chart!

The verb **ser** appears 7 times in
this reading. It has been
underlined in the Teacher's
Edition.

PUERTO RICO

**Sra. García:** Me llamo
10 Anita García. También
soy de Puerto Rico pero
trabajo como doctora en
Miami.

MÉXICO

**Sr. García:** Buenos días.
15 Yo me llamo Juan García.
Soy de México. Vivo en
Miami con mi familia.

CUBA

**Sr. Estrada:** Hola. Me
llamo Felipe Estrada.
20 Yo soy de Cuba, pero
vivo en Miami.

**Arturo:** Hola. Me llamo
Arturo. <u>Soy</u> estudiante
en Miami, pero <u>soy</u>
25 de la República
Dominicana.

REPÚBLICA DOMINICANA

**Alma:** Mi nombre <u>es</u>
Alma. <u>Soy</u> de Colombia,
pero también vivo
30 en Miami.

CENTRO Y SUDAMÉRICA

**APUNTES**

**CHALLENGE** Why do you think a person would choose to move to another country? Write down some ideas below. (Draw Conclusions)

*Sample answers:*
for professional or employment opportunities; for educational opportunities; to be with family members

# Vocabulario de la lectura

**Palabras clave**

**Centroamérica**  *Central America*
**el (la) doctor(a)**  *doctor*
**Estados Unidos**  *United States*
**el (la) estudiante**  *student*
**hay**  *there are*

**el hombre**  *man*
**México**  *Mexico*
**la mujer**  *woman*
**República Dominicana**  *Dominican Republic*
**Sudamérica**  *South America*

**A.** Complete each sentence with the correct **Palabra clave.**

1. La señora García trabaja de _doctora_.

2. Arturo no es doctor; él es _estudiante_.

3. El _hombre_ de México es el papá de Francisco.

4. La _mujer_ de México es la mamá de Francisco.

5. En Estados Unidos _hay_ muchas personas de México, Puerto Rico y Cuba.

**B.** Fill in each blank with the correct **Palabra clave.**

Los latinos de ___Estados Unidos___ son de muchos países diferentes.
                              (1)
Francisco y su papá son de ___México___. Arturo es de la
                              (2)
___República Dominicana___. Alma es de Colombia, un país de
         (3)
___Sudamérica___. Muchas otras personas son de Costa Rica, El Salvador,
         (4)
Guatemala, Honduras, Nicaragua o Panamá; ellas son de ___Centroamérica___.
                                                              (5)

# ¿Comprendiste?

**1.** ¿De dónde es la doctora? ¿Cómo se llama?

La doctora es de Puerto Rico. Se llama Anita García.

**2.** ¿De dónde es el señor García?

El señor García es de México.

**3.** ¿Cómo se llama el señor de Cuba?

El señor de Cuba se llama Felipe Estrada.

**4.** ¿De dónde es la chica?

La chica es de Colombia.

**5.** ¿Cómo se llama el estudiante? ¿De dónde es?

El estudiante se llama Arturo. Es de la República Dominicana.

# Conexión personal

Choose a person from the reading that you would like to meet. What questions would you like to ask him or her? Write a few questions in Spanish.

Persona: Sra. García

Preguntas:

¿Le gusta ser doctora?

¿Dónde vive ahora?

¿Habla inglés y español?

# Para leer   *Las celebraciones del año*

## Reading Strategy

**LOOK FOR COGNATES** These are words that look alike and have similar meanings in both English and Spanish, such as **europeo** and **artificiales**. What other cognates can you find in **Las celebraciones del año**? List them below.

*Cognates may include: celebraciones, importantes, formas, tradiciones, diferentes,*

*octubre, europeo, cultura, latinoamericana, noviembre, personas, familias, decoran,*

*famosas, tradicional.*

_____

_____

_____

_____

_____

_____

## What You Need to Know

There are many important holidays in Spanish-speaking countries. Some, such as Christmas or Mother's Day, are observed in many parts of Latin America as well as the United States. Many dates of historical significance, such as Mexican Independence Day, are celebrated primarily in one country. Spanish-speaking communities in the United States continue to observe many traditional holidays, such as **el Día de los Muertos** (the Day of the Dead), which is celebrated annually by Mexican Americans.

This reading can also be found on pages 86–87 of the Level 1 Pupil Edition. The audio is on CD 3, Tracks 6–7.

**READING TIP** Remember that, in Spanish, dates are written with the number of the day first, then the number of the month. For example, 4/1 means January 4.

**APUNTES**

# Las celebraciones del año

Hay muchas fechas importantes durante el año. Los países hispanohablantes celebran estas fechas de varias formas. Algunas[1] celebraciones son **iguales** que las de Estados

5 Unidos, pero también hay tradiciones diferentes.

El Día de la Raza

## octubre

**12/10 El Día de la Raza** En este día no hay trabajo. Hay muchos **desfiles.** El día celebra

10 el encuentro[2] del **indígena** con el europeo y el africano. Hoy esta mezcla[3] de razas[4] y tradiciones forma la cultura latinoamericana.

[1]some [2]meeting [3]mixture [4]races

**PALABRAS CLAVE**
**igual** *the same*          **el (la) indígena** *native (Indian)*
**el desfile** *parade*

**CHALLENGE** Why do you think that Mexicans have special holidays for remembering ancestors and deceased relatives and for honoring their families? Write down some notes, then talk about your ideas in small groups. **(Discuss)**

*Answers will vary. Sample answer: The concept of family is an important part of Mexican culture.*

## A pensar...

**1.** Which of the holidays described are the same in both Spanish-speaking countries and the U.S.? Which holidays are celebrated primarily by persons from Spanish-speaking countries? **(Compare and Contrast)**

*La Nochevieja and el Año Nuevo are celebrated in both Latin America and the U.S. El Día de la Raza, el Día de Todos los Santos, el Día de los Muertos, and el Día de los Reyes are celebrated primarily by people from Spanish-speaking countries.*

**2.** Name two different ways in which **la Nochevieja** is celebrated in Spain and Latin America. Then tell about a custom observed on New Year's Eve that is typical of the United States or of your community. **(Connect)**

*Answers will vary. Sample answer: Ecuadorians celebrate New Year's Eve by burning symbols of past years at midnight. In Spain it is traditional to eat twelve grapes. In the United States...*

## noviembre

15 **1/11 El Día de Todos los Santos y**
**2/11 el Día de los Muertos**[5] En estos días todos honran a las personas de su familia. En México las familias decoran las tumbas de sus **antepasados** con flores bonitas.

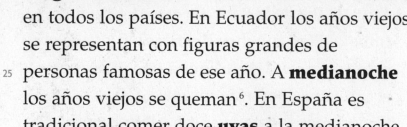

La Nochevieja

## diciembre y enero

20 **31/12 La Nochevieja y**
**1/1 el Año Nuevo** Hay **fuegos artificiales**, desfiles o celebraciones en todos los países. En Ecuador los años viejos se representan con figuras grandes de
25 personas famosas de ese año. A **medianoche** los años viejos se queman[6]. En España es tradicional comer doce **uvas** a la medianoche.

---

[5] Dead      [6] are burned

**PALABRAS CLAVE**
el (la) antepasado(a)  *ancestor*      la medianoche  *midnight*
la Nochevieja  *New Year's Eve*      la uva  *grape*
los fuegos artificiales  *fireworks*

READER'S
SUCCESS
STRATEGY  As you read, pay
attention to the pictures that
accompany the text. They
may help you understand
some of the unfamiliar words.

# enero

**6/1** **El Día de los Reyes**  Es el día tradicional

30  para dar regalos[7] de Navidad en los países

latinos.

---

[7] give gifts

MÁRCALO  GRAMÁTICA
Circle all of the dates that
appear in the article. Then
write each of them below, in
numbers and in words.

**Modelo:** 13/4, el trece de abril

12/10, el doce de octubre
1/11, el primero de noviembre
2/11, el dos de noviembre
31/12, el treinta y uno de diciembre
1/1, el primero de enero
6/1, el seis de enero

# Vocabulario de la lectura

**Palabras clave**

el año   *year*

el (la) antepasado(a)   *ancestor*

el desfile   *parade*

la fecha   *date*

los fuegos artificiales   *fireworks*

igual   *the same*

el (la) indígena   *native (Indian)*

la medianoche   *midnight*

la Nochevieja   *New Year's Eve*

la uva   *grape*

**A.** Complete each sentence with the correct form of a **Palabra clave.**

1. Hay doce meses en un _____año_____.

2. La _____fecha_____ de hoy es diez de octubre.

3. La _____uva_____ es un tipo de fruta.

4. Mis _____antepasados_____ son de España.

5. El treinta y uno de diciembre es la _____Nochevieja_____.

6. En Estados Unidos, hay _____fuegos artificiales_____ el cuatro de julio.

**B.** Fill in each blank with the correct form of a **Palabra clave.**

Los países hispanohablantes celebran varias _____fechas_____ durante el año. El
                                                      (1)

Día de la Raza, los latinoamericanos honran el encuentro del _____indígena_____,
                                                                       (2)

el europeo y el africano. Las familias mexicanas decoran las tumbas de sus

_____antepasados_____ con flores en el Día de los Muertos. En la _____Nochevieja_____,
          (3)                                                                        (4)

los españoles comen doce uvas a la _____medianoche_____. Algunas celebraciones
                                              (5)

de España y Latinoamérica son diferentes de las de Estados Unidos, pero otras,

como la Navidad, son _____iguales_____.
                              (6)

# ¿Comprendiste?

**1.** ¿Cómo celebran los latinoamericanos el Día de la Raza?

No hay trabajo. Hay muchos desfiles.

**2.** ¿Cuáles son las fechas en que los mexicanos honran a su familia?

Son el primero y el dos de noviembre.

**3.** Describe dos tradiciones del Año Nuevo.

(Two of the following): Hay fuegos artificiales; hay desfiles; los años se representan con

figuras grandes y los años se queman; comer doce uvas.

**4.** ¿En qué fecha dan regalos de Navidad las personas de los países latinos? ¿Cómo se llama ese día?

Dan regalos de Navidad el seis de enero. Se llama el Día de los Reyes.

# Conexión personal

Choose one of your favorite holidays. What words or phrases come to mind when you think of this day? Write them down in the word web.

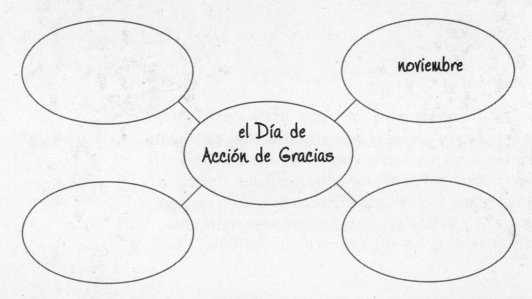

el Día de Acción de Gracias

noviembre

# Para leer   *Una estudiante de Nicaragua*

## Reading Strategy

**LOOK FOR COGNATES**  Words in Spanish that look like words in English are called cognates. They will help you understand readings in Spanish. One example of a cognate in this reading is **estudiante**. What do you think it means? Scan the reading and jot down all the other cognates you can find.

*Cognates may include estudiante, programa, académico, internacional, practicar, inglés, tímida, aeropuerto, contenta, oficiales, bilingües, familia, norteamericana, emoción.*

## What You Need to Know

International exchange programs offer students the opportunity to experience the day-to-day life of another culture. Many participants choose to live with a host family, where they can be part of a home, learn new customs, and participate in family activities. Students in exchange programs also attend local schools or enroll in language study programs. This reading is about an exchange student from Nicaragua who goes to live with a family in Miami, Florida.

This reading can also be found on pages 46–47 of the Level 1a Pupil Edition. The audio is on the Bridge CD, Tracks 1–2.

# Una estudiante de Nicaragua

Una chica viaja sola[1] en **avión** a Miami. Se llama Eva. Eva es de Nicaragua, pero este año estudia en
5 Estados Unidos. Eva es estudiante del programa del Intercambio Académico Internacional. A Eva le gusta viajar y le gusta practicar el inglés. Pero ahora Eva está un poco tímida.

[1] travels alone

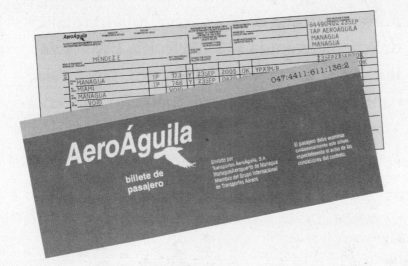

**PALABRAS CLAVE**
**el avión** *airplane*

**READING TIP** The girl in this story is from the country of Nicaragua. Look at a map or an atlas to locate Nicaragua.

The audio CD for this reading can be found in the Middle School Bridging Packet.

**READER'S SUCCESS STRATEGY** Often you can understand a story better if you place yourself in the situation of the characters. Imagine that you are going to spend the next year living in another country as an exchange student. How would you feel as you arrived at the airport and were about to meet your host family?

**APUNTES**

**▌▌▌ MÁRCALO ▷ GRAMÁTICA**
Underline the passage in the reading that tells what country Eva is from. Then write a sentence below saying what country you are from.

*(Yo) soy de...*

# A pensar...

**1.** Why does Eva feel shy as she arrives at the airport in Miami? Mark passages in the text that support your answer. **(Infer)**

*Sample answer: Eva feels shy because she is traveling alone from Nicaragua to the United States. Her first language is Spanish, and as an exchange student she will live with a family she has never met before.*

**2.** How does she feel after she sees her host family, and why? **(Infer)**

*Sample answer: Upon seeing her host family, Eva feels happy and relieved, because they are smiling and holding a welcome sign with her name on it.*

**CHALLENGE** Write a dialog between Eva and her new family. Then act it out in small groups. **(Extend)**

*Answers will vary.*

10 En el aeropuerto internacional de Miami los **letreros** están en inglés ¡y español! Eva se siente[2] más contenta. Los oficiales de la **aduana** también son **bilingües** y muy simpáticos. Eva ya tiene confianza[3] y va

15 a la **sala de espera**. Una simpática familia norteamericana la espera con un letrero que dice, «¡Bienvenida Eva! Welcome Eva!» Eva llora[4] de gusto y de emoción. «Sí, voy a estar contenta. ¡Voy a pasar un buen año aquí en

20 Miami!»

---
[2] feels    [3] has confidence    [4] cries

**PALABRAS CLAVE**

| | |
|---|---|
| **el letrero** *sign* | **bilingüe(s)** *bilingual* |
| **la aduana** *customs* | **la sala de espera** *waiting room* |

# Vocabulario de la lectura

## Palabras clave

**la aduana** *customs*          el (la) **estudiante** *student*
**el avión** *airplane*          la **familia** *family*
**bilingüe(s)** *bilingual*      **el letrero** *sign*
la **chica** *girl*              **la sala de espera** *waiting room*

**A.** Complete each sentence with the best **Palabra clave**. Use each word only once.

Eva, una _____chica_____ de Nicaragua, es una _____estudiante_____ del
　　　　　　　(1)　　　　　　　　　　　　　　　　　　　　(2)

programa de Intercambio Académico Internacional. Viaja sola en

_____avión_____ a Miami. Los oficiales de la _____aduana_____ del aeropuerto
　　　　(3)　　　　　　　　　　　　　　　　　　　　　(4)

son _____bilingües_____; hablan inglés y español. En la ___sala de espera___ hay
　　　　　(5)　　　　　　　　　　　　　　　　　　　　　　(6)

una _____familia_____ norteamericana con un _____letrero_____ que dice
　　　　(7)　　　　　　　　　　　　　　　　　　　　(8)

«¡Bienvenida Eva!»

**B.** Choose two **Palabras clave** and write a sentence with each one.

_____

_____

_____

_____

# ¿Comprendiste?

**1.** ¿Quién es Eva?

Eva es estudiante.

**2.** ¿De dónde es ella?

Es de Nicaragua.

**3.** ¿Adónde viaja?

Viaja a Miami.

**4.** ¿Qué le gusta?

Le gusta viajar y practicar el inglés.

# Conexión personal

You are going to participate in an international exchange program. Write a letter to your host family introducing yourself. Say what town or city you are from, what kind of home you live in, and what you like to do.

¡Hola! Me llamo...

# Para leer
## Los Ángeles: Una carta del pasado

## Reading Strategy

**PICTURE CLUES** Looking at the pictures that accompany a reading can help you understand the reading better. Look at the illustrations on these pages. What do you think the reading will be about? Write your ideas in the space below.

_____

_____

_____

_____

_____

## What You Need to Know

In 1769 Gaspar de Portolá, a soldier in the Spanish army, and Juan Crespi, a Catholic priest, led an expedition up the California coast to an area that is now part of Los Angeles. They camped by a river, which they named **El Río de Nuestra Señora la Reina de los Ángeles de Porciúncula. Porciúncula** was a chapel in Italy. In 1781 the Spanish government recruited a group of eleven families in northern Mexico to move to the area and establish a **pueblo,** or town. The settlers, known as **los pobladores,** consisted of 11 men, 11 women, and 22 children. They named their new home **El Pueblo de Nuestra Señora la Reina de los Ángeles de Porciúncula** after the nearby river. The letter you are about to read is by a boy who lived in the settlement of Los Angeles just three years after the original founding families arrived there.

# Los Ángeles: Una carta del pasado[1]

**A**quí tienes un fragmento de una carta de Miguel José Guerra, un chico español, que vivía[2] en Los Ángeles en ¡1784!

5   2 de agosto de 1784

**Querido** primo:

¿Cómo estás? ¿Cómo está toda la familia allá en Málaga? Aquí en el Pueblo de Nuestra Señora de Los Ángeles

10   estamos contentos. ¡Hoy mi familia y yo no trabajamos!

Generalmente, mi hermana y yo trabajamos en el campo[3] con mamá y papá. (Mi hermana ya tiene 15 años y

15   yo tengo 13, pero mi papá es muy viejo —¡él tiene 36 años!) Papá es fuerte y

---
[1]past   [2]lived   [3]fields

**PALABRAS CLAVE**
la carta   *letter*                    querido(a)   *dear*

¡En español! Level 1

muy moreno por el sol⁴ del campo.
Mamá es muy fuerte también y siempre
muy bonita.

20 Hoy es el día de Nuestra Señora de Los
Ángeles, la patrona de mi pueblo.
Hay celebración y fiesta. Llevo mi ropa
elegante y mi hermana también.
Vamos a la capilla⁵ con mamá y papá
25 y con los tíos y los primos de aquí.
Hay música y danzas tradicionales y
¡mucha buena **comida**!

Un **abrazo** de tu primo,
Miguel José

---

⁴sun    ⁵*Vamos…capilla* We go to chapel

**PALABRAS CLAVE**
la comida  *food*          el abrazo  *hug*

# A pensar…

**1.** Why does Miguel have a cousin and other relatives in Spain? **(Infer)**

*Answers will vary. Sample answer: Miguel is of Spanish descent. It is probable that his family lived in Spain before they moved to the settlement of Los Angeles.*

**2.** Why do you think that even the children in Miguel's family had to work? **(Draw Conclusions)**

*Answers will vary. Sample answer: In 1784, the town of Los Angeles was still very young, and much of the surrounding land was unsettled. The pioneer families who lived there had to build their own houses, establish their own businesses, and grow their own food.*

**CHALLENGE** Why do you think a family would make the decision to leave their own country and move far away to a new, unsettled place? **(Make Judgments)**

*Answers will vary.*

# Vocabulario de la lectura

**Palabras clave**

| | | |
|---|---|---|
| **el abrazo** *hug* | **la comida** *food* | **querido(a)** *dear* |
| **agosto** *August* | **la hermana** *sister* | **los tíos** *uncle(s) and aunt(s)* |
| **la carta** *letter* | **el (la) primo(a)** *cousin* | |

**A.** Complete the following letter with the correct **Palabras clave.**

16 de _____agosto_____
            (1)

_____Querido_____ primo:
        (2)

¿Cómo estás? Aquí en Málaga estoy muy contenta. Me gusta
esta ciudad. Picasso, el artista, es de aquí. Hoy mis padres y yo
vamos a visitar el Museo Picasso. Esta noche, vamos a un
restaurante que sirve _____comida_____ típica de España. ¡Qué
                         (3)
chévere! Te escribo otra _____carta_____ pronto.
                              (4)
Un _____abrazo_____ de tu _____prima_____,
        (5)              (6)

Manuela

**B.** Complete each sentence with the correct form of a **Palabra clave.**

1. El hijo de tus tíos es tu _____primo_____.

2. La hija de tus tíos es tu _____prima_____.

3. Los padres de tus primos son tus _____tíos_____.

4. La hija de tus padres es tu _____hermana_____.

# ¿Comprendiste?

**1.** ¿Quién escribe la carta?

Miguel José Guerra, un chico español, escribe la carta.

**2.** ¿A quién le escribe? ¿Dónde vive esa persona?

Le escribe a su primo. El primo vive en Málaga, España.

**3.** ¿Por qué está contento?

Hay celebración y fiesta. No hay trabajo hoy.

**4.** ¿Cuántos miembros de la familia hay? ¿Quiénes son?

Hay cuatro (pero también hay tíos y primos). Son el padre, la madre, la hermana y Miguel José.

**5.** ¿Cómo celebran el día?

Hay música y danzas tradicionales y buena comida.

# Conexión personal

Write a letter to a pen pal, real or imaginary, describing yourself and your family.

Querido(a)...

# Para leer — *Una encuesta escolar*

## Reading Strategy

**USE CONTEXT CLUES** You can use the context to guess the meaning of unfamiliar words. Context includes what is written before and after the word. Pictures often contribute to the context too. What do you think the highlighted words mean? Write your answers in the chart below.

• Una encuesta **escolar**

• El papel sale de la impresora con los **resultados** de la encuesta.

| Word | Definition |
|------|-----------|
| escolar | |
| resultados | |

## What You Need to Know

In Mexico, children are required to attend public or private school through grade nine. There are six grades of primary education and three grades of secondary education. The school day for the primary grades is usually from 9 A.M. to 12:30 P.M. and for the secondary grades it is from 7:30 A.M. to 2:30 P.M. Most Mexican students attend public schools, although in the cities many attend private schools. Students who wish to continue their education beyond the secondary level take college preparatory classes for three more years or they attend vocational school, after which they may apply to a university. Both public and private universities in Mexico have highly competitive entrance exams, which applicants must pass in order to gain admission.

This reading can also be found on pages 116–117 of the Level 1 Pupil Edition. The audio can be found on CD 4, Tracks 6–7.

# *Una encuesta escolar*

**R**icardo tiene que hacer una **encuesta** en la escuela. Él prepara una lista de preguntas. Ricardo habla con los otros estudiantes y escribe sus **respuestas** en un (cuaderno.) En

5 casa escribe las respuestas en la (computadora.) Con una (calculadora) suma[1] el total de respuestas. El (papel) sale[2] de la (impresora) con los resultados de la encuesta. Ricardo usa los resultados de la encuesta para hacer un

10 **proyecto** en la clase de matemáticas.

[1] he adds    [2] comes out

**PALABRAS CLAVE**
la encuesta    *survey*        el proyecto    *project*
la respuesta   *response*

**READING TIP** This article employs chronological order to keep track of the steps Ricardo follows, from preparing his survey to utilizing the results. As you read, ask questions about what happens first, next, and last.

**MÁRCALO VOCABULARIO**
Reread the boxed text. How many words name classoom objects? Circle each one.

Students should circle **cuaderno, computadora, calculadora, papel, impresora.**

**APUNTES**

# A pensar...

1. Reread Ricardo's survey, then take the survey yourself. Fill in the blanks and place checkmarks in the boxes as appropriate. If you have classes not listed on the form, write them in.
**(Assess)**

2. In groups, compare your individual responses to the survey. Then prepare the survey results for your group using a format like Ricardo's, as shown on the next page. Were there any questions to which all members of your group had the same response? What did you learn from the results of this survey?
**(Tabulate/Summarize)**

APUNTES

## Mi clase favorita es...

Soy estudiante de la escuela secundaria _____.

Tengo clases de...

15
- ❏ arte
- ❏ ciencias
- ❏ computación
- ❏ educación física
- ❏ inglés

- ❏ estudios sociales
- ❏ historia
- ❏ literatura
- ❏ matemáticas
- ❏ música

Tengo mucha tarea en la clase de _____.

20 Saco una buena nota en la clase de _____.

Siempre hablo en la clase de _____.

Nunca hablo en la clase de _____.

Siempre escucho en la clase de _____.

Nunca escucho en la clase de _____.

25 Mi clase más difícil es _____.

Mi clase más fácil es _____.

Mi clase favorita es _____.

## Los resultados

### Una encuesta a 50 estudiantes

30 Clase con más tarea: matemáticas
(*25 estudiantes*)

Los estudiantes sacan más buenas notas en la clase de: música
(*35 estudiantes*)

Los estudiantes hablan más en la clase de: literatura
35 (*30 estudiantes*)

Los estudiantes nunca hablan en la clase de: inglés
(*25 estudiantes*)

Los estudiantes escuchan más en la clase de: ciencias
(*40 estudiantes*)

40 Los estudiantes nunca escuchan en la clase de: historia
(*20 estudiantes*)

La clase más difícil es: ciencias
(*35 estudiantes*)

La clase más fácil es: arte
45 (*45 estudiantes*)

La clase favorita es: literatura
(*30 estudiantes*)

**READER'S SUCCESS STRATEGY** Use a chart like the one below to compare and contrast the courses offered at Ricardo's school with the courses offered at your school.

| Ricardo's School |
| --- |
|  |

| My School |
| --- |
|  |

**CHALLENGE** Look at the results of Ricardo's survey. Note in the heading how many students he surveyed in all. Then convert the number of students listed in each subcategory to the percentage of all students surveyed. (**Calculate**)

Modelo: Clase con más tarea: matemáticas (25 estudiantes: 50%)

(35 estudiantes: 70%)

(30 estudiantes: 60%)

(25 estudiantes: 50%)

(40 estudiantes: 80%)

(20 estudiantes: 40%)

(35 estudiantes: 70%)

(45 estudiantes: 90%)

(30 estudiantes: 60%)

# Vocabulario de la lectura

**Palabras clave**

| | | |
|---|---|---|
| **la calculadora** *calculator* | **la encuesta** *survey* | **el proyecto** *project* |
| **la computadora** *computer* | **la impresora** *printer* | **la respuesta** *response* |
| **el cuaderno** *notebook* | **el papel** *paper* | |

**A.** Fill in each blank with the correct form of a **Palabra clave.**

Ricardo prepara una lista de preguntas para su ___encuesta___ escolar.
                                              (1)

Primero, escribe las ___respuestas___ de los otros estudiantes en un
                        (2)

___cuaderno___. Cuando llega a casa, escribe las respuestas en la
    (3)

___computadora___. Usa una ___calculadora___ para sumar el total de
     (4)                      (5)

respuestas. El ___papel___ sale de la ___impresora___ con los
                  (6)                    (7)

resultados. Ricardo usa los resultados de su encuesta para un ___proyecto___
                                                                  (8)

que tiene que hacer en la clase de matemáticas.

**B.** Choose two **Palabras clave** and write a sentence with each one.

_____

_____

_____

_____

_____

_____

# ¿Comprendiste?

**1.** ¿Qué tiene que hacer Ricardo?

Tiene que hacer una encuesta escolar.

**2.** ¿Qué usa Ricardo para escribir la encuesta?

Usa una computadora.

**3.** ¿Los estudiantes hablan mucho o poco en la clase de inglés?

Hablan poco.

**4.** ¿Es difícil la clase de música o arte en la escuela de Ricardo?

No, son fáciles.

**5.** ¿Qué clase es la clase favorita de los estudiantes?

La clase favorita de los estudiantes es la literatura.

# Conexión personal

What is your favorite class? Why do you like it? Write your answers in the web below.

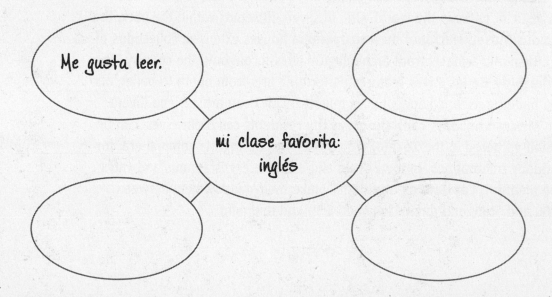

Me gusta leer.

mi clase favorita: inglés

# Para leer · *México y sus jóvenes*

## Reading Strategy

**SKIM** Before reading a long passage, it is helpful to read quickly to get a general idea of its content. Skim the paragraphs, noting clues that indicate the central theme or topic. By skimming, you can tell quickly what a reading is about. Then it will be easier to do a more careful reading. After skimming **México y sus jóvenes**, write down some words or phrases below that indicate what it is about.

*Answers may include: jóvenes, escuela, tarea, teatros, museos, tiendas,*

*parques, fines de semana, viernes, sábados, domingos, libres, descansar.*

## What You Need to Know

Mexico City offers a variety of attractions for residents and visitors alike. **El Bosque de Chapultepec**, at nearly three square miles, is one of the largest city parks in the world. One of seven museums within the park, the famous **Museo Nacional de Antropología** houses extensive collections of pre-Hispanic artifacts from archeological sites throughout the country. The **Palacio de Bellas Artes** features performing arts from opera to ballet, and the building itself is known for its murals by Mexican artist Diego Rivera. On Mexican holidays **capitalinos**, as city residents call themselves, can be found gathered in the **Zócalo**, the city's center during the colonial era, for outdoor celebrations. In the **Zócalo** and elsewhere, restaurants and cafés are plentiful. **Capitalinos** traditionally take their midday meal between 3:00 and 5:00, and dinner between 8:30 and midnight.

This reading can also be found on pages 160–161 of the Level 1 Pupil Edition. The audio is on CD 6, Tracks 6–7.

# México y sus jóvenes

¿**Q**ué hacen los mexicanos jóvenes? De lunes a viernes los muchachos que tienen **menos de** 18 años van a la escuela.

5 Tienen muchas materias — a veces tienen hasta ocho clases en un día. Y también tienen mucha tarea. Por eso, después de clases

10 muchos de los estudiantes van a sus casas para hacer la tarea y después descansar.

15 En la Ciudad de México hay muchos teatros, museos, tiendas y parques. En **cada** lugar es posible ver a muchos jóvenes, especialmente los fines de semana.

**PALABRAS CLAVE**
**menos de**  *less than*          **cada**  *every*

**READING TIP**  Cover the definitions of the **Palabras clave** at the bottom of the page, and see if you can determine what the words mean on your own. Clues to meaning are often offered by the context of a sentence. If you guessed a word correctly, ask yourself how you figured out what it meant.

_____

_____

_____

_____

_____

**CHALLENGE**  Imagine that you are interviewing an exchange student from Mexico City. What would you like to know about what life is like in the capital of Mexico? You might want to ask about a typical school day, what teenagers do for fun with their friends, what activities they share with their families, or something else you are interested in. In Spanish, write three interview questions below. (**Connect**)

**Preguntas**

1._____

2._____

3._____

Las chicas comen una merienda mexicana.

El hombre toca la guitarra.

La gente pasea en el parque.

▮▮▮ MÁRCALO ⟫ VOCABULARIO

You have just learned words and phrases to describe leisure activities. Using this vocabulary, write a caption for each of the photographs on these pages.

Sample answers appear below the photographs.

APUNTES

_____

_____

_____

A pensar...

Consider what you have learned about how teenagers in Mexico City spend time on the weekends. Do you and your friends enjoy the same types of activities in your free time? Name some activities you have in common with Mexican teenagers and some activities that differ from theirs.
(Compare and Contrast)

Answers will vary.

Los viernes por la tarde, los sábados y los
20 domingos son los días principales en que los
jóvenes mexicanos están **libres.** Los domingos
hay mucha gente en los parques. Andan en
bicicleta, practican **deportes** o tocan un
instrumento. De vez en cuando, para el
25 almuerzo, van a un restaurante con sus
familias. El domingo es el día principal para
pasear y descansar.

Los jóvenes pasan un rato con los amigos.

Para el almuerzo, esta familia va a un restaurante.

El muchacho camina con los perros.

**PALABRAS CLAVE**
libre  *free*                      **los deportes**  *sports*

# Vocabulario de la lectura

**Palabras clave**

| | | | | | |
|---|---|---|---|---|---|
| **cada** | *every* | **menos de** | *less than* | **el teatro** | *theater* |
| **los deportes** | *sports* | **el museo** | *museum* | **la tienda** | *store* |
| **libre** | *free* | **el parque** | *park* | | |

**A.** For each **Palabra clave** in the first column, find the sentence in the second column that best describes it. Write the corresponding letter in the blank.

___B___ 1. tienda      A. Es donde la gente pasea y descansa.

___A___ 2. parque      B. Venden cosas aquí.

___E___ 3. teatro      C. Incluyen patinar, nadar y andar en bicicleta.

___D___ 4. museo      D. Tiene cosas muy viejas.

___C___ 5. deportes      E. Es donde va la gente para ver ballet y escuchar música.

**B.** Fill in each blank with the correct form of a **Palabra clave.**

1. Julio descansa los sábados y los domingos, los días principales en que

   está _____libre_____.

2. Los viernes por la tarde, me gusta practicar _____deportes_____ en el parque con los amigos.

3. Normalmente hay muchas personas en el museo, pero hoy hay

   _____menos de_____ diez.

4. A María le gusta hacer ejercicio; anda en bicicleta _____cada_____ día.

5. Mamá va a la _____tienda_____ de ropa para comprar una falda nueva.

# ¿Comprendiste?

**1.** ¿Qué hacen los jóvenes de lunes a viernes?

Van a la escuela. Hacen mucha tarea.

**2.** ¿Adónde van muchos jóvenes los fines de semana en la Ciudad de México?

Van a los teatros, a los museos, a las tiendas y a los parques.

**3.** ¿Qué actividades hacen los domingos?

Andan en bicicleta, practican deportes o tocan un instrumento.

**4.** ¿Qué hace a veces una familia los domingos?

Va a un restaurante para el almuerzo.

# Conexión personal

How would you describe an ideal Saturday? Write some of your favorite weekend activities in the space at the right.

Los sábados, me gusta...

1. andar en bicicleta
2.
3.
4.

# Para leer

## Una leyenda azteca: El origen de la Ciudad de México

## Reading Strategy

**LOOK FOR CONTEXT CLUES** At first glance, there may appear to be many words in the reading you can't seem to understand. To improve your comprehension, use this strategy: Read each sentence as a whole rather than translating word for word.

## What You Need to Know

It is believed that the people who founded the Aztec capital of Tenochtitlán migrated south from a place called Aztlan in the area of present-day northern Mexico or southern Arizona. The name Aztec comes from the word *Aztlan*. Tenochtitlán, the largest city in the Aztec empire, was built on a lake and linked to the mainland by three large causeways. By the early 1400s, the Aztecs had one of the most advanced civilizations in the world. Although they were met with fierce resistance, the Spanish finally destroyed Tenochtitlán in 1521 and built Mexico City on the site of the Aztec capital. The Mexican flag, which shows an eagle standing on a nopal cactus with a rattlesnake in its mouth, was inspired by the Aztec legend about Tenochtitlán that is the subject of this reading.

The audio CD for this reading can be found in the Middle School Bridging Packet.

# Una leyenda azteca

## El origen de la Ciudad de México 🎧

**L**os aztecas, una tribu de **guerreros,** deciden dejar[1] su casa en el norte por necesidades económicas. Caminan todos los días por mucho tiempo buscando un lugar nuevo.

5  Pasan por muchos lugares pero no encuentran[2] el lugar perfecto. Esperan ansiosos la señal[3] de su **dios,** Huitzilopochtli.

Pasa mucho tiempo y están los aztecas muy
10  cansados[4]. Llegan a un **lago** donde miran la señal en medio del lago. Está un **águila** sobre un **cacto,** ¡con
15  una **serpiente** en la **boca!** Todos miran y hablan.

---
[1] leave   [2] find   [3] sign   [4] tired

**PALABRAS CLAVE**

| | | |
|---|---|---|
| **el guerrero** *warrior* | | **el cacto** *cactus* |
| **el dios** *god* | | **la serpiente** *snake* |
| **el lago** *lake* | | **la boca** *mouth* |
| **el águila** (f.) *eagle* | | |

—¡Ésta es la señal que esperamos! ¡Ésta es la señal de (nuestro) dios!

20 —¡Aquí es donde preparamos (nuestra) ciudad!

Y así, en el lago de Texcoco, los aztecas empiezan a construir (su) ciudad. Usan tierra y raíces [5] para crear pequeñas **islas.** Construyen (sus) casas en las islas.

25 Y así fue la creación, en el año 1325, de la gran Tenochtitlán, que ahora es la maravillosa Ciudad de México.

[5] earth and roots

**PALABRAS CLAVE**
**la isla** *island*

## A pensar...

**1.** What do the Aztecs begin to do after they see the eagle on a cactus with a snake in its mouth, and why? **(Clarify)**

*Sample answer:* They begin to build Tenochtitlán. The god Huitzilopochtli told the Aztecs to build their city in the place where they found an eagle on a cactus eating a snake.

**2.** Look at the picture of the Mexican flag. What is the symbol on the flag? What is its significance? **(Clarify)**

*Sample answer:* The Mexican flag shows an eagle standing on a cactus eating a snake, the sign the Aztecs were told to look for by Huitzilopochtli.

**CHALLENGE**  What can you infer about the role of religion in Aztec life from reading this legend? Mark any passages that support your ideas. **(Infer)**

*Answers will vary. Sample answer:* Religion was important in Aztec life. The Aztec people in the legend were looking for a sign from their god to tell them where to live.

# Vocabulario de la lectura

**Palabras clave**

**el águila** (f.)  *eagle*    **esperar**  *to wait for, to expect*    **el lago**  *lake*

**la boca**  *mouth*    **el guerrero**  *warrior*    **mirar**  *to watch, to look at*

**el cacto**  *cactus*    **la isla**  *island*    **la serpiente**  *snake*

**el dios**  *god*

**A.** Fill in each blank with the correct form of a **Palabra clave**.

Los aztecas _____esperan_____ una señal de Huitzilopochtli. Huitzilopochtli es el
(1)

_____dios_____ de los aztecas. La señal es un _____águila_____ sobre un
(2)                                                      (3)

cacto. El águila tiene una _____serpiente_____ en la _____boca_____. Un día,
(4)                           (5)

los aztecas _____miran_____ la señal en medio de un lago. Usan tierra y raíces
(6)

para crear _____islas_____ en el lago. Construyen Tenochtitlán en las islas del
(7)

_____lago_____ de Texcoco.
(8)

**B.** Complete each sentence with the correct form of a **Palabra clave**.

1. Los aztecas son un tribu de _____guerreros_____.

2. El _____dios_____ de los aztecas se llama Huitzilopochtli.

3. En un lago, hay un _____águila_____ con una serpiente en la boca.

4. El águila está sobre un _____cacto_____.

5. Los aztecas empiezan a construir pequeñas _____islas_____.

6. El _____lago_____ en que los aztecas construyen las islas se llama Texcoco.

# ¿Comprendiste?

**1.** ¿Quiénes son los aztecas?

Son una tribu de guerreros.

**2.** ¿Qué buscan?

Buscan un lugar nuevo.

**3.** ¿Cuál es la señal que reciben?

En medio de un lago hay un águila sobre un cacto con una serpiente en la boca.

**4.** ¿Qué es Tenochtitlán?

Es la ciudad de los aztecas. Hoy es la Ciudad de México.

# Conexión personal

Suppose you are part of an archaeological dig on the site of an Aztec civilization. What would you most like to find? Make a list on the right.

Busco...

casas

# Para leer
## Una leyenda mexicana: La Casa de los Azulejos

## Reading Strategy

**FOLLOWING PLOT** Use a chart to help you follow what happens in this legend. Show the beginning, middle, and end of the story. What do the father and the son do at each point of the story?

|  | Beginning | Middle | End |
|---|---|---|---|
| **Father** |  |  |  |
| **Son** |  |  |  |

## What You Need to Know

In 1737, the Count and Countess of Orizaba Valley ordered a reconstruction of their house in Mexico City and covered it with blue and white tiles. Tiled houses were a sign of success in Mexico during the colonial era, and were already popular in the town of Puebla, where the countess had lived before moving to Mexico City. **La Casa de los Azulejos,** or the House of Tiles, as the count and countess's former home is known today, is one of Mexico City's oldest landmarks. Its two-story courtyard is now a restaurant, and the second-floor stairwell contains a mural by the famous Mexican artist Orozco. The following legend gives one account of the history of **La Casa de los Azulejos.**

# Una leyenda mexicana

## La Casa de los Azulejos 🎧

En la Ciudad de México hay una casa muy famosa. Hay muchas leyendas de esta casa. Una de ellas va así...

En la **época**
5 **colonial**, el señor
**conde** de Valle
tiene un hijo que
no trabaja y no
estudia. Sólo va a
10 muchas fiestas de
noche y descansa de
día. Sólo quiere llevar
ropa elegante. Su padre está muy **triste.**
Piensa[1] que su hijo nunca va a hacer nada[2]
15 bueno. Por fin, un día dice: —Veo, hijo mío,
que tú nunca vas a trabajar, nunca vas a
estudiar y nunca vas a hacer tu casa de
azulejos como la gente buena de esta ciudad.

[1] He thinks  [2] *nunca...nada* is never going to do anything

**READER'S SUCCESS STRATEGY** In Spanish, dashes are often used to indicate dialog, a conversation between two or more persons. As you read this selection, make note of who is speaking the words that follow the first dash, and who is speaking the words that follow the second dash.

The audio CD for this reading can be found in the Middle School Bridging Packet.

**READING TIP** Note that the first and last paragraphs of this reading are an introduction and a conclusion to the legend. They describe a building that still stands in Mexico City today.

**CHALLENGE** How do you think this legend began? Exchange ideas in small groups. **(Make Judgments)**

*Answers will vary.*

**PALABRAS CLAVE**
**el azulejo**  *ceramic tile*
**la época colonial**  *colonial period, the time during which Spain ruled Mexico*
**el conde, la condesa**  *count, countess*
**triste**  *sad*

**||||MÁRCALO⟩ GRAMÁTICA**
Circle the verb in line 25. Then conjugate it in the space below.

Students should conjugate **hacer: hago, haces, hace, hacemos, hacen.**

## A pensar…

**1.** Why is the count displeased with his son at the start of the story? **(Clarify)**

*Sample answer:* The count's son spends most of his time relaxing and going to parties. His father wants him to be more industrious.

**2.** Why does the count's son decide to build a house of tiles? **(Cause and Effect)**

*Answers will vary. Sample answer:* He feels responsible for his father's unhappiness and wants to show respect for his father's feelings.

**3.** Check two sentences below that are *facts* about **La Casa de los Azulejos. (Differentiate)**

☑ There are many legends about its origin.

☐ It has always been a restaurant.

☑ The house is still standing in Mexico City.

El hijo escucha con atención las palabras de su
20 papá por primera vez y contesta: —Lo veo a usted muy triste por mi culpa[3]. Quiero **cambiar** mi vida. Voy a abandonar mi vida de perezoso y voy a trabajar.

Entonces, el hijo empieza a trabajar mucho.
25 Hace una casa grande y bonita con azulejos **por dentro** y ¡**por fuera**! Es para enseñarle a su papá que sí escucha sus palabras.

¡Y todavía existe esta casa! Si vas a la
30 Ciudad de México, puedes visitarla. Es un restaurante muy bonito y famoso.

[3] fault

**PALABRAS CLAVE**
**cambiar** *to change*          **por fuera** *outside*
**por dentro** *inside*

# Vocabulario de la lectura

### Palabras clave

**el azulejo** *ceramic tile*     **la gente** *people*    **por fuera** *outside*

**cambiar** *to change*    **por dentro** *inside*    **primero** *first*

**el conde, la condesa** *count, countess*    **por fin** *finally*    **triste** *sad*

**entonces** *then, so*

**la época colonial** *colonial period, the time during which Spain ruled Mexico*

**A.** Complete each sentence with the correct form of a **Palabra clave.**

El señor _____*conde*_____ de Valle vive en la Ciudad de México durante la
(1)

_____*época colonial*_____. Está _____*triste*_____ porque su hijo perezoso no trabaja y
(2)                 (3)

no estudia. El hijo ve a su padre muy descontento y por fin decide

_____*cambiar*_____ su vida. Hace una casa bonita con _____*azulejos*_____ por
(4)                                       (5)

dentro y _____*por fuera*_____.
(6)

**B.** On the line next to each word pair, write whether the words are synonyms or antonyms. Synonyms are words with the same or similar meaning. Antonyms are words with opposite meanings.

1. primero–final ___*antonyms*___

2. descontento–triste ___*synonyms*___

3. por fuera–por dentro ___*antonyms*___

4. triste–feliz ___*antonyms*___

5. personas–gente ___*synonyms*___

# ¿Comprendiste?

**1.** ¿Cómo es el hijo del conde?

Es perezoso.

**2.** ¿Qué hace todos los días?

No trabaja y no estudia. Sólo va a fiestas y quiere llevar ropa elegante.

**3.** ¿Qué piensa el padre?

Piensa que su hijo nunca va a hacer nada bueno.

**4.** Por fin, ¿qué hace el hijo?

Empieza a trabajar mucho y hace una casa con azulejos por dentro y por fuera.

# Conexión personal

If you were the son or daughter of a wealthy nobleman, how would you spend your time? List some things you would do in the space on the right.

ir al teatro

# Para leer   *Bomba y plena*

## Reading Strategy

**SCAN** Reading very quickly to get a specific piece of information, like a football score or a movie time, is called scanning. Scan the poster on page 47 and decide whether you could attend the festival if you had baseball practice on Saturday, October 16, at 2:00 P.M. Write down your answer below.

_____

_____

_____

## What You Need to Know

Puerto Rico has developed unique musical traditions reflecting the convergence of indigenous, African, and European cultures. Some instruments still used in Puerto Rican music are believed to have originated with the **taínos.** Most notable among these is the **güiro**, a hollow gourd with grooves carved into its surface used in the forms of Puerto Rican music and dance called **bomba** and **plena. Maracas,** percussive instruments originally made from the fruit of the **higuera** tree, also date to the **taínos** and are an important part of Caribbean **salsa** music. **Conga** drums, also used by salsa bands, trace their roots to African instruments made from hollow logs covered with animal skins. A stringed instrument adapted from the Spanish classical guitar, the four-stringed **cuatro** is unique to Puerto Rico and a central presence in a wide variety of traditional and contemporary Puerto Rican music.

This reading can also be found on pages 190–191 of the Level 1 Pupil Edition. The audio is on CD 7, Tracks 6–7.

**READING TIP** As you read, look at the photographs or illustrations to see if you can identify the instruments mentioned in the text.

**APUNTES**

_____

_____

_____

_____

**MÁRCALO GRAMÁTICA**
Find and underline each form of the verb **tener** that appears in the article. Then conjugate **tener** and **venir** below.

The word **tienen** in the first sentence and the word **tiene** in the last sentence should be underlined.
**tener:** tengo, tienes, tiene, tenemos, tienen
**venir:** vengo, vienes, viene, venimos, vienen

## A pensar...

The article refers to the musical traditions of three world cultures. What are they? What is their relation to the subject of the reading? **(Analyze)**

Sample answer: The article refers to the music of Puerto Rico, Africa, and Spain. The **bomba** and **plena** and the instruments used to accompany them represent a blending of these cultural influences.

# Bomba y plena

La bomba y la plena son danzas típicas de Puerto Rico. Tienen sus orígenes en la música africana. Los instrumentos originales para tocar esta música alegre son los **tambores,**
5 las **panderetas,** las maracas y el cuatro. El cuatro es un tipo de guitarra española pequeña, originalmente con cuatro **cuerdas.** Las personas que bailan estas danzas llevan ropa de muchos colores. La música tiene
10 mucho **ritmo** y las personas ¡mueven todo el **cuerpo**!

**PALABRAS CLAVE**
**el tambor**   drum
**la pandereta**   type of tambourine
**la cuerda**   string
**el ritmo**   rhythm
**el cuerpo**   body

# ¡TODOS A BAILAR!

## Concierto espectacular de
## BOMBA y PLENA
### ¡Músicos sensacionales!

Claudio de Mata: maracas

Rubén López: cuatro

Lucio Escobar: tamborín

¡Y la actuación especial de los bailarines
## Lilián y Alberto!

Sábado 16 de octubre
a las 5 de la tarde
en el Instituto de Cultura

**PALABRAS CLAVE**
el (la) músico(a)   *musician*
la actuación   *performance*
el (la) bailarín/bailarina   *dancer*

READER'S SUCCESS STRATEGY   While reading the poster for the concert, ask yourself the questions Who? What? When? Where? Look for the answers in the poster and write them down below.

| Who? | músicos, bailarines |
| What? | concierto de bomba y plena |
| When? | sábado 16 de octubre a las 5 de la tarde |
| Where? | el Instituto de Cultura |

**CHALLENGE**   What kind of music or dance do you like? Using the Venn diagram, compare this music or dance to **la bomba** and **la plena**. Where the circles are separate, write in differences. Where they intersect, write in similarities.

Bomba y plena

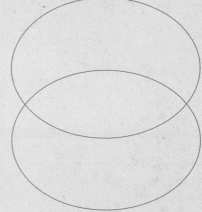

Other music/dance:

# Vocabulario de la lectura

**Palabras clave**

la **actuación**  *performance*

el (la) **bailarín/bailarina**  *dancer*

el **concierto**  *concert*

la **cuerda**  *string*

el **cuerpo**  *body*

el (la) **músico(a)**  *musician*

la **pandereta**  *type of tambourine*

el **ritmo**  *rhythm*

el **tambor**  *drum*

**A.** For each **Palabra clave** in the first column, find the phrase in the second column that is closest in meaning. Write the corresponding letter in the blank.

___C___ 1. cuerdas

___A___ 2. ritmo

___E___ 3. tambor

___B___ 4. bailarín

___D___ 5. músico

A. elemento de la música

B. persona que se dedica al baile

C. parte de una guitarra

D. persona que toca un instrumento

E. instrumento de percusión

**B.** Fill in each blank with the correct form of one of the **Palabras clave.** Then unscramble the boxed letters to complete the sentence below the puzzle.

1. Viernes, 11 de julio, hay un __c__ __o__ __n__ __c__ __i__ __e__ __r__ __t__ |o| de bomba y plena en el teatro.

2. La __a__ __c__ __t__ __u__ __a__ __c__ |i| __ó__ __n__ de los bailarines, Silvana y Jaime, va a ser fenomenal.

3. Los |m| __ú__ __s__ __i__ __c__ __o__ __s__ tocan las maracas y el cuatro.

4. También tocan la __p__ __a__ __n__ __d__ __e__ __r__ __e__ |t| __a__, un tipo de tamborín.

5. La bomba y la plena son danzas alegres, y las personas ¡mueven todo

   el __c__ __u__ __e__ |r| __p__ __o__!

   La música de bomba y plena tiene mucho __r__ __i__ __t__ __m__ __o__.

# ¿Comprendiste?

**1.** ¿Cuándo es el concierto?

El concierto es el sábado dieciséis de octubre, a las cinco de la tarde.

**2.** ¿En qué tienen sus orígenes la bomba y la plena?

Tienen sus orígenes en la música africana.

**3.** ¿Es una música triste o alegre?

Es una música alegre.

**4.** ¿Qué es el cuatro?

Es un tipo de guitarra española pequeña, originalmente con cuatro cuerdas.

**5.** ¿Qué otros instrumentos hay?

Hay tambores, panderetas y maracas.

**6.** ¿Qué ropa llevan las personas que bailan?

Llevan ropa de muchas colores.

# Conexión personal

Design your own poster in Spanish advertising a school event or a local cultural event, either real or imagined. Your goal is to try to entice people to attend the event. Be sure to include the name of the event, the names of any performers, and the date, time, and place.

# Para leer  *El coquí*

## Reading Strategy

**DISTINGUISH DETAILS** Find out what **coquíes** are. What features do they have? Use the word web to describe a **coquí** and name its identifying characteristics.

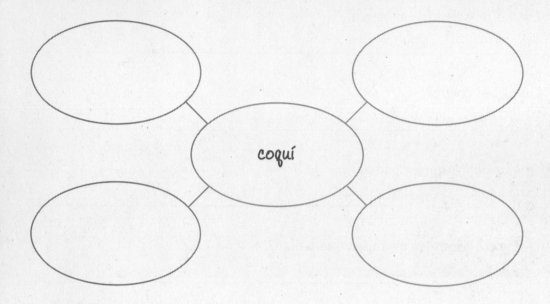

## What You Need to Know

The only rain forest in the U.S. National Forest Service is found on the island of Puerto Rico, in the **Sierra de Luquillo,** 25 miles from San Juan. Twenty-eight thousand acres in size, **El Bosque Nacional del Caribe,** commonly called **El Yunque,** is home to 240 species of trees and plants, some of which are found nowhere else in the world. The highly diverse wildlife of **El Yunque** includes 16 types of **coquíes**; 11 types of bats; and the Puerto Rican boa, a snake that can grow to over eight feet in length. Hunting is not allowed at El Yunque, which is a wildlife refuge and the habitat for eight endangered species, including the extremely rare **loro puertorriqueño,** or Puerto Rican Parrot.

This reading can also be found on pages 234–235 of the Level 1 Pupil Edition. The audio is on CD 9, Tracks 6–7.

# El coquí 🎧

No muy lejos de[1] San Juan está el Bosque Nacional del Caribe. En este bosque tropical, El Yunque, hay animales y plantas que no ves en ninguna otra parte[2] del mundo. El coquí, el animal más conocido de todo Puerto Rico, vive **protegido** en El Yunque.

[1] Not far from   [2] any other part

*El Yunque, el Bosque Nacional del Caribe*

**PALABRAS CLAVE**
**protegido(a)** *protected*

▥ **MÁRCALO** ▷ **VOCABULARIO**
Imagine that you are planning a trip to El Yunque. You know that the park's daytime temperature ranges from approximately 65°F to 78°F, it rains frequently, and at higher elevations visitors can swim in the pools. Make a list of clothing and accessories you should bring with you.

*Answers will vary. Sample answer: gorro, impermeable, shorts, traje de baño, bronceador, gafas de sol, paraguas*

**APUNTES**

READER'S
SUCCESS
STRATEGY  Make a list of facts
that you learned about the
**coquí** from reading this
article. For example: **Coquíes**
live in trees.

## A pensar...

Why do you think certain
species of the **coquí** are in
danger of becoming extinct?
(Cause and Effect)

*Answers will vary. Sample answer:*
*Some types of* **coquíes** *are*
*endangered because of*
*deforestation. When the natural*
*habitat of the* **coquí** *is destroyed,*
*their eggs are lost and their food*
*supply is diminished.*

**CHALLENGE**  Write a brief
paragraph about an animal of
your own choosing. Describe
the animal's appearance, say
where it is found, and discuss
what the weather is like in the
animal's habitat. (Extend)

*Answers will vary.*

El coquí es
una (rana) de
(tamaño)
10 pequeño
que vive en
los árboles.
Los coquíes
son de diferentes colores. Hay coquíes (grises,)
15 marrones, amarillos y verdes. Reciben su
nombre por su (canto) característico. Hay 16
(especies) de coquíes en Puerto Rico, pero sólo
dos producen el canto típico «coquí». Dos
están en (peligro) de extinción. Casi todos los
20 coquíes empiezan a cantar cuando llega la
noche.

Si visitas Puerto Rico, vas a ver imágenes del
coquí en muchos lugares — en nombres de
tiendas, artículos de promoción y libros. La
25 tradición puertorriqueña es que si ves un
coquí vas a tener mucha suerte. Y si quieres
tener un bonito recuerdo[3] de Puerto Rico es
posible comprar un
coquí verde de
juguete[4], símbolo
de la isla.

[3] souvenir        [4] toy

**PALABRAS CLAVE**
**la rana**   *frog*          **el canto**   *song*
**el tamaño**   *size*      **la especie**   *species*
**gris**   *grey*           **el peligro**   *danger*

# Vocabulario de la lectura

**Palabras clave**

| | | |
|---|---|---|
| **el árbol** *tree* | **gris** *grey* | **protegido(a)** *protected* |
| **el bosque** *forest* | **el peligro** *danger* | **la rana** *frog* |
| **el canto** *song* | **la planta** *plant* | **la extinción** *extinction* |
| **la especie** *species* | | |

**A.** Fill in the blanks with the most appropriate **Palabra clave.**
Use each word only once.

El Yunque es un ___bosque___ tropical de Puerto Rico. Aquí hay
　　　　　　　　(1)

___plantas___ que no ves en ninguna otra parte del mundo. El coquí,
　　(2)

una ___rana___ pequeña, vive ___protegido___ en los
　　　(3)　　　　　　　　　　　(4)

___árboles___ del parque. Los coquíes reciben su nombre por su
　　(5)

___canto___ típico «coquí». Hay coquíes marrones, amarillos, verdes y
　　(6)

___grises___ . Hay 16 ___especies___ de coquí en Puerto Rico,
　　(7)　　　　　　　　(8)

pero dos están en ___peligro___ de ___extinción___ .
　　　　　　　　　(9)　　　　　　(10)

**B.** What did you learn from the article about **El Yunque**? Use at least two of the
**Palabras clave** in your answer.

_____

_____

_____

_____

# ¿Comprendiste?

**1.** ¿Dónde vive el coquí?

Vive en El Yunque.

**2.** ¿Qué es el coquí? ¿Por qué se llama coquí?

El coquí es una rana. Recibe su nombre por su canto característico.

**3.** ¿Cómo es el coquí?

Es de tamaño pequeño. Hay coquíes grises, marrones, amarillos y verdes.

**4.** ¿Cuándo canta el coquí?

Canta cuando llega la noche.

**5.** ¿Por qué es bueno ver un coquí?

Los puertorriqueños piensan que si ves un coquí vas a tener mucha suerte.

# Conexión personal

Describe a national park or wilderness area that you have been to or that you would like to visit. What are its geographical characteristics? What is the weather like there? Why would you like to go to this place?

Me gustaría ir a Yosemite, un parque nacional de California...

# Para leer   *El bohique y los niños*

## Reading Strategy

**USING CONTEXT** You can use context to understand a word's meaning. Context includes what is written before and after the word. Write the words that help you understand what these words mean.

| Word | Context |
|------|---------|
| voz | |
| areito | |

## What You Need to Know

When Christopher Columbus arrived in Puerto Rico in 1493, the island was inhabited by **taínos. Taíno** villagers lived in round, straw huts **(bohíos)** arranged around a central plaza, where the village chief, or **cacique,** had his headquarters. The chief governed the village with the help of the **bohique,** a respected member of **taíno** society who acted as an oracle, or prophet. The **bohique** knew the medicinal properties of herbs and trees and was also considered to be a healer. Even before the arrival of the Spanish, the survival of the **taínos** had been threatened by the warlike Caribs, an indigenous people of South America. By the mid-1500s, however, the **taínos** had been virtually annihilated by the Europeans.

This reading can also be found on pages 218–219 of the Level 1a Pupil Edition. The audio is on the Bridge CD, Tracks 9–10.

## READING TIP
Remember the concept of false cognates, words that look alike in Spanish and English but have different meanings. Can you find the false cognate in line 2 of this reading? What English word does it look like?

The false cognate is **rato** (while), which resembles the English word rat.

The audio CD for this reading can be found in the Middle School Bridging Packet.

## A pensar...

**1.** Which sentence below is *not* true of the **bohique?** Cross it out. (Clarify)

He is a respected member of **taíno** society.

~~He relates his knowledge in writing.~~

He sings songs that tell stories.

He explains **taíno** history.

**2.** How are historical knowledge and cultural traditions passed down by the **taíno** people? (Summarize)

Sample answer: History and traditions are passed down orally from generation to generation.

# El bohique[1] y los niños

Hace sol[2] en las islas del Caribe. Unos niños taínos[3] pasan un buen rato en la **playa.** Enseñan a hablar a los **loros.** El bohique está en su casa. El bohique es una persona muy

5  importante. Es la persona que sabe toda la historia de su **pueblo.** Es la persona que comunica la historia a su pueblo. El bohique empieza[4] a contar[5] un areito. Un areito es una **canción,** leyenda o historia.

10  Cuando los niños escuchan la voz del bohique, uno dice[6]: —Vamos a ir a la casa del bohique. ¡Va a contar un areito! ¡Va a contar la historia de nuestra gente!

---

[1] storyteller [2] It's sunny [3] original inhabitants of Puerto Rico
[4] begins [5] to tell [6] says

**PALABRAS CLAVE**
**la playa** *beach*          **el pueblo** *people, civilization*
**el loro** *parrot*          **la canción** *song*

—¡Sí! —dicen todos los niños—. ¡Vamos a
15 escucharlo!

—¡Escuchen! Acaba de empezar el bohique.
Escucho los **tambores.**

—Y tocan las maracas también.

—¡Vamos a cantar con el bohique!

20 —A mí me gustan los areitos. Me gusta bailar
cuando canta el bohique.

—¡Escuchen! El bohique empieza a contar el
areito.

El bohique empieza: «Dicen que de las
25 primeras personas, los taínos, el sol crea todo
el mundo...»

Gracias al bohique que cuenta las historias,
los niños aprenden de la vida de su pueblo.

**PALABRAS CLAVE**
**el tambor** *drum*

READER'S
SUCCESS
STRATEGY As you have
learned, dashes are often
used in Spanish to indicate
dialog, or conversation. In
addition to dashes, this
selection also contains
Spanish quotation marks
(see lines 24 and 26),
which are used to set off
quoted material.

▌▌▌MÁRCALO ❯ GRAMÁTICA
You know how to use the verb
**gustar** with an infinitive to talk
about what a person likes to
do. In this reading, one of the
children uses a form of **gustar**
with the infinitive **bailar**. Find
this phrase and circle it. Then
write three similar sentences
using **gustar** with an infinitive
to tell three things that you like
to do.

*Answers will vary and should begin*
*with* Me gusta.

_____

_____

_____

_____

**CHALLENGE** Why do you
think the **taíno** children
enjoyed hearing the **bohique**
tell his stories through songs?
**(Draw Conclusions)**

*Answers will vary. Sample answer:*
*The songs were entertaining and*
*easy to remember.*

_____

_____

Unidad 3, Etapa 1
El bohique y los niños          **57**

# Vocabulario de la lectura

**Palabras clave**

**la canción** *song*      **la playa** *beach*      **el tambor** *drum*

**el loro** *parrot*      **el pueblo** *people, civilization*

**A.** For each **Palabra clave** in the first column, find the phrase in the second column that is closest in meaning. Write the corresponding letter in the blank.

___E___ 1. loro        A. una composición musical

___B___ 2. tambor      B. un instrumento musical

___D___ 3. playa       C. un grupo de personas que forma una comunidad

___A___ 4. canción     D. donde vas para nadar

___C___ 5. pueblo      E. un tipo de pájaro

**B.** Complete each sentence with the correct form of a **Palabra clave.**

1. Un areito es un tipo de ___canción___ taína.

2. El bohique sabe la historia de su ___pueblo___.

3. En las islas del Caribe hay muchas ___playas___.

4. Los niños taínos enseñan a hablar a los ___loros___.

5. Les gusta bailar cuando oyen los ___tambores___.

# ¿Comprendiste?

**1.** ¿Dónde están los niños taínos?

Están en la playa.

**2.** ¿Qué hacen?

Enseñan a hablar a los loros.

**3.** ¿Qué hace el bohique?

Comunica la historia a su pueblo.

**4.** ¿Qué aprenden los niños gracias al bohique?

Los niños aprenden de la vida de su pueblo.

# Conexión personal

Not all teachers are found in school. The children in the reading learn history from the **bohique.** Who are the important teachers in your life? In the boxes below, name two. Describe some things you have learned from each person. An example has been done.

| Abuela | | |
|---|---|---|
| Me dice la historia de nuestra familia También me enseña canciones. | | |

# Para leer   *Una leyenda taína*

## Reading Strategy

**SKIM** Skimming a reading before you begin can give you valuable information about what you are going to read. Skim this selection and write down what you learn by looking at these things.

| Look at | Learn |
|---|---|
| title | |
| pictures | |
| text | |

## What You Need to Know

When the Spanish explorers arrived in the New World, the **taínos** inhabited Cuba, Jamaica, Puerto Rico, and the island of Hispaniola, which is now Haiti and the Dominican Republic. Religion played a central role in **taíno** culture, and the **taínos** worshipped various gods and spirits. The **taínos** told many myths and legends, such as the one you are about to read, that explained the world around them. After visiting Hispaniola, Christopher Columbus commissioned a Spanish scholar to live with the **taínos** and record their myths. Many **taíno** myths and legends are still a part of Caribbean cultural tradition.

This reading can also be found on pages 270–271 of the Level 1a Pupil Edition. The audio is on the Bridge CD, Tracks 11–12.

# Una leyenda taína

**E**n las islas del Caribe los bohiques cuentan[1] una leyenda de la creación del mundo. Dicen[2] que de las primeras personas, los taínos, el sol crea todo el mundo.

5 Los taínos viven en **cuevas** en las montañas. En una de las cuevas vive un hombre que se llama Marocael. Marocael cuida la cueva de su gente.

Un día el sol le habla a Marocael: —Marocael,
10 Marocael, ¡te invito a mi casa!

Marocael está **aterrorizado** y contesta: —Muchas gracias, pero tengo que cuidar la cueva de mi gente.

El sol habla otra vez y dice:
15 —Por favor, vamos a pasar buen rato.

—No, muchas gracias —contesta Marocael—. Estoy muy contento en mi cueva.

[1] tell    [2] they say

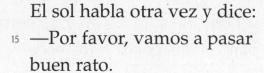

**PALABRAS CLAVE**
**la cueva** *cave*
**aterrorizado(a)** *terrified*

**READER'S SUCCESS STRATEGY** This legend is a myth, an ancient story that serves to explain the origin of natural things. As you read, try to imagine how the story evolved. To what questions does it provide answers?

The audio CD for this reading can be found in the Middle School Bridging Packet.

**MÁRCALO GRAMÁTICA**
Circle the direct object pronoun in the boxed sentence on this page and the next page. Then underline the noun that it is replacing.

On this page, students should circle **te** and underline **Marocael**. On the next page, students should circle **lo** and underline **Marocael**.

**CHALLENGE** What can historians learn about a previous civilization by studying its myths and legends? **(Extend)**

Answers will vary. Sample answer: Myths and legends can provide insight into a civilization's gods, religious beliefs, physical environment, and social structure.

READING TIP Remember the vocabulary you have already learned for animals, **pájaro** and **pez**.

APUNTES

_____

_____

_____

_____

_____

## A pensar...

**1.** Write the numbers 1, 2, 3, 4, and 5 to show the order in which the following things occur. **(Sequence of Events)**

_4_ The sun turns Marocael into a stone.

_3_ The sun becomes furious and takes Marocael away.

_2_ Marocael is terrified and prefers to stay in his cave.

_5_ The people of the cave become plants, birds, fish, and trees.

_1_ The sun invites Marocael to its house.

**2.** What does this legend indicate about the role of the sun in **taíno** culture? **(Infer)**

Answers will vary. Sample answer: The sun was regarded with fear and respect. It may have been considered a god or a supernatural power.

_____

_____

_____

20 Y Marocael empieza a regresar a su cueva cuando el sol, **furioso,** habla fuerte y dice: —¡Ahora vienes conmigo, Marocael!— Y el sol lleva a Marocael de la cueva a su casa.

Cuando la gente de la cueva se despierta[3],
25 busca a Marocael pero no lo encuentra[4]. El sol convierte a Marocael en una de las primeras **piedras** de la **tierra.** Y cuando la gente sale[5] de la cueva, el sol convierte a cada uno de ellos en algo diferente. Así de la primera gente, el
30 sol crea no sólo las piedras pero también las plantas, los pájaros, los peces y los árboles.

[3] wake up    [4] find    [5] go out

**PALABRAS CLAVE**
**furioso(a)** _furious_          **la tierra** _earth_
**la piedra** _stone_

_¡En español!_ **Level 1**

# Vocabulario de la lectura

**Palabras clave**

| | | | | | |
|---|---|---|---|---|---|
| **el árbol** | *tree* | **furioso(a)** | *furious* | **el sol** | *sun* |
| **aterrorizado(a)** | *terrified* | **la piedra** | *stone* | **la tierra** | *earth* |
| **la cueva** | *cave* | **la planta** | *plant* | | |

**A.** For each **Palabra clave** in the first column, find the phrase in the second column that is closest in meaning. Write the corresponding letter in the blank.

____D____ 1. sol

____C____ 2. cueva

____A____ 3. furioso

____E____ 4. planta

____B____ 5. árbol

A. Significa «enojado».

B. Es marrón y verde y más alto que una planta.

C. Es donde vive Marocael.

D. Es grande y amarillo.

E. Una flor es una...

**B.** Complete each sentence with the correct form of a **Palabra clave.**

Marocael está _____aterrorizado_____ cuando el sol lo invita a su casa. Dice que está
             (1)

muy contento en su _____cueva_____ . Furioso, el sol convierte a Marocael
             (2)

en una _____piedra_____ . De las otras personas, el sol crea las
     (3)

_____plantas_____ , los _____árboles_____ , los pájaros y los peces.
  (4)           (5)

# ¿Comprendiste?

**1.** ¿Dónde tiene lugar *(take place)* la leyenda?

Tiene lugar en una isla del Caribe.

**2.** Según la leyenda, ¿dónde viven los taínos?

Los taínos viven en cuevas.

**3.** ¿Quién cuida la cueva?

Marocael cuida la cueva.

**4.** ¿Qué le dice el sol al señor?

Dice: —¡Te invito a mi casa!

**5.** ¿Qué hace el sol con el señor?

El sol lo convierte en una de las primeras piedras de la tierra.

# Conexión personal

The sun played an important role in the life of the **taínos.** How does the sun play a part in your life? Using vocabulary you have learned to describe the weather, name some things you like to do when it's sunny outside.

Cuando hace sol, me gusta...

# Para leer    *¡Visita Oaxaca! Un paseo a pie*

## Reading Strategy

**COMBINE STRATEGIES** Put together the reading strategies you have practiced.

1. Look at the title, photos, and graphics to predict the reading's theme.

2. Skim the reading to get a general idea of the content.

3. Use context clues to help you make intelligent guesses about new words.

These steps make it easier for you to read Spanish.

| Predict | Theme: |
|---|---|
| Skim | General Idea: |
| Use context clues | New Words: |

## What You Need to Know

The city of Oaxaca, in southern Mexico, was founded by Aztec warriors in 1485 and taken over by the Spaniards in 1521. The majority of Oaxaca's present-day population is of Zapotec or Mixtec heritage, and many city residents speak an indigenous language as well as Spanish. Located near some of Mexico's most important archaeological sites, Oaxaca is also known for its examples of European colonial architecture. Of additional interest to travelers are the woodcarvings, textiles, and pottery of local artisans, and Oaxaca's cuisine. **Chapulines**, or fried grasshoppers, are a popular Oaxacan dish available in the city's restaurants and **mercados**. Many types of **mole**, spicy sauces often made with chocolate, also originated in Oaxaca.

# ¡VISITA OAXACA! UN PASEO¹ A PIE

La ciudad de Oaxaca es un monumento histórico nacional. Hay **arquitectura** colonial, iglesias y museos muy importantes. Para verla mejor tienes que conocer Oaxaca a pie.

5 **❶** <u>Empieza</u> en el Zócalo, el centro de Oaxaca. Es el lugar ideal para ver a los **oaxaqueños**. Hay muchos cafés y restaurantes aquí.

¹walk

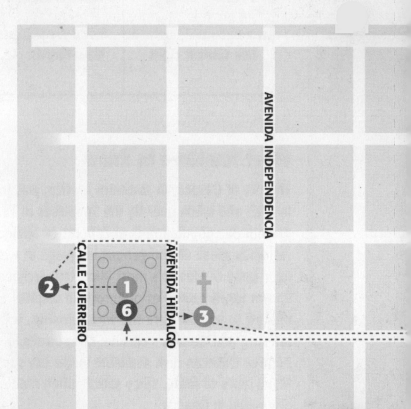

**PALABRAS CLAVE**
  **la arquitectura** *architecture*
  **oaxaqueño(a)** n., adj. *Oaxacan*

10 **2** Ahora <u>cruza</u> la calle Guerrero y <u>entra</u> en el Palacio de Gobierno[2]. <u>Mira</u> el mural sobre la historia y la cultura

15 de Oaxaca.

**3** Al salir del Palacio, <u>camina</u> hasta llegar a la avenida Hidalgo. Cruza la avenida para

20 ver la catedral. A veces hay conciertos aquí.

[2] Government Palace, State Capitol

CALLE NICOLÁS BRAVO

CALLE IGNACIO ALLENDE

CALLE GARCÍA VIGIL

CALLE MACEDONIO ALCALÁ

APUNTES

## A pensar...

**1.** Based on what you know from the article, which of the following can be found in Oaxaca? Check four. **(Summarize)**

☐ aeropuerto

☑ palacio

☑ centro

☐ metro

☑ iglesias

☑ museos

**2.** Reread the boxed paragraph. What is Monte Albán? How do you know? **(Infer)**

*Answers will vary. Sample answer: Monte Albán is an archaeological site near Oaxaca. There are artifacts from Monte Albán in a museum in Oaxaca that contains other objects from the area's early cultures.*

**CHALLENGE** You and your family are on vacation in Oaxaca. Choose a place that you would like to visit, and try to persuade a family member to accompany you. **(Convince)**

*Reasons to visit_____:*

1.

2.

3.

❹ Detrás de la catedral está la avenida Independencia. <u>Sigue</u>
25 por la avenida y <u>dobla</u> a la izquierda en la calle Macedonio Alcalá.

Allí hay unas tiendas excelentes y varias casas coloniales. <u>Sigue</u> derecho cuatro cuadras
30 para ver la iglesia de Santo Domingo. <u>Mira</u> el interior.

❺ Al lado de la iglesia queda el Museo Regional de Oaxaca. En el museo hay objetos
35 **arqueológicos** de Monte Albán. También hay ropa, artículos textiles y otros artículos de las primeras culturas de la región.

❻ <u>Regresa</u> al Zócalo.
40 Si hace buen tiempo, hay conciertos aquí a las siete de la tarde. ¿Tienes hambre? Entonces, <u>cena</u> en uno
45 de los restaurantes oaxaqueños. ¡<u>Come</u> algo típico y <u>pasa</u> un rato con tus amigos!

**PALABRAS CLAVE**
**arqueológico(a)** *archaeological*

# Vocabulario de la lectura

**Palabras clave**

**a pie**  *on foot*

**arqueológico(a)**  *archaeological*

**la arquitectura**  *architecture*

**el café**  *restaurant*

**la calle**  *street*

**cruzar**  *to cross*

**la cuadra**  *block*

**derecho**  *straight ahead*

**doblar**  *to turn*

**la iglesia**  *church*

**oaxaqueño(a)** n., adj.  *Oaxacan*

**quedar (en)**  *to be (in a specific place)*

**A.** Complete the following dialog with the correct **Palabras clave.**

**Turista:**  Perdona, ¿puedes decirme dónde ___queda___ el Palacio
de Gobierno? (1)

**Oaxaqueño:**  ¡Cómo no! Sigue por la calle Macedonio Alcalá y

___dobla___ a la derecha en la calle Guerrero. (2)

___Cruza___ la calle para ver el palacio. (3)

**Turista:**  ¿Queda lejos? No tengo carro. Voy ___a pie___. (4)

**Oaxaqueño:**  No queda lejos. Está a solamente tres ___cuadras___ de aquí. (5)

**Turista:**  ¡Tengo hambre! ¿Hay un ___café___ cerca del palacio? (6)

**Oaxaqueño:**  Al salir del palacio, cruza la ___calle___ Guerrero y sigue (7)

___derecho___ para llegar al Zócalo. Allí hay unos cafés (8)
excelentes.

**B.** Fill in each blank with the correct form of a **Palabra clave.**

1. En Oaxaca hay mucha ___arquitectura___ colonial.

2. La ___iglesia___ de Santo Domingo es un ejemplo de arquitectura europea.

3. En el Museo Regional de Oaxaca, puedes ver objetos ___arqueológicos___ de
Monte Albán.

4. Si quieres comida típica, regresa al Zócalo y cena en un restaurante

___oaxaqueño___.

# ¿Comprendiste?

**1.** ¿Dónde empieza el paseo?

El paseo empieza en el Zócalo, el centro de Oaxaca.

**2.** ¿Dónde ves un mural sobre la historia y la cultura de Oaxaca?

Ves un mural sobre la historia y la cultura de Oaxaca en el Palacio de Gobierno.

**3.** ¿Dónde está la catedral?

La catedral está en la avenida Hidalgo.

**4.** ¿Qué hay en la calle Macedonio Alcalá?

En la calle Macedonio Alcalá hay unas tiendas excelentes y varias casas coloniales.

**5.** ¿Dónde está el Museo Regional de Oaxaca?

El Museo Regional de Oaxaca está al lado de la iglesia de Santo Domingo.

# Conexión personal

On the grid below, draw a simple map of your neighborhood or local area. Use the symbols in the key to identify places and landmarks. If you need additional symbols, create your own and add them to the key.

| REFERENCIAS | | | |
|---|---|---|---|
| 🏠 casa o apartamentos | 🏫 escuela | ═══ calle | 📖 biblioteca |
| ✉ correo | 🏷 tienda | 🌳 parque | |

# Para leer    *Andrés, joven aprendiz de alfarero*

## Reading Strategy

**GATHER AND SORT INFORMATION AS YOU READ** Do you and your friends have jobs after school or on weekends? Fill out this chart about jobs by interviewing two people. Then use this chart to gather information about Andrés as you read.

| Preguntas | Persona | | Andrés |
|---|---|---|---|
| | **1** | **2** | |
| ¿Dónde trabajas? | | | |
| ¿Cuándo? | | | |
| ¿Qué haces? | | | |
| ¿Trabajas en algo que te puede servir en el futuro? | | | |

## What You Need to Know

The distinctive black pottery found in markets and stores throughout Mexico originated in the town of San Bartolo Coyotepec, south of the city of Oaxaca, where in 1953 a woman named doña Rosa discovered a method of firing clay that made it black. The pottery previously produced in the area had been a light grayish brown color. After the pottery was fired, doña Rosa rubbed it with quartz to give it a metallic sheen. Some of doña Rosa's original pieces may be seen at the **Museo del Barro Negro de Coyotepec.** The family of doña Rosa still produces black pottery using her techniques.

READING TIP Look at the ¿Comprendiste? questions before you begin the article. Then read the selection with these questions in mind.

APUNTES

Which of the following might you find for sale at **Alfarería Doña Rosa**? Check five.

- ☑ jarras
- ☐ joyas de plata
- ☑ platos
- ☑ cerámica
- ☐ botas
- ☑ artesanías
- ☐ artículos de cuero
- ☑ ollas

**CHALLENGE** What has changed over the years about the pottery business first started by doña Rosa? What has stayed the same? Underline passages in the text to support your answer. **(Compare and Contrast)**

*Answers will vary. Sample answer: The pottery is still made using doña Rosa's original methods. The business has grown in size; today, ceramics from San Bartolo Coyotepec are sold throughout Mexico.*

ALFARERIA DOÑA ROSA

This reading can also be found on pages 308–309 of the Level 1 Pupil Edition. The audio is on CD 12, Tracks 6–7.

# Andrés, joven aprendiz de alfarero

¡Hola! Me llamo Andrés Real. Vivo en San Bartolo Coyotepec, un pueblo cerca de la ciudad de Oaxaca. *Coyotepec* significa [1] «montaña de los coyotes». La verdad es que
5 ya no hay muchos de estos animales. Mi pueblo no es muy grande, pero es muy famoso. La cerámica negra que ves en tiendas y mercados por todo México es de aquí. Si algún día ves una olla de **barro** negro
10 que parece [2] metal, probablemente es de San Bartolo Coyotepec.

[1] means     [2] that looks like

**PALABRAS CLAVE**
**el alfarero** *potter*
**el barro** *clay*

*¡En español!* Level 1

READER'S
SUCCESS
STRATEGY   Be aware of time
jumps in the article. Use a
chart like the one below to
keep track of the current
action of the reading and the
events that occurred at an
earlier time.

| Past Events | Current Action |
|---|---|
| Doña Rosa hace la cerámica negra. | Andrés es estudiante de alfarero. |

La **Alfarería** *Doña Rosa* es donde yo trabajo después de salir de la escuela. En la alfarería hacemos la cerámica de barro. Esta alfarería se
15 llama *Doña Rosa* en honor a mi abuela doña Rosa Valente Nieto de Real. Ella inventó[3] este tipo de cerámica. Mi abuela murió[4] en 1979, pero mi familia todavía[5] usa su método para hacer la cerámica.

20 Yo soy aprendiz, o estudiante, de alfarero. Mi papá, mi mamá y mis tíos me enseñan este arte. No hago ollas grandes pero hago animalitos, como coyotes. Mis **animalitos** no siempre salen bien porque estoy aprendiendo.
25 Como mi abuela, algún día voy a vender los artículos de barro negro de Coyotepec por todo el mundo.

[3]invented    [4]died    [5]still

**PALABRAS CLAVE**
la alfarería   *pottery-making
factory; ceramics shop*

el animalito   *small animal*

## A pensar...

1. Write the numbers 1, 2, and 3 to show the order in which the following events occurred. **(Sequence of Events)**

   3  Andrés hace animalitos en la alfarería.

   2  Los padres de Andrés aprenden el arte de hacer artesanías de barro negro.

   1  Doña Rosa inventó la cerámica negra que parece metal.

2. Do you think the tradition of making pottery using the techniques of doña Rosa will continue to be maintained by future generations of her family? Why or why not? **(Predict)**

   *Answers will vary. Sample answer: Yes, because the business started by doña Rosa has become very successful.*

# Vocabulario de la lectura

**Palabras clave**

**la alfarería**   *pottery-making factory; ceramics shop*
**el alfarero**   *potter*
**alguno(a)**   *some*

**el animalito**   *small animal*
**el barro**   *clay*
**el pueblo**   *town, village*

**A.** For each **Palabra clave** in the first column, find the sentence in the second column that best describes it. Write the corresponding letter in the blank.

___C___ 1. animalitos

___A___ 2. barro

___D___ 3. alfarero

___E___ 4. alguno

___B___ 5. alfarería

A. Lo usas para hacer la cerámica.

B. Hacen ollas de barro aquí.

C. Son animales pequeños.

D. Es una persona que hace la cerámica.

E. **Algún** es una forma abreviada de esta palabra.

**B.** Fill in each set of blanks with the correct form of a **Palabra clave.**
Then unscramble the boxed letters to complete the sentence below.

1. Andrés Real es aprendiz, o estudiante, de   a  l  f  a  r  e  r  o .

2. No hace ollas grandes; hace   a  n  i  m  a  l  i  t  o  s ,
   como coyotes.

3. Andrés vive en el   p  u  e  b  l  o   de San Bartolo Coyotepec.

4. Después de la escuela, Andrés trabaja en la

   A  l  f  a  r  e  r  í  a   Doña Rosa.

5.  A  l  g  ú  n   día, Andrés quiere vender artículos de barro negro,
   como su abuela.

San Bartolo Coyotepec es famoso por la cerámica   n  e  g  r  a .

# ¿Comprendiste?

**1.** ¿Dónde vive Andrés?

Andrés vive en el pueblo de San Bartolo Coyotepec.

**2.** ¿Por qué es famoso su pueblo?

Su pueblo es famoso por la cerámica negra.

**3.** ¿Quién es su abuela? ¿Por qué es famosa?

Su abuela es doña Rosa Valente Nieto de Real. Es famosa porque ella inventó un método para

hacer la cerámica de barro negro.

**4.** ¿Qué hace Andrés en la alfarería?

En su trabajo, Andrés aprende a hacer la cerámica. Hace animalitos.

**5.** ¿Qué quiere hacer Andrés algún día?

Algún día va a vender los artículos de barro negro de Coyotepec por todo el mundo.

# Conexión personal

Have you ever had an after-school or weekend job that you enjoyed?
What kind of work have you liked least? In the chart below list jobs you
have liked and disliked. Explain why you feel the way you do.

| Trabajo que me gusta | Me gusta porque... |
|---|---|
| ser mesero(a) en un restaurante | es buen ejercicio. |
|  |  |
| **Trabajo que no me gusta** | **No me gusta porque...** |
|  |  |
|  |  |

# Para leer

*Benito Juárez;
un oaxaqueño por excelencia*

## Reading Strategy

**RECOGNIZING SEQUENCE** Charts can help you remember the events of a story in the order they happen. For example, when you read a biography, you can list the events in the person's life chronologically. As you read this selection complete a chart like the one below.

| Benito Juárez | |
| --- | --- |
| **Event** | **Stage in Life** |
| loses parents | 3 years old |
| worked as a shepherd | a boy |
| | |
| | |
| | |

## What You Need to Know

Benito Juárez (1806–1872) was one of Mexico's great political leaders. He fought for the rights of indigenous communities, organized education reform, and issued laws that separated church and state. He was elected governor of the state of Oaxaca in 1847 and president of Mexico in 1861. Born to a poor Zapotec family, Juárez left his native village of San Pablo Guelatao at age 12 and traveled alone to the city of Oaxaca, where he hoped to acquire an education. There he met Antonio Salanueva, a scholar and theologian who made Juárez his godson and sent him to school. Juárez studied at the local seminary in Oaxaca and later attended law school. As a lawyer and throughout his political career he defended the rights of the poor.

This reading can also be found on pages 104–105 of the Level 1b Pupil Edition. The audio is on the Bridge CD, Tracks 31–32.

# Benito Juárez,

## *un oaxaqueño por excelencia* 🎧

**E**n 1806 (mil ochocientos seis), en un pueblo del **estado** de Oaxaca, nace[1] un niño. Se llama Benito. Cuando Benito tiene sólo tres años, su mamá y su papá se mueren[2]. Un tío lleva

5 a Benito a vivir a su casa, pero Benito tiene

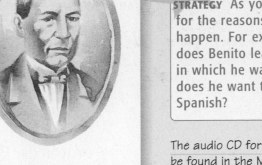

que trabajar porque la familia es **pobre.** El tío le <u>dice</u>: —Benito, tienes

10 que cuidar a los corderitos[3] en la montaña.

---

[1] is born  [2] die  [3] young sheep

**PALABRAS CLAVE**

**el (la) oaxaqueño(a)** *Oaxacan*  **pobre** *poor*
**el estado** *state*

---

**READER'S SUCCESS STRATEGY** As you read, look for the reasons why things happen. For example, why does Benito leave the village in which he was born? Why does he want to learn Spanish?

The audio CD for this reading can be found in the Middle School Bridging Packet.

📏 **MÁRCALO** ▷ **GRAMÁTICA**
Find and underline the form of **decir** that is used in the article. Then conjugate the verb **decir** in the space below.

*Students should underline **dice**.*
**decir: digo, dices, dice, decimos, dicen**

**READING TIP** Like the U.S., Mexico is divided into states. Look at a map that shows the 31 Mexican states. Identify Oaxaca, the state in which Benito Juárez was born.

**CHALLENGE** In Mexico, Benito Juárez is a national hero. What makes someone a hero? Who are some national heroes of the United States or of other countries? (**Make Judgments**)

*Answers will vary.*

## A pensar...

**1.** In the list below, mark a "T" beside each true statement and an "F" beside each false one. **(Main Idea and Details)**

_F_ Benito came from a wealthy family.

_T_ Orphaned at age three, Benito went to live with his uncle.

_T_ Benito's native language was Zapotec.

_F_ Benito spoke Spanish all his life.

_T_ After serving as governor of Oaxaca, Benito became president of Mexico.

**2.** How did Antonio Salanueva help Benito? **(Summarize)**

_Sample answer:_ Mr. Salanueva taught Benito to speak, read, and write Spanish. Previously, Benito had spoken only Zapotec, his native language.

**3.** How do you think Benito's childhood influenced his decision to work for the rights of the poor? **(Cause and Effect)**

_Answers will vary. Sample answer:_ Benito spent much of his childhood living and working in a poor Mexican village. He understood from personal experience the difficulties faced by Mexico's indigenous communities.

Y entonces, Benito trabaja todos los días de **pastorcito.** Un día, decide salir del pueblo
15 porque quiere una vida mejor. Llega a la capital y conoce a un buen hombre, Antonio Salanueva. El señor Salanueva le enseña a Benito a hablar español (antes, sólo hablaba zapoteco, el **idioma** nativo regional).
20 El señor Salanueva también le enseña a leer y a escribir. Después de muchos años de estudio, llega
25 a ser **abogado.** Se dedica a ayudar a la gente pobre.

Los mexicanos conocen a Benito como un hombre bueno, serio y muy trabajador y ¡lo
30 quieren para **gobernador** del estado! Trabaja mucho e, increíblemente, llega a ser presidente de toda la República Mexicana.

¡Así es que el humilde Benito va de pastorcito a presidente!

**PALABRAS CLAVE**
el pastorcito *shepherd boy*
el idioma *language*
el (la) abogado(a) *lawyer*
el (la) gobernador(a) *governor*

# Vocabulario de la lectura

**Palabras clave**

el (la) abogado(a)   *lawyer*
decir   *to say, to tell*
el estado   *state*
el (la) gobernador(a)   *governor*
el idioma   *language*

el (la) oaxaqueño(a)   *Oaxacan*
el pastorcito   *shepherd boy*
pobre   *poor*
salir   *to go out, to leave*

**A.** For each **Palabra clave** in the first column, find the sentence in the second column that best describes it. Write the corresponding letter in the blank.

___D___ 1. estado

___C___ 2. idiomas

___E___ 3. pobre

___A___ 4. abogado(a)

___B___ 5. oaxaqueño

A. Es una persona que sabe de cuestiones legales.

B. Un hombre de Oaxaca es un...

C. El español y el inglés son dos.

D. Oaxaca es el nombre de una ciudad y un...

E. Se refiere a una persona que tiene poco dinero.

**B.** Complete each sentence with a **Palabra clave**.
Use the correct form of the verbs.

Benito Juárez es un niño pobre de un pueblo del ____estado____ de Oaxaca.
(1)

Trabaja todos los días de ____pastorcito____ y quiere una vida mejor. Un día,
(2)

decide ____salir____ de su pueblo a pie para la ciudad. Allí conoce a un
(3)

buen hombre, el señor Salanueva, que le ____dice____ a Benito que le
(4)

enseñe a hablar español. Benito estudia mucho. Primero, llega a ser

____abogado____, luego ____gobernador____ de Oaxaca, y por fin, presidente
(5)                          (6)

de México.

# ¿Comprendiste?

**1.** ¿De dónde es Benito?

Es de un pueblo del estado de Oaxaca.

**2.** ¿De qué trabaja de niño?

Trabaja de pastor.

**3.** ¿Cuál es su profesión de adulto?

Es abogado.

**4.** ¿Qué idiomas habla?

Habla español y zapoteco.

**5.** ¿Qué llega a ser?

Llega a ser presidente de México.

# Conexión personal

Benito Juárez overcame many obstacles to realize his dreams. What goals or dreams do you have for yourself, your community, or your country? List one important goal, and name something you would have to do in order to make it a reality.

Me gustaría ayudar a los niños de

mi comunidad que no hablan inglés...

# Para leer
## Una leyenda oaxaqueña: El fuego y el tlacuache

## Reading Strategy

**MAKING A STORY MAP** To help you remember characters and events in a story, use a story map like the one below. This will help you organize the main ideas in this legend.

| Characters: | | |
|---|---|---|
| 1. _mujer vieja_ | 2. _____ | 3. _____ |
| **Problem:** Los vecinos quieren... | | |
| **Solution:** El tlacuache... | | |

## What You Need to Know

The Sierra Mazateca, located in northern Oaxaca state, is a beautiful part of Mexico with tall mountain peaks, deep valleys, waterfalls, and lush vegetation including orchids and many other colorful flowers. The **mazatecas**, an indigenous group who make their living mainly by farming and weaving, occupy the Sierra Mazateca region of Oaxaca and parts of the neighboring states of Guerrero and Veracruz. Animals have long played important roles in **mazateca** rites and beliefs. Many **mazateca** textiles are decorated with animal figures. The following legend about an opossum is part of **mazateca** folklore.

**▥ MÁRCALO ⟩ GRAMÁTICA**
Find and underline the verb **pedir** in the legend. Remember that it is an **e→i** stem-changing verb. Then conjugate **pedir** in the space below.

Pedir: pido, pides, pide, pedimos, piden

**CHALLENGE** In groups, pretend you are characters in the legend. Prepare a version of the action and present it to the class. **(Extend)**

Presentations will vary.

# Una leyenda oaxaqueña

## El fuego y el tlacuache[1]

La gente mazateca, que vive en la región norte de Oaxaca, les cuenta esta leyenda a sus hijos.

Una noche una mujer vieja atrapa la lumbre[2]
5  al caerse de una **estrella.** Todos sus **vecinos** van a la casa de la vieja a <u>pedir</u> lumbre. Pero la vieja no quiere darle lumbre a la gente.

En ese momento,
llega un tlacuache
10  y les dice
a los vecinos:
—Yo, tlacuache,
voy a darles la
lumbre si ustedes
15  prometen no
comerme.

Todos se ríen[3] cuando oyen las palabras del tlacuache. Pero el tlacuache les repite que él sí va a compartir la lumbre con
20  todo el mundo.

---

[1] opossum      [2] fire, light      [3] laugh

**PALABRAS CLAVE**
el fuego   *fire*                    el (la) vecino(a)   *neighbor*
la estrella   *star*

READING TIP **Tlacuache** is a word from the indigenous language of the **mazatecas**. Listen to the audio to see how it is pronounced.

APUNTES

Entonces, el tlacuache va a la casa de la vieja y le dice: —Buenas tardes, señora Lumbre, ¡qué frío hace! Si me permite, quiero estar un rato al lado de la lumbre para calentarme[4].

25 La vieja le permite al tlacuache acercarse[5] a la lumbre porque sabe que sí hace un frío terrible. En ese momento el animalito avanza y pone la **cola** en la lumbre. Entonces, sale rápidamente de la casa y les da la lumbre
30 a todas las casas de la región.

Es por eso que hasta ahora los tlacuaches tienen la cola **pelada**.

[4] warm myself    [5] approach

**PALABRAS CLAVE**
**la cola** *tail*              **pelado(a)** *hairless*

## A pensar...

**1.** Write the numbers 1, 2, 3, 4, 5, and 6 to show the order in which the events below occurred. **(Sequence of Events)**

__5__ The opossum puts his tail in the light.

__2__ The woman's neighbors ask her for light, but she will not give them any.

__1__ A woman traps the light coming from a star.

__6__ The opossum gives light from his tail to all the neighbors.

__3__ The opossum asks the woman if he can come in and get warm.

__4__ The woman lets the opossum come in.

**2.** Check the phrase that best completes the following sentence. **(Main Idea)** This legend explains why...

☐ stars shine at night.

☐ the climate is cool in northern Oaxaca.

☑ the opossum has a hairless tail.

☐ the opossum is a generous animal.

# Vocabulario de la lectura

**Palabras clave**

| | | |
|---|---|---|
| **la cola** *tail* | **el fuego** *fire* | **pelado(a)** *hairless* |
| **la estrella** *star* | **pedir** *to ask for* | **el (la) vecino(a)** *neighbor* |

**A.** For each **Palabra clave** in the first column, find the sentence in the second column that best describes it. Write the corresponding letter in the blank.

<u> B </u> 1. estrellas       A. Es alguien que vive cerca.

<u> A </u> 2. vecino(a)       B. Las ves por la noche.

<u> E </u> 3. colas       C. Se refiere a algo que no tiene pelo.

<u> C </u> 4. pelado(a)       D. Es muy caliente.

<u> D </u> 5. fuego       E. Los perros y los gatos las tienen.

**B.** Write two sentences about the legend using two or more of the **Palabras clave.**

_____

_____

_____

_____

_____

_____

_____

_____

_____

# ¿Comprendiste?

**1.** ¿Quién atrapa la lumbre?

Una mujer vieja la atrapa.

**2.** ¿Quiere darle la lumbre a alguien?

No, no quiere darle la lumbre a nadie.

**3.** ¿Qué les dice el tlacuache a los vecinos?

El tlacuache les dice que va a traer la lumbre, pero sólo si la gente no lo come.

**4.** ¿Cómo puede el tlacuache entrar a la casa de la vieja? ¿Qué le dice a ella?

Le dice que tiene mucho frío y que quiere calentarse al lado de la lumbre.

**5.** ¿Cómo es que la gente recibe el fuego?

El tlacuache pone la cola en la lumbre y sale de la casa. Le da la lumbre a la gente.

# Conexión personal

Have you ever wondered why some animals look the way they do? Make a list of animals and their physical characteristics that could be the subject of a legend explaining their appearance.

| Animales | Características |
|----------|----------------|
| tigre    | rayas          |
|          |                |
|          |                |
|          |                |
|          |                |
|          |                |
|          |                |
|          |                |

# Para leer    *Una exhibición especial de Picasso*

## Reading Strategy

**SCAN FOR CRUCIAL DETAILS** Before you decide to visit the exhibit "Picasso y los retratos" there is some practical information you need to know. Look quickly to pick up certain details. Can you find the answers in the article? If so, write them in below.

| ¿En qué museo está la exhibición? | ¿Cuándo termina? |
| --- | --- |
| | |

## What You Need to Know

**El Museo Picasso** occupies five medieval palaces in Barcelona's Gothic Quarter. It contains works from all of Picasso's periods but is best known for its collection of paintings and drawings completed during the artist's early years when he was living in Barcelona. Born in Málaga, Spain, in 1881, Pablo Picasso was painting by the age of fourteen. He worked in a wide range of styles, and over time his art became increasingly abstract. Among his favorite subjects were musical instruments, still-life objects, and people. In 1904 Picasso moved to France, where he remained until his death in 1973.

This reading can also be found on pages 338–339 of the Level 1 Pupil Edition. The audio is on CD 13, Tracks 6–7.

# Una exhibición especial de Picasso

Si te levantas el sábado y tienes ganas de ir a un museo, hay una **exhibición** especial en el Museo Picasso de Barcelona. Es una colección de **retratos** de Pablo Picasso. La exhibición se
5 llama «Picasso y los retratos». Es posible verla hasta el 31 de julio.

Las **pinturas** de la exhibición «Picasso y los retratos» son de varios **estilos.** En algunos retratos, por ejemplo *Retrato de Jaime Sabatés,*
10 usa un estilo **tradicional.** En otros retratos vemos el desarrollo[1] de la pintura **moderna** en la composición de las partes del cuerpo: la cara, las orejas, los brazos y las piernas. Un ejemplo es *Maya con una muñeca.*

---
[1] development

**PALABRAS CLAVE**
la exhibición   *exhibit*
el retrato   *portrait*
la pintura   *painting*

el estilo   *style*
tradicional   *traditional*
moderno(a)   *modern*

---

**READING TIP** Remember to look for cognates, words that look alike in English and Spanish and have similar meanings. What cognates can you find in **Una exhibición especial de Picasso?** Underline them in the text.

*Answers may include* **exhibición, especial, museo, colección, posible, julio, varios, estilos, tradicional, moderna, composición, partes, ejemplo, idea, privada, importantes, visita, pintor.**

**▌▌▌ MÁRCALO ⟩ VOCABULARIO**
You have just learned vocabulary for parts of the body. How many words for parts of the body do you recognize in the boxed text? Find and underline each one.

*Students should underline* **cara, orejas, brazos** *and* **piernas.**

## A pensar...

1. Check three items in the list below that describe what you can see at the exhibit **"Picasso y los retratos."** (Summarize)

   ☑ portraits of Picasso's friends
   ☐ landscapes by Picasso
   ☐ photographs
   ☑ traditional works
   ☑ modern painting

2. What can we learn about Picasso's life from the subjects he chose for his portraits? (Clarify)

   *Sample answer: We can learn about some of the people who were important to Picasso, because he did many portraits of friends and family.*

READER'S
SUCCESS
STRATEGY Compare and
contrast the two portraits by
Picasso. Use the Venn
diagram to organize your
ideas. Where the circles are
separate, write in differences.
Where they intersect, write in
similarities.

**Retrato de Jaime Sabatés**

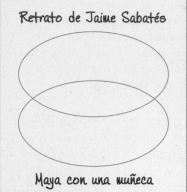

**Maya con una muñeca**

APUNTES

CHALLENGE What makes
*Maya con una muñeca* an
example of what the article
calls modern painting?
(Evaluate)

*Answers will vary. Sample answer:
Many elements of the picture are
not realistically represented. The
parts of the body of the girl and
doll are isolated and geometric.
Instead of using a natural
perspective, Picasso has
portrayed the image on flat
surfaces, or planes.*

Retrato de Jaime Sabatés, *1899–1900*
*Un retrato de Jaime Sabatés, gran
amigo de Picasso. Sabatés le dio⁴ su
colección de* **obras** *de Picasso al museo.*

Maya con una muñeca, *1938*

15 Los retratos de Picasso también nos dan una
idea de su vida privada. Hay retratos de sus
amigos, sus hijos y las mujeres importantes
en su vida.

Si vas a la exhibición, aprovecha² tu visita
20 para ver otras obras de este **pintor** español
en nuestro Museo Picasso. ¡Hay más de
tres mil³!

---

²take advantage of       ³thousand       ⁴gave

**PALABRAS CLAVE**
   **el (la) pintor(a)**  *painter*          **la obra**  *work*

*¡En español!* Level 1

# Vocabulario de la lectura

**Palabras clave**

| | | |
|---|---|---|
| **el estilo** *style* | **la obra** *work* | **el retrato** *portrait* |
| **la exhibición** *exhibit* | **el (la) pintor(a)** *painter* | **tradicional** *traditional* |
| **moderno(a)** *modern* | **la pintura** *painting* | |

**A.** For each **Palabra clave** in the first column, find the word or phrase in the second column that is closest in meaning. Write the corresponding letter in the blank.

   _C_   1. estilo       A. del período histórico actual; contemporáneo(a)

   _E_   2. exhibición       B. clásico(a)

   _A_   3. moderno(a)       C. manera de expresarse artísticamente

   _H_   4. pintura       D. representación de la cara o la figura entera de una persona

   _D_   5. retrato       E. colección de arte que puede ver el público

   _B_   6. tradicional       F. creación artística

   _F_   7. obra       G. artista

   _G_   8. pintor       H. el arte de pintar; obra del que pinta

**B.** Fill in each blank with the correct form of a **Palabra clave.**
Use each word only once.

El Museo Picasso de Barcelona tiene más de tres mil ___obras___
(1)
de Picasso, el ___pintor___ español. Hay una ___exhibición___ especial
(2)             (3)
en el museo hasta el 31 de julio. Se llama «Picasso y los ___retratos___».
(4)
Picasso usa ___estilos___ variados. *Retrato de Jaime Sabatés*
(5)
es del estilo ___tradicional___, pero *Maya con una muñeca* es
(6)
un ejemplo de pintura ___moderna___. Picasso es más famoso por
(7)
sus ___pinturas___, pero su obra también incluye la escultura y la cerámica.
(8)

# ¿Comprendiste?

**1.** ¿Cómo se llama la exhibición especial del Museo Picasso de Barcelona?

Se llama «Picasso y los retratos».

**2.** ¿Cuáles son dos estilos de retratos de la exhibición?

El estilo tradicional y el estilo moderno.

**3.** ¿De quiénes son los retratos de la exhibición?

Los retratos son de sus amigos, sus hijos y las mujeres importantes en su vida.

**4.** ¿Cómo se llama el amigo que Picasso pintó?

Se llama Jaime Sabatés.

**5.** ¿Cuántas obras de Picasso hay normalmente en el Museo Picasso de Barcelona?

Hay más de tres mil.

# Conexión personal

Imagine that you are a portrait artist. Whom would you choose to paint? Would your subject be real or imaginary? Why would you like to paint this person? How do you imagine your painting would look? Write in your answers on the right.

Yo voy a pintar...

# Para leer  *Los favoritos de la cocina española*

## Reading Strategy

**REORGANIZE INFORMATION TO CHECK UNDERSTANDING** A family friend gave you a copy of this recipe from her favorite cookbook. She has asked you to write it down as a recipe for her card file. Read "Los favoritos de la cocina española" and fill out the recipe card for her.

| Paso | Ingredientes | Cantidad | Instrucciones |
|------|--------------|----------|---------------|
| | **LA PAELLA VALENCIANA** | | |
| 1. | Aceite | $\frac{1}{4}$ taza | Pon en la sartén. |
| 2. | | | |
| 3. | | | |
| 4. | | | |

## What You Need to Know

**Paella** originated in Valencia, a region of Spain next to Cataluña. It got its name from the pan in which it is prepared, the **paellera.** The traditional iron **paellera** is round and shallow, with handles on either side and a thick, flat base. Historically, Valencians used the **paellera** to cook rice and other locally obtainable ingredients such as tomatoes, onions, snails, rabbit, or duck. Most paella dishes of today contain chicken, sausage, and different types of seafood, typically squid, shrimp, and mussels.

**READER'S SUCCESS STRATEGY** When reading instructions, look for time-order words such as **primero** and **luego** that indicate you are moving on to the next step.

**APUNTES**

## A pensar...

Write the numbers 1, 2, 3, 4, and 5 to show the order in which you should do the following steps according to the recipe. **(Sequence of Events)**

5 Sirve la paella.

4 Cocina el arroz.

2 Fríe el pollo y la salchicha.

1 Pon el aceite en la sartén.

3 Pon las verduras en la sartén.

# LOS FAVORITOS
## de la cocina española

De la *cocina de Maruja Serrat, cocinera*[1] del *restaurante Tibidabo de Barcelona*

Ésta es la receta[2] de un plato muy especial, la paella valenciana. Es importante usar los ingredientes más frescos[3] posibles. Y busca el mejor **azafrán.** El azafrán da sabor[4] y color a
5  la paella. Si no hay azafrán, no hay paella. A todo el mundo le gusta tanto la paella que generalmente no queda[5] nada. Pero si queda algo, ponlo en el frigorífico para mañana.

[1] chef   [2] recipe   [3] freshest   [4] flavor   [5] remains

**PALABRAS CLAVE**
**el azafrán**   *saffron*

# Paella valenciana

10     para cuatro personas

**Ingredientes**

     1/4 taza de aceite de oliva

     1/2 kilo de pollo

     1/4 kilo de salchicha

15     1 cebolla

     2 **dientes de ajo**

     1 tomate

     1/2 taza de **guisantes**

     1 **pimentón**

20     1/4 kilo de calamares

     200 gramos de **gambas**

     sal y pimienta

     1 1/2 taza de arroz

     1/2 cucharadita de azafrán

25     3 tazas de agua

## Instrucciones

Primero pon el aceite de <u>oliva</u> en la sartén[6]. Corta[7] el (pollo) y la (salchicha) en pedazos. Fríelos[8] por diez minutos. Luego corta la

30 <u>cebolla</u>, el <u>ajo</u>, el <u>tomate</u> y el <u>pimentón</u>. Ponlos en la sartén junto con los guisantes. Ahora añade[9] los (calamares) y las (gambas,) la sal y la pimienta. En otra sartén o en una **paellera,** cocina el arroz en el agua. Luego añade el

35 pollo, la salchicha, los calamares, las gambas, las verduras y el azafrán. Cocínalo otros veinte minutos. Sirve la paella en la paellera.

[6] frying pan     [7] cut     [8] fry them     [9] add

**PALABRAS CLAVE**

| | |
|---|---|
| **los dientes de ajo** *cloves of garlic* | **las gambas** *shrimp* |
| **los guisantes** *green peas* | **la paellera** *paella pan* |
| **el pimentón** *sweet red pepper* | |

**READING TIP** In the United States we use a different set of units for measuring weight than many other countries, such as Spain, which uses the metric system. In this recipe you will notice that the meats are measured in **kilos** (kilograms) or **gramos** (grams) instead of in pounds or ounces.

**APUNTES**

**▥ MÁRCALO ⟩ VOCABULARIO**
Reread the boxed text. Circle the words that name a kind of meat, poultry, or seafood. Underline the names of vegetables or fruits.

Students should circle **pollo, salchicha, calamares,** and **gambas.** They should underline **oliva, cebolla, ajo, tomate,** and **pimentón.**

**CHALLENGE** Do you think this is an easy recipe? (Evaluate)

*Answers will vary.*

# Vocabulario de la lectura

**Palabras clave**

el aceite   *oil*

el azafrán   *saffron*

la cebolla   *onion*

los dientes de ajo   *cloves of garlic*

las gambas   *shrimp*

los guisantes   *green peas*

la paellera   *paella pan*

el pimentón   *sweet red pepper*

la salchicha   *sausage*

el tomate   *tomato*

la verdura   *vegetable*

**A.** Fill in each blank with the correct **Palabra clave.**

Para hacer paella, primero pon el _____aceite_____ en la sartén. Luego,
                                          (1)

corta el pollo y la _____salchicha_____ en pedazos, y fríelos. Ahora corta la
                               (2)

_____cebolla_____ , el ajo, el _____tomate_____ y el pimentón. Ponlos en la
        (3)                              (4)

sartén con los guisantes, y añade los calamares y las _____gambas_____ .
                                                                (5)

Cocina el arroz en una _____paellera_____ y añade los otros ingredientes.
                              (6)

**B.** Match the **Palabra clave** in the first column with the sentence that best describes it in the second column. Write the corresponding letter in the blank.

___E___ 1. ajo

___A___ 2. pimentón

___F___ 3. gambas

___B___ 4. azafrán

___D___ 5. guisantes

___C___ 6. verduras

A. Es una verdura roja.

B. Es algo amarillo.

C. Esta categoría incluye cebollas y zanahorias.

D. Son verdes.

E. Necesitas dos dientes de este ingrediente para hacer paella.

F. Vienen del mar.

# ¿Comprendiste?

**1.** ¿Por qué es importante el azafrán?

El azafrán le da sabor y color a la paella.

**2.** Si hay demasiada paella, ¿qué debes hacer?

Debes ponerlo en el frigorífico para mañana.

**3.** ¿Qué haces con el pollo y la salchicha?

Los cortas en pedazos.

**4.** ¿Qué pones en la segunda sartén?

Pones el arroz en el agua.

**5.** Después de poner el azafrán, ¿cuánto tiempo cocinas la paella?

Cocinas la paella otros veinte minutos.

# Conexión personal

Do you have a favorite recipe? Write the ingredients and steps for a simple recipe in the space below. If you don't remember the exact quantities of ingredients, use approximations.

RECETA PARA HACER _____

| Paso | Ingredientes | Cantidad | Instrucciones |
|------|-------------|----------|---------------|
| 1. | | | |
| 2. | | | |
| 3. | | | |
| 4. | | | |

# Para leer    *La Tomatina: una rara tradición española*

## Reading Strategy

**PREDICT** Look at the title and the illustrations that go with this reading selection. What do you think this piece might be about? Write your predictions in a grid like this. After you've completed the reading, fill out the right side.

| Prediction | What I Found Out |
|---|---|
| 1. | 1. |
| 2. | 2. |
| 3. | 3. |

## What You Need to Know

Spain is famous for its fiestas, observed locally and nationwide. Unlike the majority of Spanish festivals, the tradition of **la Tomatina** has no known religious or historical significance, and no one is exactly sure how it began. **La Tomatina** takes place every year in the town of Buñol, 25 miles west of Valencia. On the morning of the last Wednesday of August, thousands of revelers flock to the town square wearing T-shirts, shorts, and eye goggles. As they wait for a firecracker to begin the festivities, participants shout **"¡Tomate! ¡Tomate! ¡Queremos tomate!"** The article you are about to read explains what happens next.

# La Tomatina:
## una rara tradición española

¿**Q**ué haces cuando hay demasiados tomates en el **jardín**? A ver... puedes regalárselos a los vecinos. Puedes hacer salsa para la pasta. Tal vez haces salsa ranchera

5 mexicana, ¿verdad?

Pues, en el pueblo español de Buñol, con el exceso de tomates la gente hace la «Tomatina». Llega un

10 **camión lleno** de tomates **maduros** que se depositan en el centro del pueblo. ¡Y todo el mundo se cubre[1] con ellos! Ocurre al final de una fiesta que se celebra cada año a fin de agosto.

[1] is covered

**PALABRAS CLAVE**
**raro(a)** *strange*       **lleno(a)** *full*
**el jardín** *garden*     **maduro(a)** *ripe*
**el camión** *truck*

**READING TIP** Although **maduro** and the word *ripe* are not cognates, **maduro** can be easily remembered because it looks like the English word *mature*, which has a similar meaning.

The audio CD for this reading can be found in the Middle School Bridging Packet.

**⫿⫿⫿ MÁRCALO ⫸ GRAMÁTICA**
Imagine you are participating in **la Tomatina**. Write two positive **tú** commands and two negative **tú** commands about things to do or not do during the festival.

*Answers will vary. Sample answers: ¡Corre! ¡Lava tu camisa! ¡No comas los tomates! ¡No seas malo!*

**CHALLENGE** Each year tourists from around the world travel to Buñol to take part in **la Tomatina**. Why do you think this festival is so popular? **(Draw Conclusions)**

*Answers will vary. Sample answers: La Tomatina is a fun and exciting festival during which many common rules of behavior are suspended. People are curious to see such an unusual event.*

As you read **La Tomatina**, look for words and phrases that help you visualize the action. Mark them with a highlighter.

**APUNTES**

_____

_____

_____

_____

_____

_____

# A pensar...

**1.** Cross out the statement that is *not* true about **la Tomatina**. (Clarify)

It takes place in Buñol, Spain.

Thousands of people participate.

~~The festival is a religious celebration.~~

Participants throw tomatoes at one another.

Everyone cleans up afterwards.

**2.** Why do you think this festival takes place in August? (Infer)

_Answers will vary. Sample answer: The festival takes place in August because large crops of tomatoes are ripe at that time._

_____

_____

15 Durante una hora hay una **verdadera guerra** de tomates. Esta locura[2] empezó[3] en Buñol hace más de 50 años[4] entre unos jóvenes del pueblo. Pero ahora llega gente de todas partes—¡vienen más de 20.000 personas!

20 ¿Cómo queda el pueblo después de todas estas festividades? Todo el mundo empieza a limpiar y el pueblo queda bonito y limpio como siempre. ¡Olé!

_____

[2] madness     [3] began     [4] *hace... años* more than 50 years ago

**PALABRAS CLAVE**
**verdadero(a)** _true, veritable_      **la guerra** _war_

# Vocabulario de la lectura

**Palabras clave**

| | | |
|---|---|---|
| **el camión** *truck* | **limpiar** *to clean* | **maduro(a)** *ripe* |
| **la guerra** *war* | **limpio(a)** *clean* | **raro(a)** *strange* |
| **el jardín** *garden* | **lleno(a)** *full* | **verdadero(a)** *true, veritable* |

**A.** Fill in each set of blanks with the correct form of a **Palabra clave.**
Then unscramble the boxed letters to answer the question below the puzzle.

1. Puedes comer la fruta; es m a d u r a .

2. Hay tomates y lechuga en el j a r d í n .

3. Mi cuarto está muy sucio; lo voy a l i m p i a r .

4. Di si las oraciones son v e r d a d e r a s o falsas.

5. El día de la Tomatina, llega un camión l l e n o de tomates.

6. Durante la Tomatina, hay una verdadera g u e r r a de tomates.

¿En qué estación hacen la Tomatina? v e r a n o

**B.** Pretend you are at **la Tomatina**. Describe what you see using at least four
of the **Palabras clave.**

_____

_____

_____

_____

_____

_____

# ¿Comprendiste?

**1.** ¿Dónde se hace la Tomatina?

Se hace en Buñol.

**2.** ¿Qué hace la gente del pueblo con los tomates?

Todo el mundo se cubre de ellos. Hace una guerra de tomates.

**3.** ¿De dónde vienen los participantes?

Vienen de todas partes.

**4.** ¿Cómo está el pueblo después de esta fiesta?

Está limpio.

# Conexión personal

Do you know of any festivals having to do with food in your town or elsewhere? What foods are featured? Describe the event in the space on the right.

En julio mi comunidad tiene un festival de comida mexicana. Hay platos típicos de...

# Para leer   *Correo electrónico desde Barcelona*

## Reading Strategy

**NOTING DETAILS** The e-mail on page 103 describes **festes**, cultural celebrations that take place in Cataluña. As you read, use a web to note details about the celebrations.

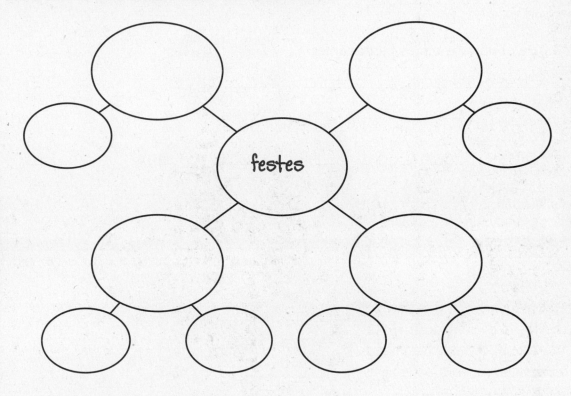

## What You Need to Know

Located on the Mediterranean Sea in the northeast of Spain, Barcelona is the capital of the region of Cataluña. One of Europe's oldest cities, Barcelona has celebrated various festivals since the Middle Ages. The city's largest celebration, **Festes de la Mercè**, takes place in September and honors one of the city's patron saints. Festivities last for a week and include a swimming race across the harbor, outdoor music concerts, traditional folk dancing, and spectacular parades. This reading describes some of the exciting elements typical of **Festes de la Mercè** and other **catalán** traditions.

**READING TIP** This reading contains some words in **catalán**, a language spoken in the Cataluña region of Spain. Listen to the audio to hear how they are pronounced. Note that the **catalán** word *castells* and the English word *castles* are cognates.

**APUNTES**

The audio CD for this reading can be found in the Middle School Bridging Packet.

▥▥▥ **MÁRCALO** ⟩ **GRAMÁTICA**
You have learned how to form the preterite of regular **-ar** verbs. Read the boxed paragraph and underline the **-ar** preterite verbs. Which of the verbs you underlined is spelled the same in both the present and the preterite?

**Caminamos** is the same in the present and the preterite.

**CHALLENGE** Imagine that you are in Barcelona participating in this festival. How would you like to join in? **(Connect)**

*Answers will vary.*

# Correo electrónico desde Barcelona 🎧

**A**quí tienes un mensaje que escribió un grupo de estudiantes norteamericanos que viajaron a España con su maestra de español.

**PALABRAS CLAVE**
 el correo electrónico   *e-mail*

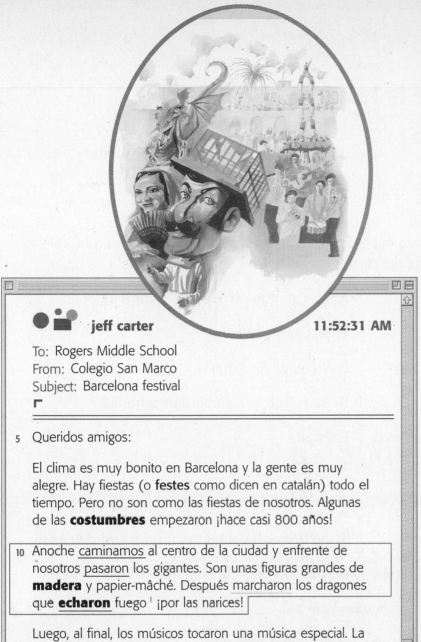

**jeff carter**      11:52:31 AM

To: Rogers Middle School
From: Colegio San Marco
Subject: Barcelona festival

5   Queridos amigos:

El clima es muy bonito en Barcelona y la gente es muy alegre. Hay fiestas (o **festes** como dicen en catalán) todo el tiempo. Pero no son como las fiestas de nosotros. Algunas de las **costumbres** empezaron ¡hace casi 800 años!

10   Anoche <u>caminamos</u> al centro de la ciudad y enfrente de nosotros <u>pasaron</u> los gigantes. Son unas figuras grandes de **madera** y papier-mâché. Después <u>marcharon</u> los dragones que **echaron** fuego[1] ¡por las narices!

Luego, al final, los músicos tocaron una música especial. La
15   gente empezó a formar los **castells** (**torres** humanas). Un grupo de personas formó la base y otro grupo subió encima del[2] primero. Luego otro grupo subió encima del segundo[3] grupo, etc., etc. Entonces, el niño más **chico** subió hasta lo más alto. Ahora nosotros queremos aprender a hacer los
20   **castells** al regresar a Estados Unidos la semana próxima.

Con el cariño de siempre,

Jeff, Susan, Amy, Emily, Josh, Frank

---

[1] fire     [2] *subió encima del* climbed to the top of     [3] second

**PALABRAS CLAVE**

| | | | |
|---|---|---|---|
| **la costumbre** | custom | **la torre** | tower |
| **la madera** | wood | **chico(a)** | small |
| **echar** | to shoot out, emit | | |

**READER'S SUCCESS STRATEGY** As you read, look for the illustrations that depict or suggest the following words: **correo electrónico, gigantes, dragón,** *castells.*

**APUNTES**

---

# A pensar...

1. Based on what you know from the e-mail, which of the following did the students see in Barcelona? Check three. (**Summarize**)

   ☑ fire-breathing dragons
   ☐ flamenco dancers
   ☑ pâpier-maché figures
   ☑ human towers
   ☐ flower sellers

2. What do the students want to do when they get home? Underline the answer below. (**Clarify**)

   organize a local parade

   study **catalán**

   <u>learn how to make **castells**</u>

3. What is one way in which the fiestas of Barcelona are different from celebrations of the U.S.? (**Compare and Contrast**)

   *Answers will vary. Sample answer: Some of the festivals in Barcelona date back almost 800 years. The holidays and celebrations of the U.S. have a shorter history.*

# Vocabulario de la lectura

**Palabras clave**

anoche  *last night*    **la costumbre**  *custom*    **la madera**  *wood*

**chico(a)**  *small*    **echar**  *to shoot out, emit*    **la torre**  *tower*

**el correo electrónico**  *e-mail*

**A.** For each **Palabra clave** in the first column, find the sentence in the second column that best describes it. Write the corresponding letter in the blank.

___B___ 1. chico          A. Es algo que escribes en la computadora.

___E___ 2. torre          B. Significa pequeño.

___D___ 3. costumbre    C. Viene de los árboles.

___C___ 4. madera       D. Se refiere a una tradición cultural.

___A___ 5. correo electrónico    E. Es alta.

**B.** Fill in the blanks with the correct form of a **Palabra clave**.

Algunas de las ____costumbres____ de Barcelona empezaron hace casi 800 años.
              (1)

Las ____torres____ humanas, llamadas ***castells,*** son una tradición catalana.
     (2)

Muchas personas forman la base y un niño ____chico____ queda encima de
                          (3)

todas. ____Anoche____ mis amigos y yo caminamos al centro de la ciudad para
      (4)

ver la fiesta. Primero miramos los gigantes, figuras enormes de ____madera____
                                       (5)

y pâpier-maché. Luego pasaron dragones que ____echaron____ fuego por las
                           (6)

narices.

# ¿Comprendiste?

**1.** ¿Quiénes mandaron el mensaje?

Un grupo de estudiantes norteamericanos que están en Barcelona lo mandaron.

**2.** ¿Cómo es Barcelona?

Barcelona tiene un clima muy bonito y la gente es muy alegre.

**3.** ¿Qué hay en las fiestas de Barcelona?

Hay gigantes, dragones, castells y música.

**4.** ¿Qué les gustó más de todo a los muchachos?

Les gustaron más los castells.

# Conexión personal

Write an e-mail similar to the one in the reading to a real or imaginary pen pal in Spain. Tell your pen pal about a local celebration in your area. The Spanish terms for *From* (**De**), *To* (**Para**), and *Subject* (**Asunto**) have been provided.

De:
Para:
Asunto: _____

Querido(a) _____ :

# Para leer    *Saludos desde Quito*

## Reading Strategy

**RECOGNIZE PLACE NAMES** It is easy to be confused by unfamiliar place names, but often there are simple words nearby to explain them. As you read each of the following place names, identify the word nearby that explains what it is.

| NOMBRE | LUGAR |
| --- | --- |
| **Amazonas** | avenida |
| **La Carolina** | parque |
| **La Compañía** | iglesia |
| **El Ejido** | parque |
| **Pichincha** | volcán |

## What You Need to Know

Quito, the capital of Ecuador, was founded on the ruins of an Incan city in 1534. It is named for the Quitu people, an indigenous group that inhabited the area prior to the Incas. The second highest capital in Latin America after La Paz, Bolivia, Quito enjoys a majestic setting amidst the snow-capped Andean mountains, and a springlike climate year-round. Many houses and churches from the Spanish colonial era still survive in the city's historic district, known as **Quito Colonial,** or Old Town. In the city's commercial center, to the north in modern Quito, or New Town, there are hotels, banks, businesses, restaurants, and shopping centers.

This reading can also be found on pages 412–413 of the Level 1 Pupil Edition. The audio is on CD 16, Tracks 6–7.

# Saludos desde Quito

**U**n grupo de estudiantes está de visita en Quito, Ecuador. Aquí hay unas tarjetas que ellos les escribieron a sus amigos.

Quito

5 ¡Hola! Hoy llegamos a Quito. ¡Estamos a sólo 24 kilómetros de la **línea ecuatorial**! Fuimos en taxi al Cerro[1] Panecillo. Allí fue posible ver toda la ciudad. La ciudad es bonita y el **paisaje** es maravilloso.
10 Quito queda al lado del **volcán** Pichincha. Hoy, la cima se cubrió[2] de nieve, ¡pero en la ciudad la temperatura fue de 80 grados!

Alfonso

John Vivas
4231 Avenue M
Galveston, TX  77550
EE.UU.

[1] hill    [2] the peak was covered

**PALABRAS CLAVE**
**la línea ecuatorial**  equator          **el volcán**  volcano
**el paisaje**  landscape

You have learned that the verbs **ir** and **ser** have the same preterite forms. Look again at the postcards by Alfonso and Lucila. Underline the preterite forms that indicate the verb **ir**, and draw a circle around those that indicate the verb **ser**.

Students should underline **fuimos** and circle **fue** as indicated.

APUNTES

## A pensar...

How are **Quito Colonial** and Quito's **sector moderno** the same? How are they different? Use the Venn diagram to organize your ideas. (**Compare and Contrast**)

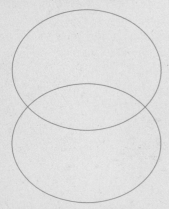

Quito Colonial

sector moderno

La Compañía

15  ¡Saludos desde Quito! Ayer paseamos por el Quito Colonial. (Fue) bonito caminar por las calles estrechas y ver las casas antiguas. Fuimos a la Plaza de la Independencia para ver la
20  Catedral y el Palacio de Gobierno. ¡Allí sacamos muchas fotos! Después fuimos a la iglesia jesuita de la Compañía. Es famosa por su arte y su decoración de oro. Luego, en el Museo
25  Arqueológico aprendí mucho sobre el arte **precolombino**. Mañana vamos al sector moderno. ¡Hasta pronto!
Lucila

Elena Martínez
59 Collins Ave.
Corona, CA 91720
EE.UU.

ECUADOR
333 98-07- 9:39
2.600

**PALABRAS CLAVE**
**precolombino(a)**   *pre-Columbian*

Parque Carolina

30 ¿Qué tal? Hoy paseamos por el norte de Quito. ¡Qué diferencia! Las avenidas son anchas y hay parques grandes, como El Ejido y La Carolina. En el sector de la avenida Amazonas está la mayor parte de los hoteles, bancos, restaurantes caros y
35 tiendas finas. Mañana vamos a visitar la Mitad del Mundo, un complejo turístico en la línea ecuatorial. Allí hay un museo, tiendas y restaurantes. Los domingos hay música típica de los Andes. Me encanta
40 escuchar la música andina.

    ¡Hasta luego!
    Marisa

Jennifer Herrera
131 Edgewater Drive
Orlando, FL 32804
EE.UU.

| Student | Places Visited |
| --- | --- |
| Alfonso | Cerro Panecillo,... |
| Lucila | |
| Marisa | |

**APUNTES**

_____

_____

**CHALLENGE** What influences would you expect to see in the architecture of **Quito Colonial?** (Draw Conclusions)

_Answers will vary. Sample answer: Because Ecuador was a colony of Spain, the architecture of **Quito Colonial** most likely shows Spanish and European influence._

_____

_____

_____

_____

# Vocabulario de la lectura

**Palabras clave**

ancho(a)  *wide*

antiguo(a)  *old, ancient*

estrecho(a)  *narrow*

**la línea ecuatorial**  *equator*

**moderno(a)**  *modern*

**el paisaje**  *landscape*

**precolombino(a)**  *pre-Columbian*

**el volcán**  *volcano*

**A.** On the line next to each word pair, write whether the words are synonyms or antonyms. Synonyms are words with the same or similar meaning. Antonyms are words with opposite meanings.

1. antiguo–viejo          _synonyms_

2. estrecho–ancho         _antonyms_

3. nuevo–antiguo          _antonyms_

4. moderno-tradicional    _antonyms_

**B.** Complete each sentence with the correct form of a **Palabra clave.**

1. Ayer, la cima del ____volcán____ Pichincha se cubrió de nieve.

2. La Mitad del Mundo es un complejo turístico en la ____línea____ ____ecuatorial____.

3. Me gusta la ciudad, pero mi hermano prefiere el ____paisaje____ de las montañas.

4. En el Museo Arqueológico, hay arte de la era ____precolombina____.

# ¿Comprendiste?

**1.** ¿Dónde queda Quito?

Queda al lado del volcán Pichincha.

**2.** ¿Cómo es el Quito Colonial?

Es bonito y tiene calles estrechas y casas antiguas.

**3.** ¿Qué lugares puedes visitar en el Quito Colonial?

Puedes visitar la Catedral, el Palacio de Gobierno, la iglesia jesuita de la Compañía y el Museo

Arqueológico.

**4.** ¿Dónde está la parte moderna de Quito?

Está en el norte de Quito.

**5.** ¿Adónde vas para caminar por la línea ecuatorial?

Vas a la Mitad del Mundo, un complejo turístico.

# Conexión personal

If you were to visit Quito, what parts would you most like to see? Why do these places interest you? Write your answer in the space on the right.

En Quito, me gustaría ver...

# Para leer   *Un paseo por Ecuador*

## Reading Strategy

**REFLECT ON JOURNAL WRITING** Have you ever kept a journal or a diary? How are diaries organized? As you read this article about a bus trip through Ecuador, notice the place and date given for each entry. This diary-style organization of the article helps you experience each day that the writer experiences. Use the chart to record an interesting experience you read from each day.

| FECHA | LUGAR | EXPERIENCIA INTERESANTE |
|-------|-------|-------------------------|
| 17 de abril | | |
| 18 de abril | | |
| 4 de mayo | | |
| 25 de mayo | | |

## What You Need to Know

Buses are the most common means of transportation in Ecuador, where an extensive network of bus routes links towns and cities throughout the country. The most common types of buses are **colectivos** or **busetas,** used for inner-city transportation or small trips, and **autobuses** or **buses grandes,** large coaches that make longer trips. In rural or remote areas, **camionetas** (pick-up trucks) often double as buses, and passengers ride in the back. Along the coast it is common to see **rancheras,** buses with open sides and wooden seats. On buses traveling long distances, baggage is often carried on the roof. On some buses, passengers are permitted to ride on the roof as well.

This reading can also be found on pages 456–457 of the Level 1 Pupil Edition. The audio is on CD 18, Tracks 6–7.

# UN PASEO POR ECUADOR

**P**ara la **mayoría** de los ecuatorianos, el autobús es el transporte más común. Para tener una experiencia muy ecuatoriana, decidí hacer un viaje en autobús.

## 5 GUAYAQUIL, 17 de abril:

Guayaquil es el puerto principal y la ciudad más grande del país. Para conocer la costa, decidí viajar a Machala. Compré mi boleto en la terminal moderna. Los buses de larga

10 distancia tienen **cortinas** y televisores con videograbadora. Paseamos por la costa del Pacífico. Hacía[1] mucho calor y mucha humedad. Vi los cultivos de arroz, caña de azúcar y **plátanos.** Por el puerto de Machala

15 pasan más de un millón de toneladas de plátanos y **camarones** por año.

[1] It was

**PALABRAS CLAVE**

| | |
|---|---|
| **la mayoría** *majority* | **el plátano** *banana* |
| **la cortina** *curtain* | **los camarones** *shrimp* |

Look at the boxed paragraph.
Underline all the preterite
verbs and write them in the
space below. Next to each verb,
write its infinitive.

decidí: decidir
viajé: viajar
llevó: llevar
fuimos: ir

_____

_____

_____

_____

_____

_____

_____

## A pensar...

**1.** Which of the following
does the narrator see while
traveling through Ecuador?
Check three. (**Main Idea
and Details**)

☐ la costa del Atlántico

☑ volcanes

☑ el océano Pacífico

☑ plantaciones de café

☐ Quito

**2.** Which of the following are
the names of ports in
Ecuador? Check two. (**Clarify**)

☑ Guayaquil

☐ Amazonas

☑ Machala

☐ Saquisilí

# MACHALA, 18 de abril:

Decidí visitar los
pueblitos. Viajé en un
20 bus de transporte
rural de colores muy
alegres con personas
muy animadas.
El bus llevó todas sus
25 posesiones encima. Fuimos a varios pueblos y
plantaciones de café y cacao.

# LA SIERRA, 4 de mayo:

Llegué a la sierra de
Ecuador, la región
30 central de los Andes.
Hacía frío en las
montañas. Me levanté
a las cinco y subí a un
antiguo bus de escuela
35 para ir al mercado
indígena de Saquisilí.
Viajamos muy lentamente.
¡Qué frío en el bus! Todos los pasajeros
llevaron saco o poncho. Algunos se
40 durmieron. Muchas personas llevaron
productos al mercado. Vimos los volcanes de
Cotopaxi y Tungurahua. Llegamos al Saquisilí
y todos salieron del bus para trabajar o hacer
compras.

# COCA, 25 de mayo:

45

La **carretera** terminó y tuve que seguir en barco por los ríos Napo y Coca, que van al río Amazonas. Vi barcos y canoas con muchos plátanos y pasajeros. En la **selva** vive poca

50 gente, la mayoría son indígenas. Como ven, ¡se puede conocer mucho viajando en autobús!

**APUNTES**

**CHALLENGE** What have you learned about the geography or physical features of Ecuador from reading this selection? **(Analyze)**

*Sample answer:* Ecuador is on the Pacific Ocean. It has a varied geography that includes mountains, volcanoes, and rivers.

**PALABRAS CLAVE**
**la carretera** *highway*     **la selva** *jungle*

# Vocabulario de la lectura

   **los camarones** *shrimp*     **la cortina** *curtain*     **el plátano** *banana*

   **la carretera** *highway*     **la mayoría** *majority*     **la selva** *jungle*

**A.** For each **Palabra clave** in the first column, find the phrase in the second column that is closest in meaning. Write the corresponding letter in the blank.

| | | |
|---|---|---|
| __D__ 1. cortina | A. un camino grande |
| __A__ 2. carretera | B. una fruta amarilla |
| __F__ 3. selva | C. animales del mar |
| __B__ 4. plátano | D. algo para la ventana |
| __C__ 5. camarones | E. un gran número |
| __E__ 6. mayoría | F. un bosque tropical |

**B.** Choose two **Palabras clave** and write a sentence with each one.

_____

_____

_____

_____

_____

_____

# ¿Comprendiste?

**1.** ¿Cuál es el transporte más común en Ecuador?

El autobús es el transporte más común.

**2.** ¿En qué región empezó el autor?

El autor empezó en la costa.

**3.** ¿Qué productos son típicos de la costa?

El arroz, la caña de azúcar y los plátanos son típicos de la costa.

**4.** ¿Cómo es el clima de la sierra?

Hace frío.

**5.** ¿Adónde van los ríos Napo y Coca?

Van al río Amazonas.

# Conexión personal

Imagine that you and your family are on vacation in Ecuador. Write a postcard to a friend back home explaining how you spent your day. You might describe a canoe trip through the jungle, a shopping expedition in the mountains, or a visit to a large city.

¡Hola, Mary!

Hoy hicimos un viaje en autobús.

Fuimos a...

# Para leer

**Un cuento ecuatoriano:**
**El tigre y el conejo**

## Reading Strategy

**FOLLOW THE SEQUENCE** It is important to recognize the order of events in a story. The selection you are about to read has three repetitive segments. Scan the reading to try to identify what they are. Look for sequencing words in Spanish such as **un día**, **una vez más**, and **por última vez** to help you follow the story.

| Sequencing Words |
|---|
| un día |
|  |
|  |

## What You Need to Know

A fable is a short narrative that conveys a message and features animal characters that talk and act like people. The message in a fable is often a useful piece of wisdom or cautionary advice. Fables are a part of the folklore of many countries. A tiger and a rabbit are the main characters in many fables, with the small, clever rabbit typically outwitting the large, foolhardy tiger. The tiger and the rabbit continue their legendary rivalry in this fable you are about to read from Ecuador.

This reading can also be found on pages 276–277 of the Level 1b Pupil Edition. The audio is on the Bridge CD, Tracks 39–40.

# Un cuento ecuatoriano

## El tigre y el conejo

Un día Tío Tigre pasó por el bosque camino a su casa. Tenía[1] una **canasta** de comida muy rica. El amigo conejo lo vio y pensó: «¡Yo tengo hambre! ¡Quiero esa comida!» y saltó[2]
5 por el bosque y se adelantó[3] a Tío Tigre. Se echó como muerto[4]. Cuando llegó Tío Tigre, vio al conejo pero siguió el camino[5].

[1] He had
[2] hopped
[3] got ahead
[4] *Se echó…muerto.* He pretended to be dead.
[5] *siguió…camino* he continued on his way

**PALABRAS CLAVE**
el cuento    *story*
ecuatoriano(a)    *Ecuadorian*
el tigre    *tiger*
el conejo    *rabbit*
la canasta    *basket*

# A pensar...

**1.** Write the numbers 1, 2, 3, 4, and 5 to show the order in which the events below occurred. **(Sequence of Events)**

   _3_  The tiger put down his basket.

   _2_  The rabbit played dead three times.

   _5_  The rabbit stole the tiger's food.

   _1_  The rabbit saw the tiger walking through the forest with a basket of food.

   _4_  The tiger went looking for what he thought were two dead rabbits.

**2.** Which of the two animals is bigger and stronger? Which one is smarter? What does the fable imply about the relationship between physical strength and intelligence? **(Analyze)**

*Answers will vary. Sample answer: The tiger is bigger and stronger than the rabbit, but the rabbit is smarter. When the rabbit outwits the tiger, he proves that intelligence can be a greater power than physical strength.*

**3.** What is your opinion of the tiger and the rabbit? Think of three words to describe each. **(Make Judgments)**

Tiger:
*Answers will vary. Sample answer: greedy, foolish, rash*

Rabbit:
*Answers will vary. Sample answer: clever, shrewd, persistent*

---

10 El amigo conejo <u>pensó</u> y <u>dijo</u>: «Pues, voy a tratar[6] una vez más» y <u>saltó</u> y se <u>adelantó</u> otra vez a Tío Tigre. Otra vez se <u>echó</u> como muerto. Y una vez más pasó Tío Tigre, <u>vio</u> al conejo y <u>siguió</u> su camino.

15 El amigo conejo <u>pensó</u>: «Bueno, voy a tratar por última vez» y <u>saltó</u> camino adelante y otra vez se <u>echó</u> como muerto. Esta vez Tío Tigre se <u>paró</u>[7]. <u>Decidió</u> que tres conejos muertos en el camino era demasiado bueno para perder.

20 <u>Dejó</u> la canasta y <u>regresó</u> por los otros dos conejos.

Y así el amigo conejo <u>agarró</u>[8] la canasta y le <u>robó</u> al tigre su comida.

[6] to try     [7] stopped     [8] grabbed

# Vocabulario de la lectura

**Palabras clave**

| | | | |
|---|---|---|---|
| **la canasta** | *basket* | **ecuatoriano(a)** | *Ecuadorian* |
| **el conejo** | *rabbit* | **el tigre** | *tiger* |
| **el cuento** | *story* | | |

**A.** For each **Palabra clave** in the first column, find the sentence in the second column that best describes it. Write the corresponding letter in the blank.

___D___ 1. ecuatoriano(a)     A. Es un animal con rayas.

___A___ 2. tigre     B. Es algo que puedes decir o leer.

___E___ 3. conejo     C. El tigre pone su comida en una...

___B___ 4. cuento     D. Se refiere a algo o alguien nativo de Ecuador.

___C___ 5. canasta     E. Tiene orejas largas.

**B.** Choose three **Palabras clave** and write a sentence with each one.

_____

_____

_____

_____

_____

_____

# ¿Comprendiste?

**1.** ¿Por dónde pasó el tigre?

Pasó por el bosque.

**2.** ¿Qué tenía en la canasta?

Tenía comida.

**3.** ¿Qué pensó el conejo cuando vio la canasta?

Pensó: «Yo tengo hambre».

**4.** ¿Qué hizo el conejo?

Se adelantó al tigre y se echó como muerto.

**5.** ¿Cómo terminó todo?

La última vez que el conejo se echó como muerto, el tigre dejó la canasta y regresó por los

otros dos conejos.

# Conexión personal

Can you think of any memorable tiger or rabbit characters that you have read about in books or seen on TV? Choose several famous tigers, rabbits, or other animals. Write their names and give a Spanish adjective to describe each one.

| Animales famosos | Características |
|---|---|
| Brer Rabbit | inteligente |
|  |  |
|  |  |
|  |  |
|  |  |
|  |  |
|  |  |

# Para leer    *El murciélago cobarde*

## Reading Strategy

USE PICTURES  In this legend, the **murciélago** is the main character of the narrative. Skim the reading and look at the pictures to remember what a **murciélago** is. What other characters are part of this reading? Write them in the space below.

_____

_____

_____

_____

## What You Need to Know

Ecuador has three distinct land regions: the Pacific coast to the west; the Andes mountains extending north to south down the middle; and a region of tropical forests and rivers to the east. This varied geography supports a large number of habitats, and Ecuador, known for its biodiversity, has thousands of species of flora and fauna. Birdwatchers from all over the world come to Ecuador to see birds typical of the country such as condors and parrots as well as newly discovered species, which are continually being recorded. Many types of mammals are found in Ecuador as well, including monkeys, sloths, and over 100 species of bats. The legend you are about to read, in which a bat is the main character, takes place among the animals of a tropical forest in Ecuador.

**READING TIP** It may help you remember the word for bat, **murciélago**, to know that it comes from the Latin word **mus**, meaning *mouse*, and the Spanish word **cielo**, meaning *sky*. When spelling **murciélago**, keep in mind that it contains all the vowels.

The audio CD for this reading can be found in the Middle School Bridging Packet.

||||| **MÁRCALO** ✏ **GRAMÁTICA**
You are now familiar with some common irregular preterite verbs, including **decir, hacer,** and **ir**. Underline all the preterite forms of **decir, hacer,** and **ir** that you can find in this legend.

Students should underline **dijeron, fueron, dijeron, dijo, fue, fue,** and **Hicieron.**

**CHALLENGE** Do you think the bat was a coward not to take part in the fight? Why or why not? **(Make Judgments)**

Answers will vary.

# El murciélago cobarde

**U**n día, los animales del bosque y los pájaros del **cielo** decidieron **luchar**. Los animales llamaron al murciélago y le dijeron: «Ven y **pelea** con nosotros contra los pájaros.»
5  Pero el murciélago contestó: «¿No ven ustedes que soy pájaro? ¿No ven que tengo **alas**?»

Entonces, fueron los pájaros al murciélago y le dijeron: «Ven y pelea con nosotros contra los animales.» Pero el murciélago les dijo: «¿No
10  ven que soy animal? Tengo dientes y no tengo **plumas.**»

**PALABRAS CLAVE**
**el murciélago** *bat*
**cobarde** n., adj. *coward, cowardly*
**el cielo** *sky*
**luchar** *to fight*

**pelear** *to fight*
**el ala** (f.) *wing*
**la pluma** *feather*

Empezó la lucha y, viendo que ganaban[1] los animales, el murciélago <u>fue</u> con ellos. Pero los animales lo rechazaron[2]. Luego vio que los

15  pájaros ganaban y <u>fue</u> con ellos, pero los pájaros también lo rechazaron.

Por fin, **fatigados** por la lucha, los dos campos pusieron fin[3] al conflicto. <u>Hicieron</u> una fiesta para todos. El murciélago trató de[4] entrar a la

20  fiesta. Cuando todos lo vieron, se pusieron[5] furiosos y lo expulsaron de la fiesta.
Le gritaron: «¡De aquí en adelante vas a vivir en una cueva[6] y sólo vas a salir de noche porque eres un cobarde!»

25  Y así, pues, el murciélago tiene miedo de los animales y los pájaros y por eso no quiere salir de día.

---

[1] were winning    [2] rejected    [3] *pusieron fin* put an end
[4] *trató de* tried to    [5] became    [6] cave

**PALABRAS CLAVE**
fatigado(a)   *tired*

bat sides with animals
↓

↓

↓

## A pensar…

1. What physical characteristic does the bat share with the animals? What physical characteristic does he share with the birds? (**Compare and Contrast**)

The bat and the animals have teeth. Neither the bat nor the animals have feathers. The bat and the birds have wings.

2. Why do the birds and animals eject the bat from their party? (**Clarify**)

*Sample answer:* The birds and animals are angry with the bat because he made excuses to avoid fighting, and he took the side of whichever group was winning.

3. According to the legend, why do bats only come out at night? (**Main Idea**)

*Sample answer:* Bats only come out at night because they are cowards. If they came out during the day, they would have to confront the animals and birds of whom they are afraid.

# Vocabulario de la lectura

**Palabras clave**

**el ala** (f.)  *wing*
**el cielo**  *sky*
**cobarde**  n., adj.  *coward, cowardly*
**fatigado(a)**  *tired*

**luchar**  *to fight*
**el murciélago**  *bat*
**pelear**  *to fight*
**la pluma**  *feather*

**A.** Complete each analogy with one of the **Palabras clave.** In an analogy, the last two words must be related in the same way that the first two are related.

1. HOMBRE : BRAZO : : pájaro : _____ala_____

2. ALEGRE: CONTENTO : : cansado : _____fatigado_____

3. POSTRE : PASTEL : : animal : _____murciélago_____

4. ROJO: TOMATE : : azul : _____cielo_____

5. TRISTE: DEPRIMIDO : : luchar : _____pelear_____

**B.** Fill in the blank with the correct form of a **Palabra clave.**

Un día, los animales del bosque y los pájaros del _____cielo_____ deciden
                                                      (1)

luchar. Cada campo quiere la ayuda del _____murciélago_____. El murciélago les
                                         (2)

dice a los animales que es pájaro porque tiene _____alas_____. Les dice a
                                                     (3)

los pájaros que es animal porque tiene dientes y no tiene _____plumas_____.
                                                               (4)

Todos los animales están furiosos con el murciélago porque no quiere

_____luchar/pelear_____. Dicen que sólo sale de noche porque es un _____cobarde_____.
        (5)                                                                (6)

# ¿Comprendiste?

**1.** ¿Qué pasó entre los animales y los pájaros?

Ellos decidieron luchar.

**2.** ¿Qué hicieron los animales después de la lucha?

Hicieron una fiesta para todos.

**3.** ¿Qué hizo el murciélago después de la lucha?

Trató de entrar a la fiesta.

**4.** ¿Qué le dijeron los animales y los pájaros al murciélago?

Le dijeron que tiene que vivir en una cueva y salir sólo de noche porque es un cobarde.

# Conexión personal

Have you ever wondered why some animals behave as they do? Make a list of animals and their characteristics that could be the subject of a legend explaining their habits.

| Animales | Características |
|----------|----------------|
| pez | Vive en el mar. |

# Literatura adicional

In this section you will find literary readings in Spanish that range from poems to excerpts from novels, short stories, and other works. Each reading has biographical information about the author and background information about the selection. Like the **En voces** readings, the literary readings have reading strategies, reading tips, reader's success strategies, critical-thinking questions, vocabulary activities, comprehension questions, and a short writing activity to help you understand each selection. There is also a **Márcalo** feature for literary analysis of the readings.

## Para leer  *Cumpleaños*

## Reading Strategy

**QUESTION** Asking questions about a work of literature as you read is one way to understand the selection better. Use the five W's—who, what, where, when, why—to help you ask your questions. In the chart below, record questions and the answers you discover while reading "Cumpleaños" by Carmen Lomas Garza and viewing the illustration.

### "Cumpleaños"

| | |
|---|---|
| **Who** is the speaker? | a young girl |
| **What** is she describing? | a birthday party |
| **Where** does the story take place? | outside in the backyard |
| **When** is the party? | on the speaker's sixth birthday and her brother's fourth birthday |
| **Why** can't the children see the piñata? | They are blindfolded with a scarf. |

## What You Need to Know

**"Cumpleaños"** is a story from Carmen Lomas Garza's book *Cuadros de familia*, in which she describes her memories of growing up in Kingsville, Texas, near the border of Mexico. Through illustrated vignettes about family activities from making tamales to picking nopal cactus, *Cuadros de familia* relates aspects of Mexican American history and culture. In **"Cumpleaños,"** Carmen Lomas Garza remembers celebrating her sixth birthday.

## Sobre la autora

Carmen Lomas Garza, artista chicana, nació en Kingsville, Texas, en 1948. Empezó a estudiar arte a la edad de trece años. Sus pinturas, inspiradas en su niñez en el sur de Texas, son escenas típicas de la vida mexicana americana.

~~~~~~~~~~

# Cumpleaños

Ésa soy yo, pegándole[1] a la piñata en la fiesta que me dieron cuando cumplí seis años[2]. Era[3] también el cumpleaños de mi hermano, que cumplía cuatro años. Mi madre nos dio

5   una gran fiesta e invitó a muchos primos, **vecinos** y amigos.

_____

[1] hitting      [2] _cumplí seis años_ I turned six      [3] It was

Cumpleaños de Lala y Tudi _by Carmen Lomas Garza, 1989_

**PALABRAS CLAVE**
   **el (la) vecino(a)**   _neighbor_

READING TIP Review the vocabulary you have learned for family members. Then circle the words in the story that refer to the relatives of the girl who is narrating it.

APUNTES

_____

_____

_____

_____

_____

_____

||||| MÁRCALO >> ANÁLISIS
This story contains vivid descriptions, details that help the reader form a strong mental picture. Underline words or phrases in the story that help you visualize in your mind the activity and excitement of the birthday party.

_Answers will vary and may include_ una gran fiesta; muchos primos, vecinos y amigos; los ojos cubiertos; pegarle a la piñata; rompiéndola; los caramelos caerán; los niños correrán.

_____

READER'S SUCCESS STRATEGY  As you read, look for depictions of the vocabulary in the illustration. First identify the girl who is telling the story and her father. Then find the following: **la cuerda, el palo, el pañuelo, la piñata.**

### A pensar...

**1.** Whose birthday is it on the day of the party? **(Clarify)**

It is the birthday of both the narrator and her brother.

**2.** What details of Mexican American culture are described in the story? **(Main Idea)**

Answers will vary. Sample answer: The story describes a typical Mexican American birthday celebration and the tradition of the **piñata**.

**CHALLENGE** How is the birthday party described in **"Cumpleaños"** the same as or different from birthday parties you had as a child, or birthday celebrations you attended? Use the Venn diagram to record your answer. Where the circles are separate, write in differences. Where they intersect, write in similarities. **(Compare and Contrast)**

**"Cumpleaños"**

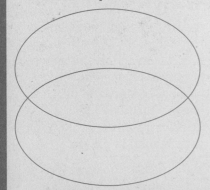

**Birthdays I Remember**

No puedes ver la piñata cuando le estás dando[4] con el **palo,** porque tienes los ojos cubiertos[5] por un **pañuelo.** Mi padre está 10 tirando[6] de la **cuerda** que **sube** y **baja** la piñata. Él se encargará[7] de que todos tengan[8] por lo menos una oportunidad de pegarle a la piñata. Luego alguien acabará rompiéndola[9], y entonces todos los **caramelos** que tiene 15 dentro caerán[10] y todos los niños correrán a **cogerlos.**

---

[4] *le estás dando* you're hitting it
[5] covered
[6] is pulling
[7] will make sure
[8] have
[9] *acabará rompiéndola* will end up breaking it
[10] will fall out

**PALABRAS CLAVE**

| | |
|---|---|
| **el palo** *stick* | **bajar** *to lower* |
| **el pañuelo** *handkerchief* | **los caramelos** *candies* |
| **la cuerda** *rope* | **coger** *to grab* |
| **subir** *to raise* | |

# Vocabulario de la lectura

**Palabras clave**

| | | |
|---|---|---|
| **bajar** *to lower* | **la cuerda** *rope* | **subir** *to raise* |
| **los caramelos** *candies* | **el palo** *stick* | **el (la) vecino(a)** *neighbor* |
| **coger** *to grab* | **el pañuelo** *handkerchief* | |

**A.** Complete the puzzle using forms of the **Palabras clave.**

**Across**

3. En general son blancos.
4. Los niños corrieron a _____ los caramelos.
5. Son dulces.
6. Es lo opuesto *(opposite)* de **bajar.**

**Down**

1. Estas personas viven en la misma comunidad.
2. Es el opuesto *(opposite)* de **subir.**
3. Rompes una piñata con este objeto.
4. La usas para subir y bajar la piñata.

**B.** Choose two **Palabras clave** and write a sentence about **"Cumpleaños"** using each one.

_____

_____

_____

_____

# ¿Comprendiste?

**1.** ¿Cuántos años tiene la narradora?

Tiene seis años.

**2.** ¿Cuántos años tiene el hermano de la narradora?

Tiene cuatro años.

**3.** ¿Quiénes asistieron la fiesta?

Asistieron muchos primos, vecinos y amigos.

**4.** ¿Por qué los niños no pueden ver la piñata cuando le pegan?

No la pueden ver porque tienen los ojos cubiertos por un pañuelo.

**5.** ¿Qué hay dentro de la piñata?

Hay caramelos.

# Conexión personal

Do you have vivid recollections of any family celebrations from your childhood? Choose a birthday, holiday, or other celebration you remember and write some details about it in the web below.

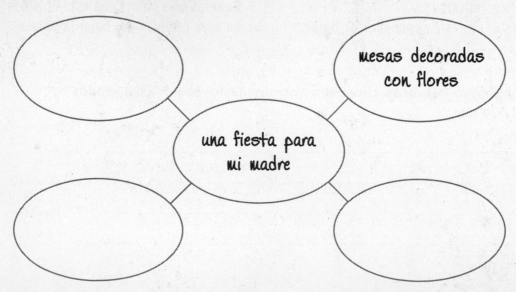

una fiesta para mi madre

mesas decoradas con flores

# Para leer    *La exclamación / En Uxmal*

## Reading Strategy

**CLARIFY THE MEANING OF A POEM** The process of stopping while reading to quickly review what has happened and to look for answers to questions you may have is called clarifying.

Complete the chart below by doing the following:

- Read the title and the first two lines of the poem.
- Stop to clarify those lines.
- Paraphrase what the lines are about in one of the boxes.
- Continue to read and clarify the rest of the poem in the same manner.

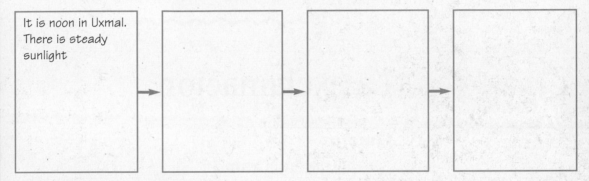

It is noon in Uxmal. There is steady sunlight

## What You Need to Know

In his Nobel lecture, Octavio Paz made the following statements:

*In Mexico, the Spaniards encountered history as well as geography. That history is still alive: It is a present rather than a past. The temples and gods of pre-Columbian Mexico are a pile of ruins, but the spirit that breathed life into that world has not disappeared; it speaks to us in the hermetic language of myth, legend, forms of social coexistence, popular art, customs. Being a Mexican writer means listening to the voice of that present, that presence.*

. . . . . . . .

*Poetry is in love with the instant and seeks to relive it in the poem, thus separating it from sequential time and turning it into a fixed present.*

Consider how these ideas are reflected in the poems that follow.

## A pensar...

**1. Form** is the placement of a poem's lines on the page. What is the significance of the way the lines are staggered on the page in **"La exclamación"**? (Draw Conclusions)

*Sample answer:* The placement of the lines mimics the darting flight of the hummingbird.

**2.** Why does Octavio Paz call this poem **"La exclamación"**? (Analyze)

*Sample answer:* He is comparing the movements of the hummingbird to an exclamation because they are both sudden and of short duration.

**MÁRCALO > ANÁLISIS**
**Repetition** is a literary technique in which sounds, words, phrases, or lines are repeated for emphasis. Reread **"La exclamación"** and circle each phrase that appears more than once. Why do you think the poet repeats these phrases one after the other?

*Sample answer:* He wants to emphasize how quickly the bird moves from one place to the next.

---

### Sobre el autor

Octavio Paz (1914–1998), poeta y ensayista que ganó el Premio Nóbel de Literatura en 1990, nació en la Ciudad de México. Durante los años cincuenta publicó *El laberinto de soledad (The Labyrinth of Solitude),* una colección de ensayos sobre la identidad mexicana, y *Libertad bajo palabra (Liberty Under Oath),* que contiene el poema «Piedra de sol» («Sunstone»). Inspirado en el calendario azteca, «Piedra de sol» es tal vez su obra más famosa. Desde 1962 hasta 1968 Octavio Paz fue embajador de México en India. Vivió en varios países y su escritura refleja una perspectiva internacional. Paz escribió sobre muchos temas, incluso sobre política, filosofía y amor.

# La exclamación

**Quieto**
no en la **rama**
en el aire
No en el aire
5  en el instante
el **colibrí**

**PALABRAS CLAVE**
**quieto(a)**  *still, motionless*       **el colibrí**  *hummingbird*
**la rama**  *branch*

**MÁRCALO ANÁLISIS**
**Personification** is a figure of speech that gives human characteristics to an object, animal, or idea. Circle the line containing personification in **"En Uxmal."** What is being personified?

*Light is being personified. In the poem, the light has the ability to blink the way people do.*

## A pensar...

**1.** Consider that this poem was inspired by the ruins of an ancient civilization. What do you think the poet means when he says a bird has stopped in the air? (**Analyze**)

*Sample answer: As the narrator views the ruins of Uxmal, he is looking at a piece of the past. Time has frozen, like a bird that has stopped in the air.*

**2.** What does the poet mean when he says time is transparent? (**Analyze**)

*Sample answer: He means that he is looking back through time to a point in the past.*

**CHALLENGE** How are these two poems similar? How are they different? (**Compare and Contrast**)

*Sample answer: Both the poems contain birds. "La exclamación" describes a real hummingbird. In "En Uxmal," the bird is symbolic.*

# En Uxmal

*Mediodía*

La **luz** no **parpadea,**

el tiempo se vacía[1] de minutos,
se ha detenido[2] un pájaro en el aire.

5  *Pleno[3] sol*

La hora es transparente:
vemos, si es invisible el pájaro,
el color de su **canto.**

[1] empties itself     [2] has stopped     [3] full

**PALABRAS CLAVE**
**la luz** *light*      **el canto** *song*
**parpadear** *to blink*

# Vocabulario de la lectura

el canto  *song*          la luz  *light*          quieto(a)  *still, motionless*
el colibrí  *hummingbird*          parpadear  *to blink*          la rama  *branch*

**A.** Complete each analogy with one of the **Palabras clave.** In an analogy, the last two words must be related in the same way that the first two are related.

1. CABEZA : PELO : : árbol : ___rama___

2. LEER : LIBRO : : cantar : ___canto___

3. PUERTA : CERRAR : : ojo : ___parpadear___

4. BEBIDA : REFRESCO : : pájaro : ___colibrí___

5. FELIZ : ALEGRE : : tranquilo : ___quieto___

**B.** Complete each sentence with the correct form of a **Palabra clave.**

1. El ___colibrí___ puede moverse con extraordinaria rapidez.

2. Apaga la ___luz___, por favor; quiero dormir.

3. Hay un pájaro raro sobre la ___rama___ de ese árbol.

4. No veo el pájaro, pero oigo su ___canto___.

5. ___Parpadear___ significa «cerrar y abrir los ojos».

# ¿Comprendiste?

**1.** ¿Qué tipo de pájaro se describe en **«La exclamación»**?

Se describe el colibrí.

**2.** ¿En qué tres lugares se encuentra el colibrí?

Se encuentra en la rama, en el aire y en el instante.

**3.** ¿A qué hora empieza el primer verso de **«En Uxmal»**?

Empieza al mediodía.

**4.** ¿En el segundo verso de **«En Uxmal»**, ¿qué palabra usa el poeta para describir la hora?

Usa la palabra **transparente**.

**5.** ¿Qué palabra usa el poeta para describir el pájaro de **«En Uxmal»**? Si el pájaro es invisible, ¿cómo sabemos que existe?

Usa la palabra **invisible**. Su canto nos dice que el pájaro existe.

# Conexión personal

If you were a poet, what would you write about? Would it be something in nature, a place you have been, or another subject? In the center of the web write a subject for your poem. Then brainstorm words you associate with it.

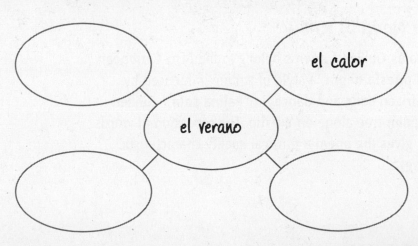

# Para leer  *Palma sola*

## Reading Strategy

**SETTING** The setting of a poem or story is the time and place where the action occurs. The setting may be a backdrop, with no effect on what happens, or it may be important to the meaning of the poem. Use the chart below to jot down lines from "**Palma sola**" that indicate setting.

| Time/Place | Meaning |
|---|---|
| bajo la luna y sol | shows the passage of time |
| en el patio | shows that the palm is a potted plant |
| el patio sellado | indicates that the patio is an enclosed space |
| guardián del atardecer | emphasizes that the palm is alone |

## What You Need to Know

Many of Nicolás Guillén's poems belong to the Afro-Caribbean genre called **poesía negra,** a style of writing influenced by traditional African song and dance. In **"Palma sola,"** Guillén describes a palm tree alone on a patio. The repetition of words and phrases gives the poem a musical quality characteristic of **poesía negra**.

## Sobre el autor

El Poeta Nacional de Cuba, Nicolás Guillén (1902–1989) es uno de los escritores latinos más conocidos. Su poesía celebra la herencia africana de la gente cubana y la historia étnica de la isla. Guillén admiró la literatura española y la poesía clásica española. Sus poemas combinan elementos de la poesía española con el lenguaje común de los cubanos. En muchas de sus obras se puede ver el ritmo de *son,* un tipo de música de origen africano y español.

〜〜〜〜〜〜〜〜

# Palma sola

La palma que está en el patio
nació[1] sola;
**creció** sin que yo la viera[2],
creció sola;

5　**bajo** la **luna** y el sol,
vive sola.

Con su largo cuerpo fijo[3],
palma sola;
sola en el patio sellado[4],

10　siempre sola,
guardián[5] del atardecer[6],
sueña[7] sola.

---

[1] was born　　[2] *sin que yo la viera* without my seeing it
[3] fixed, stationary　　[4] sealed, enclosed　　[5] watchman
[6] late afternoon　　[7] dreams

**PALABRAS CLAVE**
crecer　*to grow*　　　　**la luna**　*moon*
bajo(a)　*under*

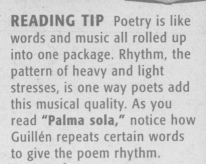
**READING TIP** Poetry is like words and music all rolled up into one package. Rhythm, the pattern of heavy and light stresses, is one way poets add this musical quality. As you read **"Palma sola,"** notice how Guillén repeats certain words to give the poem rhythm.

▥ MÁRCALO ◇ ANÁLISIS
Remember that **personification** is a literary device that gives human characteristics to something nonhuman. Circle the lines in this poem containing personification.

## A pensar...

1. What phrases does the poet use to describe the solitary existence of the palm? (Clarify)

   *Answers will vary and may include* palma sola; nació sola; creció sin que yo la viera; creció sola; vive sola; siempre sola; sueña sola; palma sola soñando.

2. How is the palm tree in the poem different from a palm tree found in nature? (Compare and Contrast)

   *Sample answer:* The plant in the poem is rooted in a pot rather than the earth. It lives on a patio instead of in its natural environment. It is isolated and disconnected from other living things.

3. Why do you think the poet repeats the words **palma** and **sola** throughout the poem? (Analyze)

   *Sample answer:* He repeats **palma** and **sola** to establish a rhythm.

**READER'S SUCCESS STRATEGY** Pay attention to the poem's descriptive details. Draw a sketch of what you imagine the palm tree to look like.

La palma sola **soñando,**
palma sola,
15 que va **libre** por[8] el viento,
libre y sola,
suelta[9] de **raíz** y **tierra,**
suelta y sola;
cazadora[10] de las nubes,
20 palma sola,
palma sola,
palma.

---

[8] through    [9] free    [10] huntress

**║ MÁRCALO ⟩ ANÁLISIS**

A **metaphor** is an implied comparison between two things. In **"Palma sola,"** **Guardián del atardecer** is a metaphor: the palm tree is being compared to a watchman. Read the last verse of the poem to find another metaphor. Underline the metaphor and name the two things being compared.

Students should underline **cazadora de las nubes.** The palm tree is being compared to a huntress. By saying the palm tree is hunting the clouds, the poet emphasizes the tree's height.

**CHALLENGE** In what ways is the palm tree captive? In what ways is it free? **(Evaluate)**

Sample answer: The palm tree is captive in that it is confined to a pot on a patio. It is free in that it makes its own dreams.

**PALABRAS CLAVE**

| | |
|---|---|
| **soñar** *to dream* | **el raíz** (pl. **raíces**) *root* |
| **libre** *free* | **la tierra** *earth* |

# Vocabulario de la lectura

**Palabras clave**

**bajo(a)** *under*      **la luna** *moon*      **soñar** *to dream*
**crecer** *to grow*      **el raíz** (pl. **raíces**) *root*      **la tierra** *earth*
**libre** *free*

**A.** Complete the puzzle using forms of the **Palabras clave.**

```
1        4                5
 l  i  b  r  e             c
 u        a                r              6
 n        í     3          r              b
 a        c     t  i  e  r  r  a
          e                c              j
       2                   e              o
          s  o  ñ  a  r
```

**Across**
1. ¿Qué haces en tu tiempo _____?
2. Lo haces cuando estás durmiendo.
3. La palma del poema es «suelta de raíz
   y _____».

**Down**
1. La ves por la noche.
4. Los árboles y las plantas los tienen.
5. Es el proceso de hacerse más grande.
6. Es lo opuesto *(opposite)* de **encima**.

**B.** Choose three of the **Palabras clave** and write a sentence with each one.

_____

_____

_____

_____

_____

_____

_____

# ¿Comprendiste?

**1.** ¿Qué es una palma?

Es un tipo de árbol.

**2.** ¿Dónde está la palma del poema?

Está en el patio.

**3.** ¿Es el patio abierto o sellado?

Es sellado.

**4.** ¿Con qué dos cosas compara la palma Nicolás Guillén?

La compara con un guardián del atardecer y una cazadora de las nubes.

**5.** ¿Qué dos palabras se repiten frecuentemente en el poema?

Se repiten **palma** y **sola**.

# Conexión personal

Nicolás Guillén chose a palm tree on a patio to represent the concept of solitude **(la soledad)**. If you were a poet, what things would you use to illustrate the state of being alone? Use the word web to jot down your ideas. Some words have been provided as examples.

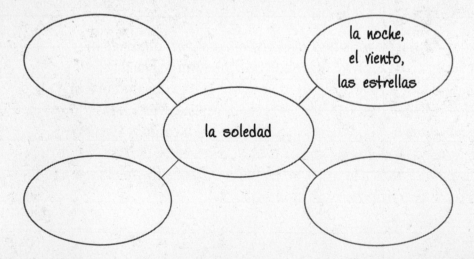

# Para leer   *Como agua para chocolate*

## Reading Strategy

**CONNECT TO YOUR OWN LIFE** You can connect the subject
of a reading to your own life. As you read the recipe from
**Como agua para chocolate**, think about foods and recipes that
have special meaning for you. Compare Laura Esquivel's recipe
for making chocolate to one of your own recipes.

| Chocolate | My Recipe |
|---|---|
| only two ingredients | lots of ingredients |

## What You Need to Know

This reading is a recipe from the novel *Como agua para chocolate* by
Mexican writer Laura Esquivel. The book is in the form of monthly
installments with food and home remedies used to describe the life and
loves of the main character. The recipe is for chocolate, which is made
from the seeds, or beans, of the cacao tree. The word **cacao** is Spanish,
from the Nahuatl word *cacahuatl*. Cacao was so prized by the Aztecs that
the beans were used as a form of currency. The Aztecs also ground the
beans to produce a rich chocolate beverage.

## Sobre la autora

Laura Esquivel nació en México en 1950. Empezó su carrera de escritora como guionista *(scriptwriter)* de películas. En 1989 publicó la novela *Como agua para chocolate,* que ganó mucha popularidad tanto en Latinoamérica como en Estados Unidos. En 1992, la película basada en la novela tuvo mucho éxito y Esquivel ganó el premio Ariel (de la Academia Mexicana de Ciencias y Artes Cinematográficas) al mejor guión.

〜〜〜〜〜〜〜

# Como agua para chocolate

## Ingredientes chocolate:

*2 libras Cacao Soconusco*
*2 libras Cacao Maracaibo*
*2 libras Cacao Caracas*
*Azúcar entre 4 y 6 libras según el gusto*

## Manaera de hacerse:

**L**a primera operación es tostar el cacao. Para hacerlo es conveniente utilizar una charola de hojalata[1] en vez del comal[2], pues el aceite que se desprende[3] de los granos se pierde entre los
5 poros del comal. Es importantísimo poner cuidado en este tipo de indicaciones, pues la **bondad** del chocolate depende de tres cosas, a saber: de que el cacao que se emplee esté sano[4] y no averiado[5], de que se mezclen[6] en su
10 **fabricación** distintas clases de cacao y, por último, de su **grado** de tueste[7].

El grado de tueste **aconsejable** es el del momento en que el cacao comienza a despedir[8] su aceite. Si se retira[9] antes, aparte de presentar
15 un **aspecto** descolorido y **desagradable,** lo hará indigesto[10]. Por el contrario, si se deja más tiempo sobre el fuego[11], el grano quedará **quemado** en gran parte y contaminará de acrimonia y aspereza al chocolate[12].

(···)

[1] *charola de holata* pan made of tin
[2] clay griddle
[3] is given off
[4] in good condition; intact
[5] damaged; spoiled
[6] are mixed
[7] toasting
[8] *comienza a despedir* starts to give off
[9] it is removed
[10] it will be indigestible
[11] flame, heat
[12] *contaminará de acrimonia y aspereza* will make bitter and acrid

### PALABRAS CLAVE

**la bondad** *goodness*
**la fabricación** *making, manufacture*
**el grado** *degree*
**aconsejable** *advisable*
**el aspecto** *appearance, aspect*
**desagradable** *disagreeable, unpleasant*
**quemado(a)** *burned*

**APUNTES**

## A pensar...

**1.** Write the numbers 1, 2, 3, 4, or 5 to show the order of steps in the recipe. **(Chronological Order)**

_5_ Divide the mass into chunks.

_2_ Separate the hulls with a sieve.

_4_ Add the sugar and pound the mixture.

_1_ Toast the beans in a pan made of tin.

_3_ Grind the beans on a metate.

**2.** What three things does the goodness of the chocolate depend on? Circle the correct answers. **(Identify Main Idea and Details)**

the bitterness of the cacao beans

( the mixing of different kinds of beans )

( the undamaged condition of the beans )

the use of a clay griddle to toast the beans

( the degree of toasting of the beans )

**3.** What happens when the cacao is not toasted enough and when it is toasted too much? **(Cause and Effect)**

_When it is not toasted enough, it will have a discolored and unpleasant appearance and be indigestible. When it is toasted too much, it will be burned and made bitter and acrid._

20 Cuando el cacao ya está tostado como se indicó, se limpia utilizando un cedazo[13] para separar la cáscara[14] del grano. Debajo del metate[15] donde se ha de **moler**[16], se pone un cajete[17] con buena lumbre[18] y cuando ya está 25 caliente el metate, se procede a moler el grano. Se mezcla entonces con el azúcar, **machacándolo** con un mazo[19] y moliendo las dos cosas juntas. En seguida se divide la masa en **trozos.** Con las manos se moldean las 30 tablillas[20], redondas o alargadas[21], según el gusto, y se ponen a orear[22]. Con la punta[23] de un cuchillo se le pueden señalar[24] las divisiones que se deseen[25].

---

| | | |
|---|---|---|
| [13] sieve | [14] hull | [15] grinding stone |
| [16] _se ha de moler_ it is to be ground | | [17] earthenware bowl |
| [18] hot fire | [19] mallet, wooden hammer | [20] tablets |
| [21] round or elongated | [22] to air | [23] tip |
| [24] to mark | [25] are desired | |

**PALABRAS CLAVE**

**moler** _to grind_          **el trozo** _chunk, piece_
**machacar** _to pound_

# Vocabulario de la lectura

**Palabras clave**

**aconsejable**  *advisable*
**el aspecto**  *appearance, aspect*
**la bondad**  *goodness*
**desagradable**  *disagreeable, unpleasant*
**la fabricación**  *making, manufacture*

**el grado**  *degree*
**machacar**  *to pound*
**moler**  *to grind*
**quemado(a)**  *burned*
**el trozo**  *chunk, piece*

**A.** Complete each sentence with a **Palabra clave**.

1. El ____grado____ de tueste es el del momento en que el cacao empieza
   a despedir su aceite.

2. El cacao presenta un ____aspecto____ descolorido si se retira antes.

3. Si se deja más tiempo sobre el fuego, el grano queda ____quemado____.

4. Se procede a ____moler____ el grano con un metate.

5. Hay que ____machacar____ el grano y el azúcar con un mazo.

**B.** On the blank line next to each group of words, write the **Palabra clave**
that goes with each set of clues.

1. cualidad; bueno          ____bondad____

2. hacer; productos, comida          ____fabricación____

3. fragmento, porción, pedazo          ____trozo____

4. feo, horrible          ____desagradable____

5. recomendable, apropiado          ____aconsejable____

# ¿Comprendiste?

**1.** ¿Cuántas libras de cacao necesitas para preparar la receta?

Necesitas seis libras.

**2.** ¿Cuál es el otro ingrediente?

Es azúcar.

**3.** ¿Qué haces primero?

Primero, tuestas el cacao.

**4.** ¿Cuándo procedes a moler el grano?

Procedes a moler el grano cuando el metate está caliente.

**5.** ¿Cómo se moldean las tablillas?

Se las moldean con las manos.

# Conexión personal

Do you like chocolate? What other foods do you like? List them in the chart and write a couple of adjectives to describe each one.

| Comida | Descripción |
|---|---|
| chocolate | dulce, marrón |
| | |
| | |
| | |
| | |

# Para leer   *Don Quijote de la Mancha*

## Reading Strategy

**UNDERSTAND CHARACTER'S MOTIVES** Motives are the emotions, wants, or needs that cause a character to act or react in a certain way. As you read this retelling of the beginning of *Don Quijote de la Mancha,* use the chart below to understand the actions of don Quijote. Next to each action, describe the reason, or motivation, he had for taking it.

| Action | Reason |
|---|---|
| 1. He wants to travel the world in search of adventure. | He wants to be like the knight-errant heroes in books of chivalry. |
| 2. He adds his region's name, *la Mancha,* to his own name. | He wants to make la Mancha famous. |
| 3. He polishes the armor that belonged to his great-grandfather. | He believes he will be fighting in battles and therefore needs armor and weapons. |
| 4. He names his horse Rocinante. | He decides that the horse of a knight-errant should have an impressive name. |
| 5. He imagines that Aldonza Lorenzo is a noble lady. | As a knight-errant, he needs a lady to whom to dedicate his heroic deeds. |

## What You Need to Know

The following selection is an adaptation of the first chapter of *El ingenioso hidalgo don Quijote de la Mancha,* the famous novel by Miguel de Cervantes. Romances of chivalry, the books that "dried out" don Quijote's brain, were popular reading between the Middle Ages and the Renaissance. Knight-errants, frequent heroes in books of chivalry, wandered in search of adventure to prove their bravery, honor, and gallantry toward women.

**APUNTES**

*Sobre el autor*

Miguel de Cervantes Saavedra (1547–1616) nació en Alcalá de Henares, España. Fue soldado y luchó en Lepanto, donde perdió el uso de la mano izquierda. Más tarde fue capturado por piratas y pasó cinco años prisionero. Escribió en todos los géneros. Algunas de sus obras son *Viaje del Parnaso* (poesía); *Comedias y entremeses* (drama); y su obra más famosa, *Don Quijote de la Mancha,* que se publicó en dos partes y puede ser la novela más importante de la literatura universal. Aunque *Don Quijote* fue un éxito inmediato, Cervantes fue pobre toda la vida.

# El famoso hidalgo don Quijote de la Mancha

Había una vez[1] un **hidalgo pobre** en un lugar de España que se llama la Mancha. En su casa había[2] muchísimos libros de **caballería** porque el pasatiempo favorito de este señor era[3] leer y leer, especialmente libros

5 de caballería. Se pasaba[4] las noches completas sin dormir, leyendo hasta el **amanecer,** y lo mismo durante el día.

---

[1] Once upon a time there was    [2] there were    [3] was    [4] He spent

**PALABRAS CLAVE**

**el (la) hidalgo(a)** *person of noble descent*      **la caballería** *chivalry*
**pobre** *poor*                                      **el amanecer** *dawn*

Leyó tantos y tantos libros que un día <u>se le</u>
10 secó el **cerebro**[5] y perdió el juicio[6]. Se
imaginó todo tipo de situaciones: batallas,
desafíos[7], encantamientos[8], heridas[9], **amores,**
tormentas[10] y muchas otras cosas imposibles.
Para él todas estas cosas eran[11] reales, tan
15 reales como su casa, el ama[12] de cuarenta
años, su sobrina de diecinueve años, su **rocín
flaco** y el mozo[13].

Un día resuelve **hacerse caballero andante.**
Decide ir por todo el mundo con sus armas y
20 caballo a buscar aventuras. Desea pelear[14] por
la justicia como los caballeros andantes de las
novelas que le gustan. Se va por el mundo a
buscar honra y fama.

Primero limpia las armas que fueron de su
25 **bisabuelo.** Después decide que el rocín de un
caballero andante tiene que tener un nombre
impresionante. «Rocinante te voy a llamar»,
le dice a su rocín. Luego cambia su propio[15]
nombre para incorporar el nombre de su
30 región y hacerla famosa. De esa forma se
convierte en[16] don Quijote de la Mancha.

---

[5] *se le secó el cerebro* his brain dried out    [6] sanity    [7] duels
[8] enchantments    [9] injuries    [10] misfortunes    [11] were
[12] housekeeper    [13] stable boy    [14] to fight    [15] own
[16] *se convierte en* he becomes

**PALABRAS CLAVE**
**el cerebro** *brain*      **hacerse** *to become*
**los amores** *love affairs*     **el caballero andante** *knight-errant*
**el rocín** *workhorse*     **el bisabuelo** *great-grandfather*
**flaco(a)** *thin*

**READING TIP** This reading
contains several plays on
words. **Quijote**, the name of
the central character, is also
the word for a piece of armor.
**Rocinante** is made up of two
words: **rocín** *(workhorse)*, and
**ante** *(before)*. **Dulcinea**, the
name of Quijote's lady, is
inspired by the word **dulce**.

**MÁRCALO** ⟩ **ANÁLISIS**
**Hyperbole** is a figure of speech
in which exaggeration is used
for emphasis or effect, as in
*This book weighs a ton.* Find
and underline an example of
hyperbole in the second
paragraph of this reading.

**APUNTES**

## A pensar...

1. Write the numbers 1, 2, 3, and 4 to show the order in which Don Quijote does the following things. **(Chronological Order)**

   _2_ He names his horse *Rocinante.*

   _4_ He decides to call Aldonza Lorenzo *Dulcinea del Toboso.*

   _3_ He changes his own name to *Don Quijote de la Mancha.*

   _1_ He polishes the armor that belonged to his great-grandfather.

2. Why does Don Quijote want to become a knight-errant? **(Clarify)**

   *Sample answer: He admires the heroic knight-errants in the books of chivalry he has been reading.*

**CHALLENGE** What does Cervantes suggest about books of chivalry? What evidence can you find in the reading to support your answer? **(Infer)**

*Answers will vary. Sample answer: Cervantes suggests that books of chivalry are addictive to some people. Don Quijote reads them throughout the night. Cervantes also pokes fun at these books. It is from reading so many of them that Don Quijote loses his mind.*

Por último, como buen caballero andante, necesita una enamorada [17] a quien dedicarle sus grandes **hazañas.** En Toboso, un lugar
35 cerca de la Mancha, hay una moza labradora [18], Aldonza Lorenzo, de la que antes estuvo **enamorado.** En su imaginación Aldonza se convierte en la **dama** de sus **sueños.** Es así como nace la figura de Dulcinea del Toboso,
40 porque así se llama el lugar donde ella vive.

---

[17] *girlfriend*    [18] *moza labradora* peasant girl

**PALABRAS CLAVE**

| | |
|---|---|
| **la hazaña** *feat; heroic deed* | **la dama** *lady* |
| **enamorado(a) (de)** *in love (with)* | **el sueño** *dream* |

# Vocabulario de la lectura

**Palabras clave**

**el amanecer** *dawn*
**los amores** *love affairs*
**el bisabuelo** *great-grandfather*
**la caballería** *chivalry*
**el caballero andante** *knight-errant*
**el cerebro** *brain*
**la dama** *lady*
**enamorado(a) (de)** *in love (with)*

**flaco(a)** *thin*
**hacerse** *to become*
**la hazaña** *feat; heroic deed*
**el (la) hidalgo(a)** *person of noble descent*
**pobre** *poor*
**el rocín** *workhorse*
**el sueño** *dream*

**A.** Complete each analogy with one of the **Palabras clave.** In an analogy, the last two words must be related in the same way that the first two are related.

1. CAMINAR : PIERNAS : : pensar : _____cerebro_____

2. CHICO: MUCHACHO : : señora : _____dama_____

3. ALTO : BAJO : : gordo : _____flaco_____

4. HIJO: PADRE : : abuelo : _____bisabuelo_____

5. MIRAR: VER : : fantasía : _____sueño_____

**B.** Complete each sentence with the correct form of a **Palabra clave.**

Don Quijote es un _____hidalgo_____ que vive en la Mancha. Tiene pocas
　　　　　　　　　　　　(1)

posesiones; es _____pobre_____. También está loco a causa de leer tantos
　　　　　　　　　(2)

libros de _____caballería_____. Pasa muchas noches sin dormir, leyendo estos
　　　　　　　(3)

libros hasta el _____amanecer_____. Un día, decide hacerse _____caballero andante_____
　　　　　　　　　　(4)　　　　　　　　　　　　　　　　　　　(5)

que se va por el mundo a buscar honra y fama. Primero, limpia las armas de su

_____bisabuelo_____. Luego, cambia el nombre de su _____rocín_____ a
　　　　(6)　　　　　　　　　　　　　　　　　　　　　　　(7)

Rocinante. Por último, imagina que Aldonza Lorenzo, una moza labradora, es la

_____dama_____ de sus sueños y la llama Dulcinea del Toboso.
　　　(8)

## ¿Comprendiste?

**1.** ¿Quién es don Quijote?

Don Quijote es un hidalgo pobre de una región de España que se llama la Mancha.

**2.** ¿Qué tipo de libros le gusta leer?

Le gusta leer libros de caballería.

**3.** ¿Por qué se le secó el cerebro?

Se le secó el cerebro porque leyó muchísimos libros de caballería.

**4.** ¿Qué resuelve hacerse don Quijote?

Resuelve hacerse caballero andante.

**5.** ¿Cómo se llama su caballo?

Su caballo se llama Rocinante.

**6.** ¿Quién es Aldonza Lorenzo? ¿Qué nombre le da don Quijote?

Aldonza Lorenzo es una moza labradora. Don Quijote le da el nombre de Dulcinea del Toboso.

## Conexión personal

Many adventure stories involve a quest, a journey that a character makes to reach a certain goal. Think of characters in books, movies, or television shows that go on quests. List them in the chart below.

| Personaje *(Character)* | De | Meta *(Goal)* |
|---|---|---|
| don Quijote | Don Quijote de la Mancha | pelear por la justicia |
|  |  |  |
|  |  |  |

## Para leer  *Oda al tomate*

## Reading Strategy

**WORD CHOICE** Writers choose their words with care in order to express their thoughts accurately. Through careful word choice, a writer can make readers feel a certain way or visualize an image. As you read **"Oda al tomate,"** think about how certain words and phrases affect you as a reader. Use the chart below to record interesting words and phrases and what they convey to you.

| Words and Phrases | Ideas and Feelings They Convey |
|---|---|
| "el tomate invade las cocinas" | expresses the abundance of tomatoes |
| "su color fogoso" | conveys an image of their bright red color |
|  |  |
|  |  |
|  |  |

## What You Need to Know

This reading is the poem **"Oda al tomate"** from the book *Odas elementales* (1954) by the Chilean poet Pablo Neruda (1904–1973). Odes are long lyric poems, usually of a serious or meditative nature and having an elevated style and formal structure. Unlike most odes, those of Pablo Neruda exalt the ordinary and the everyday, from tomatoes and artichokes to the air and rain.

**READING TIP** Read the poem aloud. Let punctuation show you where to stop or pause. How many sentences are there in the poem? A capital letter begins each one. Write your answer on the line below.

*There are four sentences.*

## APUNTES

[MÁRCALO] ANÁLISIS

Remember that **personification** is the attribution of human characteristics to an object, animal, or idea. Pablo Neruda uses personification to give life to foods. Find and circle examples of personification in the poem. Which foods are personified? Write your answer on the lines below.

*The tomato, onion, oil, parsley, and roasted meat are personified.*

**CHALLENGE** Why would the street be filled with tomatoes? **(Draw Conclusions)**

*Answers will vary. Sample answer: The street could be the location of a farmers' market.*

*Sobre el autor*

Pablo Neruda nació en Parral, Chile. Su verdadero nombre era Ricardo Neftalí Reyes. Estudió pedagogía en francés en la Universidad de Chile. Allí conoció a Albertina Azócar. A ella le dedica los primeros poemas de *Veinte poemas de amor y una canción desesperada* (1924). Para Neruda, todo puede ser poesía. En sus famosas *Odas elementales* escribió versos para el tomate, el átomo, un reloj, la pobreza y la soledad. Pablo Neruda fue diplomático en varios países de Europa y en México. En 1971 obtuvo el Premio Nóbel de Literatura.

# Oda al tomate

La calle
se **llenó** de tomates,
mediodía,
verano,
5  la luz
se parte[1]
en dos
**mitades**
de tomate,
10  corre
por las calles
el jugo.

[1] is split

**PALABRAS CLAVE**
**llenar** *to fill*     **la mitad** *half*

*¡En español!* Level 1

En diciembre
se desata [2]
15 el tomate,
invade
las cocinas,
entra por los almuerzos,
se sienta [3]
20 reposado [4]
en los aparadores [5],
entre los vasos,
las mantequilleras [6],
los saleros [7] azules.
25 Tiene
luz propia,
majestad benigna.
Debemos, por desgracia [8],
asesinarlo:
30 se hunde [9]
el cuchillo
en su pulpa **viviente,**
en una roja
víscera,
35 un sol
fresco,
profundo,

---

| | | |
|---|---|---|
| [2]breaks loose | [3]sits down | [4]relaxed |
| [5]sideboards | [6]butter dishes | [7]saltcellars |
| [8]unfortunately | [9]sinks | |

**APUNTES**

**CHALLENGE** Why is it December and yet it is summertime in the poem? (Evaluate)

*It is summertime in December because the setting of the poem is Chile, which is in the Southern Hemisphere and has seasons that are the opposite of those in the Northern Hemisphere.*

**PALABRAS CLAVE**
**viviente** *living*

## A pensar...

**1.** Why do you think the poet compares the tomato to the sun? **(Draw Conclusions)**

*Answers will vary. Sample answer: He compares the two because both are round and the sun can be red like a tomato.*

**2.** What do you think the phrase **la cintura del verano** means? **(Analyze)**

*Answers will vary. Sample answer: It means the midpoint of summer, as the waist is the middle of the body.*

### APUNTES

inagotable [10],

llena de ensaladas

40 de Chile,

se casa [11] alegremente

con la clara cebolla,

y para celebrarlo

se deja

45 caer [12]

aceite,

hijo

esencial del olivo,

sobre sus hemisferios entreabiertos [13],

50 **agrega**

la pimienta

su fragancia,

la sal su magnetismo:

son las bodas [14]

55 del día,

el perejil

levanta

banderines [15],

las papas

60 hierven [16] vigorosamente,

el **asado**

golpea [17]

---

[10] inexhaustible
[11] it marries
[12] *se deja caer* is dropped
[13] halved
[14] weddings
[15] *perejil levanta banderines* parsley hoists its flag
[16] boil, bubble
[17] beats

**PALABRAS CLAVE**
**agregar** *to add*          **el asado** *roasted meat*

con su aroma
en la puerta,
65 es hora!
vamos!
y sobre
la mesa, en la (cintura)
del verano,
70 el tomate,
astro[18] de tierra,
estrella
repetida
y **fecunda,**
75 nos muestra[19]
sus circunvoluciones[20],
sus canales,
la insigne plenitud[21]
y la abundancia
80 sin hueso[22],
sin coraza[23],
sin escamas[24] ni **espinas,**
nos entrega[25]
el regalo
85 de su color **fogoso**
y la totalidad de su **frescura.**

---

| [18] star | [19] shows | [20] convolutions, folds |
| [21] celebrated fullness | | [22] stone, pit |
| [23] shell | [24] scales | [25] delivers |

**PALABRAS CLAVE**

| **la cintura** *waist, waistline* | **fogoso(a)** *fiery* |
| **fecundo(a)** *fertile* | **la frescura** *freshness, coolness* |
| **la espina** *thorn* | |

# Vocabulario de la lectura

**Palabras clave**

| | | |
|---|---|---|
| **agregar** *to add* | **fecundo(a)** *fertile* | **llenar** *to fill* |
| **el asado** *roasted meat* | **fogoso(a)** *fiery* | **la mitad** *half* |
| **la cintura** *waist, waistline* | **la frescura** *freshness, coolness* | **viviente** *living* |
| **la espina** *thorn* | | |

**A.** On the line next to each word pair, write whether the words are synonyms or antonyms. Synonyms are words with the same or similar meaning. Antonyms are words with opposite meanings.

1. calor—frescura   _antonyms_

2. adicionar—agregar   _synonyms_

3. fértil—fecundo   _synonyms_

4. ardiente—fogoso   _synonyms_

**B.** Answer each question by writing one of the **Palabras clave** in the blank.

1. ¿Qué palabra es un tipo de carne?   _asado_

2. ¿Qué palabra significa algo que vive?   _viviente_

3. ¿Qué haces con un vaso?   _llenar_

4. ¿Qué palabra es una parte del cuerpo humano?   _cintura_

5. ¿Qué tiene una rosa?   _espinas_

6. ¿Qué palabra significa «una de dos partes»?   _mitad_

# ¿Comprendiste?

**1.** ¿En qué mes ocurre el poema?

Ocurre en diciembre.

**2.** ¿Qué tiene el tomate?

Tiene luz propia, majestad benigna.

**3.** ¿Qué no tiene el tomate?

No tiene hueso, coraza, escamas, ni espinas.

**4.** ¿Cuáles son los ingredientes de la ensalada?

Los ingredientes de la ensalada son tomates, cebolla, aceite, pimienta y sal.

# Conexión personal

Of the ordinary and the everyday, what would you write an ode to? Decide on a subject for your ode and write a list of words and phrases you would use to describe it in the notebook at the right. Include at least one example of personification.

Oda a _____

_____

_____

_____

_____

_____

_____

_____

_____

_____

_____

_____

_____

# Academic and Informational Reading

In this section you'll find strategies to help you read all kinds of informational materials. The examples here range from magazines you read for fun to textbooks to bus schedules. Applying these simple and effective techniques will help you be a successful reader of the many texts you encounter every day.

# Reading a Magazine Article

A magazine article is designed to catch and hold your interest. You will get the most from your reading if you recognize the special features of a magazine page and learn how to use them. Look at the sample magazine article as you read each strategy below.

**A** Read the **title** to get an idea of what the article is about. Scan any other **headings** to see how information in the article is organized.

**B** As you read, notice any **quotations.** Who is quoted? Is the person a reliable source on the subject?

**C** Notice information set in special type, such as **italics** or **boldface.** For example, look at the caption in the article that is set in italic type.

**D** Study **visuals,** such as charts, graphs, pictures, maps, and bulleted lists. Visuals add important information and bring the topic to life.

**MARK IT UP** Read the magazine article on the next page. Use the tips above to help you answer the following questions.

1. What is the topic of this article? This article is about the comparative sales of

    salsa and ketchup.

2. Underline the name and title of the person who speaks for Marcus Condiments.

3. Do you think the spokesperson for Restivo Tomato Products is a reliable source of information on salsa? Why or why not?

    Yes, because she's a marketing manager for a major salsa maker.

    _____

4. Circle the caption set in italic type.

5. Draw a box around the visual that compares the sales of ketchup and salsa.

# A SALSA AND KETCHUP BATTLE IT OUT FOR TOP SAUCE

When you want to add a little spice to your snack or supper, do you reach for the salsa or the ketchup? Until recently, sales figures showed that more people grabbed the ketchup bottle, slathering the tomato sauce on their hamburgers, hot dogs, French fries, mashed potatoes, scrambled eggs, green beans, and almost anything else you can imagine. Elvis Presley even used it as a topping for sweet potato pie.

In 1996, however, salsa moved into number one position, replacing ketchup as the nation's top tomato sauce. Since then, the two condiments have been battling it out, with ketchup frantically trying to play catch-up. And it seems to have **B** succeeded. "Salsa's popularity has peaked. Ketchup is back on top," boasts Peter Harrington, chief executive of the world's largest ketchup maker, Marcus Condiments.

Salsa producers do not seem overly concerned, though. Mary Sullivan, a senior marketing manager for a leading salsa maker, Restivo Tomato Products, confidently noted that salsa is perfectly able to keep pace with ketchup. It's every bit as versatile a sauce, she says. "We're not limited to hamburgers and hot dogs." Every day, more people spoon more salsa over a whole alphabet of foods, from avocados to ziti.

To increase their slim lead over salsa, Marcus Condiments is focusing on research that shows families with children use three times more ketchup than childless households.

The salsa-ketchup war probably will not be decided any time soon. And maybe it shouldn't be. After all, to update an old saying, "Variety is the spice of life"—and of tomato sauce, too.

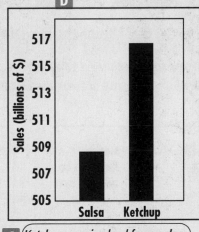

**D**

Sales (billions of $)

517
515
513
511
509
507
505

Salsa    Ketchup

**C** *Ketchup regains lead from salsa.*

# Reading a Textbook

The first page of a textbook lesson introduces you to a particular topic. The page also provides important information that will guide you through the rest of the lesson. Look at the sample textbook page as you read each strategy below.

**A** Preview the **title** and other **headings** to find out the lesson's main topic and related subtopics.

**B** Read the **key ideas** or **objectives** at the top of the page. Keep these in mind as you read. They will help you set a purpose for your reading.

**C** Look for a list of terms or **vocabulary words** at the start of each lesson. These words will be identified and defined throughout the lesson.

**D** Study **visuals** such as photographs and illustrations. Read the **captions.** Visuals can add information and interest to the topic.

**MARK IT UP** Read the sample textbook page. Then use the strategies above to help you answer the following questions.

1. What is the topic of this lesson? _This lesson is about waves and erosion._

_____

2. Circle the key idea of the lesson.

3. Draw a box around the vocabulary words that will be defined in the lesson.

4. Put a star next to the visual that shows the structure of a sea arch.

5. Using a graphic organizer can help you take notes on the textbook material you learn. Complete the chart using information on shoreline features from the lesson.

| Waves strike headlands. | → | Notch is formed. | → | Notch deepens to become sea cave. | → | Waves cut through walls of sea cave to form sea arch. | → | Roof of sea arch falls in, leaving sea stack. |

## A Shoreline Features

Ocean waves change the shape of a shoreline by eroding rock materials and by depositing sediments.

### Waves and Erosion

Breaking storm waves may strike rock cliffs with a force of thousands of kilograms per square meter. Such breakers easily remove large masses of loose sand and clay. Air and water driven into cracks and fissures may split bedrock apart. Sand and pebbles carried by the water abrade the bedrock. Waves pound loose rock and boulders into pebbles and sand. In addition, seawater dissolves minerals from rocks such as limestone.

When waves strike the headlands of a deep-water shoreline, they may cut away the rock up to the high-tide level, forming a notch. If the materials overhanging the notch collapse, a sea cliff results.

Cliffs made of soft materials such as soil and sand wear away very quickly. For example, waves washing up on Cape Cod in Massachusetts are carrying away materials from sand cliffs there so rapidly that the cliffs are receding at a rate of about one meter every year.

In cliffs made of harder rock materials, a notch may deepen until it becomes a sea cave. Waves may cut through the walls of sea caves to form sea arches. Arches may also form when waves cut through vertical cracks in narrow headlands. If the roof of a sea arch falls in, what remains is a tall, narrow rock island called a sea stack.

Sea caves, sea arches, and sea stacks can be seen on the coasts of California, Oregon, Washington, and Maine, on the Gaspé Peninsula of Canada, and in many parts of the Mediterranean Sea.

## 16.3

**B** **KEY IDEA**

Waves erode shorelines and deposit sediments in characteristic formations.

**C** **KEY VOCABULARY**
- beach
- sandbar
- fjord

**BAJA PENINSULA** Ocean waves have formed this sea stack and sea arch in Mexico.

**D**

Sea stack

Sea arch

349

# Reading a Table

Tables give a lot of information in an organized way. These tips can help you read a table quickly and accurately. Look at the example as you read each strategy in this list.

**A** Look at the **title** to find out the content of the table.

**B** Read the **introduction** to get a general overview of the information included in the table.

**C** Examine the **heading** of each row and column. To find specific information, locate the place where a row and column intersect.

**B** Water temperatures vary widely along the coasts of North America. This table shows the temperature of the water in March at eight beaches.

**A** **Average March Water Temperature at Eight Beaches (°F)**

| Location | Temperature | Location | Temperature |
|----------|-------------|----------|-------------|
| Newport, RI | 37 | Oceanside, CA | 58 |
| Ocean City, MD | 42 | Seattle, WA | 46 |
| Veracruz, Mexico | 75 | Honolulu, HI | 76 |
| Freeport, TX | 62 | Juneau, AK | 37 |

**MARK IT UP** Answer the following questions using the table of March water temperatures.

**1.** Which two beaches have the same water temperature? Circle the answers in the table.

**2.** What units are used to measure the water temperatures?

degrees Fahrenheit

**3.** If you were planning a swimming vacation in March, what two beaches might you consider visiting?

Veracruz, Mexico, or Honolulu, HI

# Reading a Map

To read a map correctly, you have to identify and understand its elements. Look at the example below as you read each strategy in this list.

**A** Read the **title** to find out what the map shows.

**B** Study the **legend,** or **key,** to find out what symbols and colors are used on the map and what they stand for.

**C** Look at **geographic labels** to understand specific places on the map.

**D** Look at the **scale** to understand how distances on the map relate to actual distances.

**E** Locate the **compass rose,** or **pointer,** to determine direction.

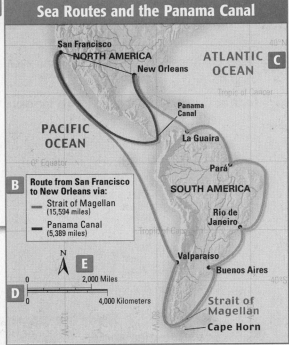

**A** Sea Routes and the Panama Canal

**C** ATLANTIC OCEAN

PACIFIC OCEAN

**B** Route from San Francisco to New Orleans via:
— Strait of Magellan (15,594 miles)
— Panama Canal (5,389 miles)

N

**E**

0          2,000 Miles

**D**

0          4,000 Kilometers

San Francisco
NORTH AMERICA
New Orleans
Panama Canal
La Guaira
Pará
SOUTH AMERICA
Río de Janeiro
Valparaíso
Buenos Aires
Strait of Magellan
Cape Horn

---

[MARK IT UP] Use the map to answer the following questions.

1. What does this map show? _It shows a sea route around South America and a sea route through the Panama Canal. It shows how the Panama Canal drastically cut the length of the sea trip from San Francisco to New Orleans._

2. How many miles is the sea route from San Francisco to New Orleans by way of the Strait of Magellan?

   _15,594 miles_

3. How many miles would you save by taking the Panama Canal from San Francisco to New Orleans rather than the route through the Strait of Magellan?

   _10,205 miles_

4. Draw a straight line from San Francisco to New Orleans. About how many miles apart are these cities by land?

   _about 2,500 miles_

# Reading a Diagram

Diagrams combine pictures with a few words to provide a lot of information. Look at the example on the opposite page as you read each of the following strategies.

**A** Look at the **title** to get an idea of what the diagram is about.

**B** Study the **images** closely to understand each part of the diagram.

**C** Look at the **captions** and the **labels** for more information.

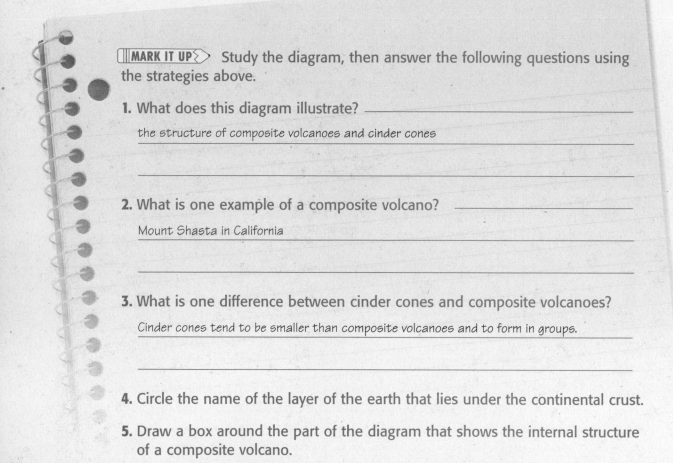

**MARK IT UP** Study the diagram, then answer the following questions using the strategies above.

1. What does this diagram illustrate? _____

   the structure of composite volcanoes and cinder cones

   _____

2. What is one example of a composite volcano? _____

   Mount Shasta in California

   _____

3. What is one difference between cinder cones and composite volcanoes?

   Cinder cones tend to be smaller than composite volcanoes and to form in groups.

   _____

4. Circle the name of the layer of the earth that lies under the continental crust.

5. Draw a box around the part of the diagram that shows the internal structure of a composite volcano.

## A Volcanic Landforms

The shape and structure of a volcano are determined by the nature of its eruptions and the materials it ejects. A cinder cone, perhaps the simplest form of volcano, forms when molten lava is thrown into the air from a vent. Cinder cones, which tend to be smaller than other types of volcanoes, typically form in groups and on the sides of larger volcanoes. Composite volcanoes develop when layers of materials from successive eruptions accumulate around a vent. The diagram shows the structure of these two types of volcanoes.

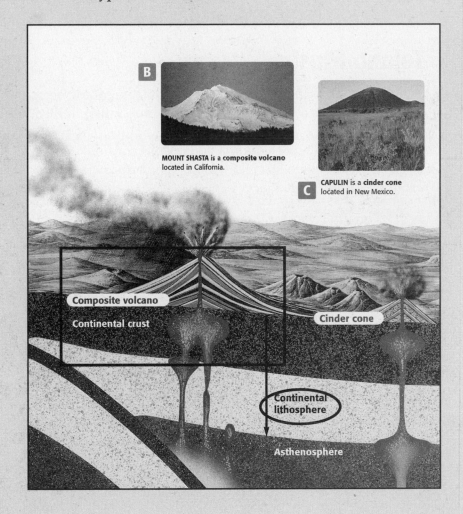

B

MOUNT SHASTA is a composite volcano located in California.

C CAPULIN is a cinder cone located in New Mexico.

Composite volcano

Continental crust

Cinder cone

Continental lithosphere

Asthenosphere

The *main idea* in a paragraph is its most important point. *Details* in the paragraph support the main idea. Identifying the main idea will help you focus on the main message the writer wants to communicate. Use the following strategies to help you identify a paragraph's main idea and supporting details.

- Look for the **main idea,** which is often the first sentence in a paragraph.

- Use the main idea to help you **summarize** the point of the paragraph.

- Identify specific **details,** including facts and examples, that support the main idea.

## Tejano Music

**Main idea** — Tejano music reflects a harmonious combination of Mexican and American lifestyles. Also known as Tex Mex or conjunto music, it blends elements of jazz, country, rock 'n' roll, and rhythm and blues. The typical tejano band, **Details** — or conjunto tejano, consists of a guitar, an accordion, and a *bajo sexto*, or large Spanish twelve-stringed guitar. The performers often wear colorful sombreros and fringed jackets.

**MARK IT UP** Read the following paragraph. Circle the main idea. Then underline the details that support the main idea.

San Antonio, Texas, is a hub of tejano music. Many radio stations compete to bring listeners the latest recording artists and songs. On any given day, articles in numerous newspapers and magazines keep fans informed about who and what is hot. A San Antonio native, Flaco Jiminez, played an important role in spreading this lively art form around the world.

# Problem and Solution

Does the proposed solution to a problem make sense? In order to decide, you need to look at each part of the text. Use the following strategies to read the text below.

- Look at the beginning or middle of a paragraph to find the **statement of the problem.**
- Find **details** that explain the problem and tell why it is important.
- Look for the **proposed solution.**
- Identify the **supporting details** for the proposed solution.
- Think about whether the solution is a good one.

## Lunchroom Language Tables Can Beef Up Students' Skills

*by Tara Blum*

**Statement of problem** — Teachers, parents, administrators, and school board members are concerned that foreign language students are not getting enough practice actually using the language in conversation.

**Details about the problem** — In their foreign language classes, students read dialogs from their textbooks and respond to questions, but rarely get a chance to just communicate their thoughts.

**Proposed solution** — One way to address this problem would be to establish language tables in the lunchroom. Students taking a specific language would eat their lunch at a designated table one day a week. The only rule would be that they must speak no English, just the foreign language.

**Details about the solution** — This plan has several advantages. First, it doesn't require any additional equipment or materials. Second, it wouldn't take time away from other classes or activities. Language students have to eat lunch just like everyone else. Finally, it would be a lot of fun.

Language tables would let students supplement their language skills while nourishing their bodies. And that's a recipe for success!

**MARK IT UP** Use the text and strategies above to answer these questions.

1. Underline the proposed solution.

2. Circle at least one reason that supports this solution.
   *Answers will vary. A sample answer has been circled.*

3. Explain why you think this is or is not a good solution to the problem.

   This is a good solution because it would get students using foreign language without a

   teacher present in a fun setting. / This is not a good solution because kids would resent

   not eating with their friends and wouldn't follow the no-English rule.

# Sequence

*Sequence* is the order in which events happen. Whether you read a story or a social studies lesson, it is important for you to understand *when* things happen in relation to one another. The tips below can help you identify sequence in any type of text.

- Look for the **main steps** or **events** in the sequence.

- Look for **words and phrases that signal time**, such as *in 1845, two days later,* and *by fall of that year.*

- Look for **words and phrases that signal order**, such as *after, first,* and *meanwhile.*

**MARK IT UP** ⟩ Read the passage about the war with Mexico on the next page. Then use the information from the article and the tips above to answer the questions.

1. Underline two words or phrases that signal time.
   Answers will vary. Possible answers have been underlined.
2. Circle two words or phrases that signal order.
   Answers will vary. Possible answers have been circled.
3. A time line can help you identify and understand a sequence of events. Use the information from the passage to complete this time line.

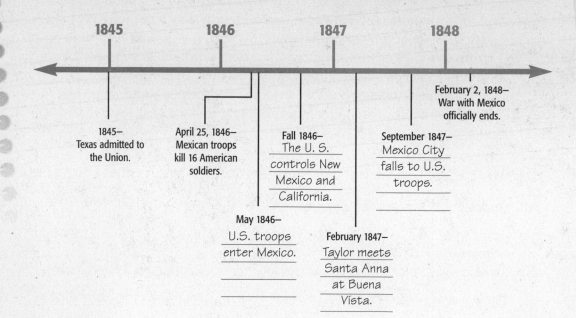

| 1845 | 1846 | 1847 | 1848 |

1845—
Texas admitted to the Union.

April 25, 1846—
Mexican troops kill 16 American soldiers.

May 1846—
U.S. troops enter Mexico.

Fall 1846—
The U. S. controls New Mexico and California.

February 1847—
Taylor meets Santa Anna at Buena Vista.

September 1847—
Mexico City falls to U.S. troops.

February 2, 1848—
War with Mexico officially ends.

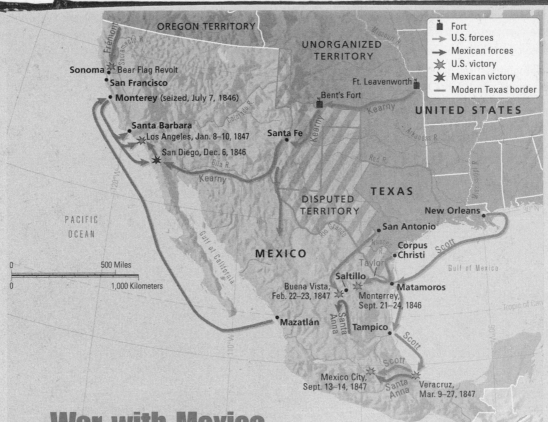

# War with Mexico

In 1845, Congress admitted Texas to the Union as a slave state, despite Northern objections to the spread of slavery. However, Mexico still claimed Texas as its own. Mexico angrily viewed this annexation as an act of war.

In a diplomatic gesture, President Polk sent an ambassador to Mexico offering $25 million for Texas, California, and New Mexico. After Mexico refused, the U.S. sent troops to the northern bank of the Rio Grande. The Mexicans responded with troops on the southern bank. On April 25, 1846, a Mexican cavalry unit crossed the Rio Grande, ambushing an American patrol and killing 16 American soldiers. Two days later, Congress declared war.

U.S. troops entered Mexico in May 1846. About the same time, troops marched toward New Mexico. They took the territory without firing a shot. They then moved westward, and by fall of that year, Americans controlled all of New Mexico and California.

The defeat of Mexico proved far more difficult. The Mexican army was much larger, but the U.S. troops were led by well-trained officers. American forces invaded Mexico from two directions. First, General Taylor battled his way south from Texas toward Northern Mexico. In February 1847, his 4,800 troops met General Santa Anna's 15,000 Mexican forces at Buena Vista. Santa Anna retreated.

Meanwhile, a fierce battle for southern Mexico was raging. Seven months after Taylor's victory in the North, Mexico City fell to U.S. troops led by General Winfield Scott.

The war officially ended on February 2, 1848 with the signing of the Treaty of Guadalupe Hidalgo. This treaty gave the U.S. the present-day states of California, Nevada, Utah, most of Arizona, and parts of New Mexico, Colorado, and Wyoming. In return, the U.S. offered Mexico $15 million and protection of the 80,000 Mexicans living in the newly acquired territories.

# Cause and Effect

A *cause* is an event that brings about another event. An *effect* is something that happens as a result of the first event. Identifying causes and effects helps you understand how events are related. Use the tips below to find causes and effects in any kind of reading.

- Look for an action or event that answers the question, "What happened?" This is the **effect.**

- Look for an action or event that answers the question, "Why did this happen?" This is the **cause.**

- Look for words or phrases that **signal** causes and effects, such as *because, as a result, therefore, consequently,* and *since.*

**MARK IT UP** Read the cause-and-effect passage on the next page. Notice that the first cause and effect are labeled. Then use the strategies above to help you answer the following questions.

1. Circle words in the passage that signal causes and effects. The first one has been done for you.

2. Some causes may have more than one effect. What are two effects of the mosquito's saliva on the body of the victim?

   It prevents blood from clotting and triggers an allergic reaction.

3. Complete the following diagram showing the cause and effects of mosquito bites.

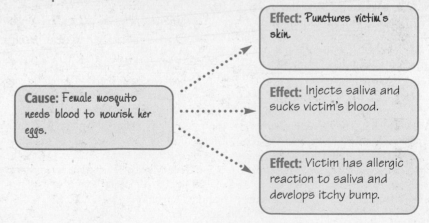

**Cause:** Female mosquito needs blood to nourish her eggs.

**Effect:** Punctures victim's skin.

**Effect:** Injects saliva and sucks victim's blood.

**Effect:** Victim has allergic reaction to saliva and develops itchy bump.

# Bzz! Slap!

**Cause**
If you spend any time outdoors in the summer, at some point you will probably find yourself covered with <u>mosquito bites</u>. The word *mosquito* means "little fly" in Spanish, but the impact these pesky insects have on people is anything but small.

**Signal Word**

**Effect**
Mosquitoes can transmit serious diseases such as yellow fever, encephalitis, and malaria. Usually, though, mosquito bites just (cause) people to develop <u>raised, red bumps that itch like crazy.</u>

This is what happens. Female mosquitoes need blood to nourish the eggs developing in their bodies. (Consequently,) they zero in on living things whose blood they can suck. Once they find a likely victim, the attack begins.

This attack is not really a bite, since a mosquito isn't able to open her jaws. Instead, she punctures the victim's skin with sharp stylets inside her mouth. The mosquito's saliva then flows into these puncture wounds. (Because) the saliva keeps the victim's blood from clotting, the mosquito can drink her fill. This can sometimes amount to 150 percent of the mosquito's weight.

Meanwhile, the mosquito's saliva sets off an allergic reaction in the

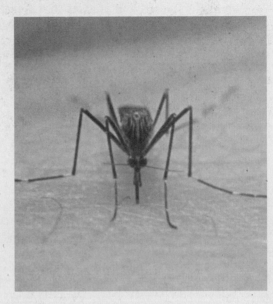

victim. (As a result,) the person develops the itchy swelling we call a mosquito bite. Ironically, if the mosquito finishes eating before the victim slaps or drives her off, there will be less saliva left in the skin. (Therefore,) the allergic reaction and itching will not be so severe.

Here are some steps you can take to help prevent mosquito bites or lessen their effect if you do get bitten.

- Don't go out at prime mosquito time—from dusk to dawn.
- Use insect repellent at all times.
- If you do get bitten, DON'T SCRATCH. Scratching just increases the allergic reaction.

# Comparison and Contrast

*Comparing* two things means showing how they are the same. *Contrasting* two things means showing how they are different. Comparisons and contrasts are important because they show how things or ideas are related. Use these tips to help you understand comparison and contrast in reading assignments such as the article on the opposite page.

- Look for **direct statements** of **comparison and contrast.** "These things are similar because…" or "One major difference is…"

- Pay attention to **words and phrases that signal comparisons**, such as *also, both, is the same as,* and *in the same way.*

- Notice **words and phrases that signal contrasts**. Some of these are *however, still, but,* and *in contrast.*

**MARK IT UP**  Read the article on the next page. Then use the information from the article and the tips above to answer the questions.

1. Circle the words and phrases that signal comparisons. A sample has been done for you.

2. Underline the words and phrases that signal contrast. Notice the sample that has been done.

3. A Venn diagram shows how two subjects are similar and how they are different. Complete this diagram, which uses information from the article to compare and contrast *la quinceañera* and a sweet sixteen party. Add one or more similarities to the center of the diagram and one or more differences to each outer circle.

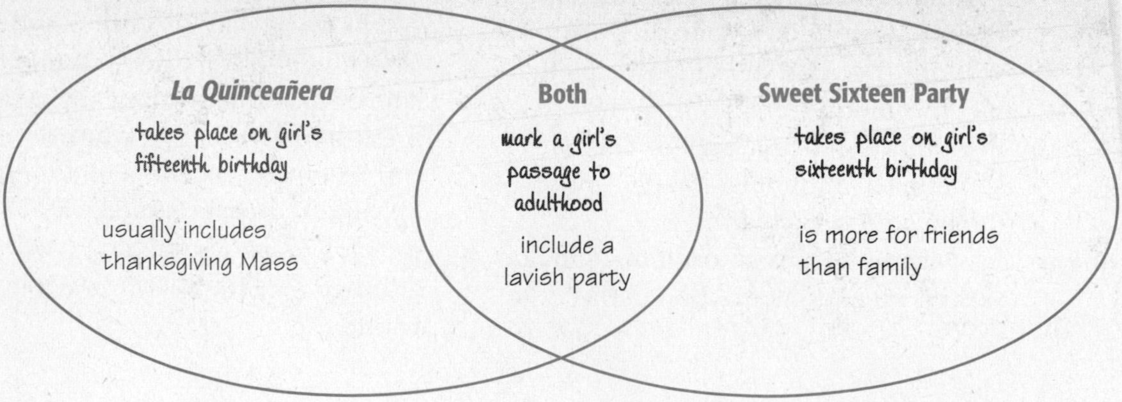

*La Quinceañera*

takes place on girl's fifteenth birthday

usually includes thanksgiving Mass

**Both**

mark a girl's passage to adulthood

include a lavish party

**Sweet Sixteen Party**

takes place on girl's sixteenth birthday

is more for friends than family

# La Quinceañera and Sweet Sixteen

¡FELICIDADES!

Almost every culture has a ceremony to mark the passage of young people from childhood to adulthood. In the Latin culture, this rite of passage for girls is *la quinceañera*. For American girls, it is the sweet sixteen birthday party.

**Comparison** Although both *la quinceañera* and the sweet sixteen birthday party commemorate a girl's passage to adulthood, they **Contrast** differ in when, where, and how the occasion is celebrated. *Quinceañera* means "fifteenth birthday," and that's when the celebration is held. In contrast, a sweet sixteen party takes place when, as the name suggests, a girl is a year older.

The origin of *la quinceañera* is uncertain, although it may have roots in the Aztec, Maya, or Toltec cultures. It generally involves celebration of a thanksgiving Mass followed by a lavish party for the extended family and friends. The *quinceañera* often dances a waltz with her father and other male relatives. In Mexico, girlfriends may give the celebrant a rag doll symbolizing her leaving childhood and its toys behind.

Sweet sixteen parties, on the other hand, do not include the religious component of *la quinceañera*. They also tend to be designed for the girl's friends rather than for her family. Like *quinceañeras*, however, they often are held in hotels or reception halls and include live bands, plentiful food, and many-tiered birthday cakes.

Both *quinceañeras* and sweet sixteeners take advantage of the opportunity to look as adult as possible. They generally deck themselves out in long dresses. *Quinceañeras* often choose frilly frocks in white or pastel colors topped by hats or headdresses. Sweet sixteen dresses can run the gamut from frothy and frilly to sleek and sophisticated.

So whether a girl celebrates *la quinceañera* or her sweet sixteen, the message is the same—"Welcome to adulthood!"

# Persuasion

To be persuasive, an opinion should be backed up with reasons and facts. After you carefully read an opinion and the reasons and facts that support it, you will be able to decide if the opinion makes sense. As you read these tips, look at the sample persuasive essay on the next page.

- Look for words or phrases that **signal an opinion**, such as *I believe, I think,* and *in my opinion.*

- Identify reasons, facts, or expert opinions that **support** the position.

- Ask yourself if the opinion and the reasons that back it up **make sense.**

- Look for **errors in reasoning,** such as overgeneralizations, that may affect the presentation of the opinion.

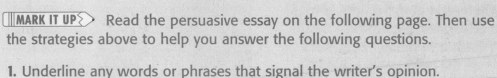 **MARK IT UP** Read the persuasive essay on the following page. Then use the strategies above to help you answer the following questions.

1. Underline any words or phrases that signal the writer's opinion.

2. Circle any words or phrases that signal the opinion of persons other than the writer.

3. The writer presents both sides of this debate. List the points supporting both sides in the chart below. One reason has been provided for you.

| For swimming pool | Against swimming pool |
|---|---|
| 1. The school has a responsibility to teach swimming. | 1. Students can take swimming lessons at the health club. |
| 2. Most students don't have money or time to take private swimming lessons. | 2. Money must be used to repair school building. |
| 3. Students' education is more important than building repairs. | |
| 4. Swimming is an excellent form of exercise. | |

# Our School Needs to Get in the Swim *by Jorge Rojo*

This school needs a swimming pool. Swimming is an important life skill and I believe it is the responsibility of the school to provide this essential part of students' education.

The school's mission is to educate the whole person—mind and body—and to prepare students to be productive citizens. In addition to our academic subjects, we are taught how to eat right, budget our money, and drive a car. But we don't learn the water safety skills that could someday save our lives.

The community and school board obviously don't feel the way I do, however. They repeatedly have refused to fund the building of a pool. In the opinion of one board member, "Students can take swimming lessons at the local health club." Other school officials think that the school has more important needs—repairing the sagging gym floor and installing new lockers, for example.

In my opinion, these reasons are not valid. First, most students cannot afford lessons at the health club. Even those who have the money don't have the time. They're busy with homework and other activities during the school year and have to work or go to summer school during vacation.

I agree that the gym floor should be replaced and wouldn't mind having a new locker. But I believe that the educational needs of the students should come first. Swimming is one of the best forms of exercise there is. Even if knowing how to swim never saves your life, it can improve its quality. Isn't that what an education is all about?

# Social Studies

Social studies class becomes easier when you understand how your textbook's words, pictures, and maps work together to give you information. Following these tips can make you a better reader of social studies lessons. As you read the tips, look at the sample lesson on the right-hand page.

**A** Read the **title** of the lesson and other **headings** to find out what the lesson is about. Smaller headings may introduce subtopics that are related to the main topic.

**B** Read the **main ideas** or **objectives** listed on the first page of the lesson. These items summarize the lesson and help set a purpose for your reading.

**C** Look at the **vocabulary terms** listed on the lesson's first page. These terms will be boldfaced or underlined where they appear in the text.

**D** Notice **how information is organized.** In social studies lessons, ideas are often presented using sequence, cause and effect, comparison and contrast, and main idea and supporting details.

**E** Carefully examine **visuals** such as photographs, boxed text, maps, charts, bulleted lists, time lines, and diagrams. Think about how the visuals and the text are related.

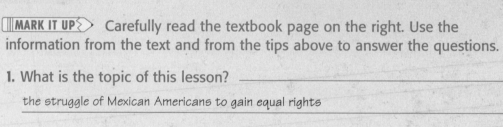

**MARK IT UP** Carefully read the textbook page on the right. Use the information from the text and from the tips above to answer the questions.

1. What is the topic of this lesson? _____

   the struggle of Mexican Americans to gain equal rights

2. Circle the main idea of the lesson.

3. List two details about César Chávez's life. _Answers will vary. Sample answer: born_

   in Yuma, Arizona, in 1927; started a union for farm workers in 1962

4. Underline the sentence that tells what farm workers did to protest poor pay.

5. What information does the quotation in the tinted box add to the text?

   details about the poor wages farm workers like Chávez and his family earned

## ③ The Equal Rights Struggle Expands

**C** TERMS & NAMES
César Chávez
National Congress of American Indians
Betty Friedan
NOW
ERA

**B** MAIN IDEA

The African-American struggle for equality inspired other groups to fight for equality.

**WHY IT MATTERS NOW**

Nonwhites and women continue to fight for equality today.

### ONE AMERICAN'S STORY

<u>César Chávez</u> was born in Yuma, Arizona, in 1927. In the 1940s, he and his family worked as migrant laborers in the California fields. (Migrant workers travel from place to place in search of work.) One time, they found work picking peas. The whole family, parents and six children, worked. Chávez described the poor pay for such hard work.

*A VOICE FROM THE PAST*

They [the managers] would take only the peas they thought were good, and they only paid you for those. The pay was twenty cents a hamper, which had to weigh in at twenty-five pounds. So in about three hours, the whole family made only twenty cents.

**César Chávez,** *César Chávez: Autobiography of* La Causa

César Chávez, head of the National Farm Workers Association, marches with striking grape pickers in the 1960s. (*Huelga* is the Spanish word for strike.)

In 1962, Chávez decided to start a union for farm workers. But the owners refused to recognize the union. Chávez used the example set by Martin Luther King, Jr., to change their minds.

**D** Responding to Chávez's call, workers went on strike. Then Chávez asked people not to buy produce harvested by nonunion workers. The tactics worked. In 1970, 26 major California growers signed a contract with the union. It gave the workers higher wages and new benefits. The victory of Chávez and his union showed how the fight for equal rights spread beyond African Americans, as you will read in this section.

### **A** Mexican Americans Organize

The farm workers' struggle inspired other Mexican Americans. By the 1960s, most Mexican Americans lived in cities in the Southwest and California. In 1970, Mexican Americans formed *La Raza Unida* (lah RAH•sah oo•NEE•dah)—"the united people." *La Raza* fought for better jobs, pay, education, and housing. It also worked to elect Mexican Americans to public office.

Mexican-American students also began to organize. They wanted reform in the school system. The students demanded such changes as

Reading a science textbook becomes easier when you understand how the explanations, drawings, and special terms work together. Use the strategies below to help you better understand your science textbook. Look at the examples on the opposite page as you read each strategy in this list.

**A** Preview the **title** and any **headings** to see what scientific concepts you will learn about.

**B** Read the **key ideas** or **objectives.** These items summarize the lesson and help set a purpose for your reading.

**C** Read the list of **vocabulary terms** that will be introduced and defined in the lesson.

**D** Notice the **boldfaced** and **italicized** terms in the text. Look for the definitions of these terms.

**E** Carefully examine any **pictures** or **diagrams.** Read the **captions** to see how the graphics help to illustrate the text.

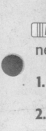

**‖MARK IT UP⟩** Use the strategies above and the science lesson on the next page to answer these questions.

**1.** Underline the title of the lesson.

**2.** Circle the list of vocabulary words that will appear in the lesson.

**3.** Draw a box around one boldfaced term in the lesson.

**4.** Examine the graph and read the text directly above it. What idea does the graph illustrate?

The graph illustrates how the elevation of the snow line changes in relation to a

given latitude.

**5.** At what latitude is the elevation of the snow line lowest?

at the North Pole

# 15.1

**B** KEY IDEAS

Glaciers are huge ice masses that move under the influence of gravity.

Glaciers form from compacted and recrystallized snow.

**C** KEY VOCABULARY

- glacier
- snow line
- firn
- valley glacier
- continental glacier
- ice cap

**A** ## What Is a Glacier?

About 75 percent of Earth's fresh water is frozen in glaciers. A **glacier** is a large mass of compacted snow and ice that moves under the force of gravity. A glacier changes Earth's surface as it erodes geological features in one place and then redeposits the material elsewhere thus altering the landscape.

## Where Glaciers Form

Glaciers form in areas that are always covered by snow. In such areas, more snow falls than melts each year; as a result layers of snow build up from previous years. Climates cold enough to cause such conditions may be found in any part of the world. Air temperatures drop as you climb high above sea level and as you travel farther from the equator.

Even in equatorial areas, however, a layer of permanent snow may exist on high mountains at high elevation. Farther from the equator, the elevation need not be so high for a layer of permanent snow to exist. In the polar areas, permanent snow may be found even at sea level. The lowest elevation at which the layer of permanent snow occurs in summer is called **D** the **snow line.** If a mountain is completely covered with snow in winter but without snow in summer, it has no snow line.

In general, the snow line occurs at lower and lower elevations as the latitudes approach the poles. The snow line also changes according to total yearly snowfall and the amount of solar exposure. Thus, the elevation of the snow line is not the same for all places at a given latitude.

**VISUALIZATIONS**
CLASSZONE.COM

Examine seasonal migration of snow cover.
*Keycode:* ES1501

**E**

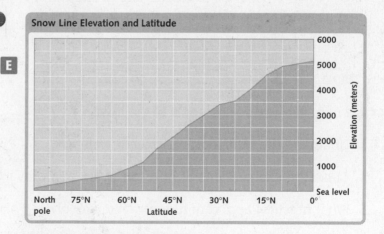

Snow Line Elevation and Latitude

VOCABULARY STRATEGY

The word *firn* comes from a German word meaning "last year's snow." The word *névé* is related to a Latin word meaning "cooled by snow."

## How Glaciers Form

Except for bare rock cliffs, a mountain above the snow line is always buried in snow. Great basins below the highest peaks are filled with snow that can be hundreds of meters thick. In these huge snowfields, buried snow becomes compressed and recrystallizes into a rough, granular ice material called **firn** (feern) or névé (nay-VAY).

# Mathematics

Reading in mathematics is different from reading in history, literature, or science. A math lesson has few words, but instead illustrates math concepts using numbers, symbols, formulas, equations, diagrams, and word problems. Use the following strategies, and the lesson on the next page, to help you better understand your math textbook.

**A** Scan the **title** and **headings** to see which math concepts you will learn about.

**B** Look for **goals, objectives** or **key ideas**. These help focus your reading.

**C** Read **explanations** carefully. Sometimes a concept is explained in more than one way to make sure you understand it.

**D** Look for **special features** such as study or technology tips or connections to real life. These provide more help or information.

**E** Study any **worked-out solutions** to sample problems. These are the key to understanding how to do the homework assignment.

**⫿MARK IT UP⫸** Use the strategies above and the mathematics lesson on the next page to answer these questions.

**1.** What is this lesson about? _____

   using scientific notation

**2.** Put a star next to the goals of the lesson.

**3.** Underline the definition of scientific notation.

**4.** Circle the explanations of how to rewrite numbers in decimal form.

**5.** What practical application does scientific notation have in the real world?

   It is used to describe and solve problems that involve large numbers, such as the amount

   of water annually discharged by the Amazon River.

# 8.4

# Scientific Notation  A

## GOAL 1 USING SCIENTIFIC NOTATION

**B** *What you should learn*

**GOAL 1** Use scientific notation to represent numbers.

★ **GOAL 2** Use scientific notation to describe **real-life** situations, such as the price per acre of the Alaska purchase in **Example 6**.

**D** *Why you should learn it*

▼ To solve **real-life** problems, such as finding the amount of water discharged by the Amazon River each year in **Example 5**.

A number is written in **scientific notation** if it is of the form $c \times 10^n$, where $1 \le c < 10$ and $n$ is an integer. **C**

> **◑ ACTIVITY**
> Developing
> Concepts
>
> ### Investigating Scientific Notation
>
> **❶** Rewrite each number in decimal form.
>
>     **a.** $6.43 \times 10^4$    **b.** $3.072 \times 10^6$    **c.** $4.2 \times 10^{-2}$    **d.** $1.52 \times 10^{-3}$
>
> **❷** Describe a general rule for writing the decimal form of a number given in scientific notation. How many places do you move the decimal point? Do you move the decimal point left or right?

**EXAMPLE 1** *Rewriting in Decimal Form*

Rewrite in decimal form.

   **a.** $2.834 \times 10^2$     **b.** $4.9 \times 10^5$     **c.** $7.8 \times 10^{-1}$     **d.** $1.23 \times 10^{-6}$

**SOLUTION** **E**

**a.** $2.834 \times 10^2 = 283.4$      Move decimal point right 2 places.

**b.** $4.9 \times 10^5 = 490,000$      Move decimal point right 5 places.

**c.** $7.8 \times 10^{-1} = 0.78$      Move decimal point left 1 place.

**d.** $1.23 \times 10^{-6} = 0.00000123$      Move decimal point left 6 places.

**EXAMPLE 2** *Rewriting in Scientific Notation*

**a.** $34,690 = 3.469 \times 10^4$      Move decimal point left 4 places.

**b.** $1.78 = 1.78 \times 10^0$      Move decimal point 0 places.

**c.** $0.039 = 3.9 \times 10^{-2}$      Move decimal point right 2 places.

**d.** $0.000722 = 7.22 \times 10^{-4}$      Move decimal point right 4 places.

**e.** $5,600,000,000 = 5.6 \times 10^9$      Move decimal point left 9 places.

# Reading an Application

To get a part-time job or to register for summer camp or classes at the local community center, you will have to fill out an application. Being able to understand the format of an application will help you fill it out correctly. Use the following strategies and the sample on the next page to help you understand any application.

**A** **Begin at the top.** Scan the application to understand the different sections.

**B** Look for special **instructions for filling out** the application.

**C** Note any **request for materials** or **special information** that must be included with the application.

**D** Watch for **sections you don't have to fill in** or **questions you don't have to answer.**

**E** Look for difficult or confusing words or abbreviations. Look them up in a dictionary or ask someone what they mean.

**MARK IT UP** Use the warranty application on the following page and the strategies above to answer the questions.

1. Why is it important to fill out and mail this warranty application?

   The completed warranty serves as confirmation of ownership in the event of theft and

   guarantees that the customer receives special offers and benefits.

2. Underline the phrase that tells when the application must be mailed.

3. What information about the product do you have to supply?

   date of purchase and retail price

4. Circle the part of the application that you do not have to fill out.

5. What purchase document must you use to fill out this application?

   sales receipt

6. **ASSESSMENT PRACTICE** Circle the letter of the correct answer.
   What amount should you include in the box marked "retail price paid"?
   A. the total amount you paid for the product
   B. the total amount you paid minus the cost of the maintenance agreement
   C. the price marked on the product
   D. the cost of extra charges, such as delivery and installation

**A** Congratulations on investing in a Calvo product. Your decision will reward you for years to come. Please complete your Warranty Registration Card to ensure that you receive all the privileges and protection that come with your purchase.

Your completed Warranty Registration Card serves as confirmation of ownership in the event of theft.

Returning the attached card guarantees you'll receive all the special offers for which your purchase makes you eligible.

---

**DETACH AND MAIL PORTION BELOW.**

| USA Limited Warranty Registration | |
|---|---|
| **123456 XXXX** | ABCDEFG7654321 |
| MODEL NUMBER | SERIAL NUMBER |

Registering your product ensures that you receive all of the benefits you are entitled to as a Calvo customer. Complete the information below in ink, and drop this card in the nearest mailbox.

**B** IMPORTANT - RETURN WITHIN TEN DAYS

**Date of Purchase**

**Your Name**
First     Initial     Last

**Address**
Street     Apt. #

City     State     ZIP Code

**C** **Retail Price Paid** $\$$ [ ] **.00**
(Excluding sales tax, maintenance agreement, delivery, installation, and trade-in allowance.) **E**

**D** **Your Phone Number** (optional)
Area Code     Phone Number

**CALVO**

# Reading a Public Notice

Public notices can tell you about events in your community and give you valuable information about safety. When you read a public notice, follow these tips. Each tip relates to a specific part of the notice on the next page.

**A** Read the notice's **title,** if it has one. The title often gives the main idea or purpose of the notice.

**B** See if there is a logo, credit, or other way of telling **who created the notice.**

**C** Ask yourself, **"Who should read this notice?"** If the information in it might be important to you or someone you know, then you should pay attention to it.

**D** Look for **contact information** that indicates where to get answers to questions.

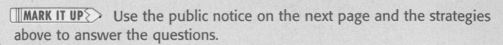 **MARK IT UP** Use the public notice on the next page and the strategies above to answer the questions.

1. What is the purpose of this notice?

   _to encourage people to get flu shots_

2. Circle the name of the organization that created the notice.

3. Who does this notice apply to?

   _anyone who wants to prevent the flu_

4. Make a star next to the contact information.

5. Who should get a flu shot earliest—health care workers or healthy people 50–64 years old?

   _health care workers_

6. **ASSESSMENT PRACTICE** Circle the letter of the correct answer.
   The best time to get a flu shot is

   **A.** your doctor's decision

   **B.** October or November

   **C.** October

   **D.** December

# When should *YOU* get your flu shot?

| C | OCT | NOV | DEC or later |
|---|---|---|---|
| **People at high risk of severe illness**<br>✓ **65 years old or older**—Even in you're in great health<br>✓ **Children 6–23 months old**—Children younger than 2 years old have one of the highest rates of hospitalizations from influenza<br>✓ **Adults and children with a chronic health condition**—Such as heart disease, diabetes, kidney disease, asthma, cancer, and HIV/AIDS<br>✓ **More than 3 months pregnant during flu season**—Typically November through March | **Best Time** | | **Not too late!** |
| **People who can give the flu to those at high risk**<br>✓ **Household contact or caregiver of someone at high risk**<br>✓ **Health care workers**<br>✓ **Household contact or caregiver of a child under 2 years old**—Infants younger than 6 months old can't get a flu shot, but they can get the flu | **Best Time** | | **Not too late!** |
| **Your child's very first flu shot**<br>✓ **Children 6 months–8 years old** getting the very first flu shot need a booster shot one month after the first dose of vaccine | **Best Time** | | **Not too late!** |
| **Healthy people 50–64 years old** | | **Best Time** | **Not too late!** |
| **Anyone who wants to prevent the flu** | | **Best Time** | **Not too late!** |

*A flu shot is your best protection against the flu.*

**For more information: Ask your health care provider or call the CDC Immunization Hotline.**
English: 1-800-232-2522 ★ Español: 1-800-232-0233    www.cdc.gov/nip/flu D

CDC B
Immunization    SAFER • HEALTHIER • PEOPLE

**Fight the Flu**

# Reading a Web Page

When you research information for a report or project, you may use the World Wide Web. Once you find the site you want, the strategies below will help you find the facts and details you need. Look at the sample Web page on the right as you read each of the strategies.

**A** Notice the page's **Web address,** or URL. Write down the Web address or bookmark it if you think you might return to the page at another time or if you need to add it to a list of sources.

**B** Read the **title** of the page. The title usually tells you what topics the page covers.

**C** Look for **menu bars** along the top, bottom, or side of the page. These guide you to other parts of the site that may be useful.

**D** Notice any **links** to other parts of the site or to related pages. Links are often highlighted in color or underlined.

**E** Many sites have a link that allows you to **contact** the creators with questions or feedback.

**F** Use a **search feature** to find out quickly whether the information you want to locate appears anywhere on the site.

**▥MARK IT UP▷** Look at the Web page on the right. Then use the information from the Web page and the tips above to answer the questions.

1. Circle the Web address of this site.

2. Draw boxes around two places you can search the site to see if it contains the information you need.

3. What is the name of the president of NLN? _Carlos Vásquez_

4. Put a star by the link you should click on to make an online contribution to NLN.

5. **ASSESSMENT PRACTICE** Circle the letter of the best answer.
   This site is designed to give information about
   **A.** issues of interest to Latinos
   **B.** Latino education
   **C.** raising Latino children
   **D.** politicians Latinos should vote for

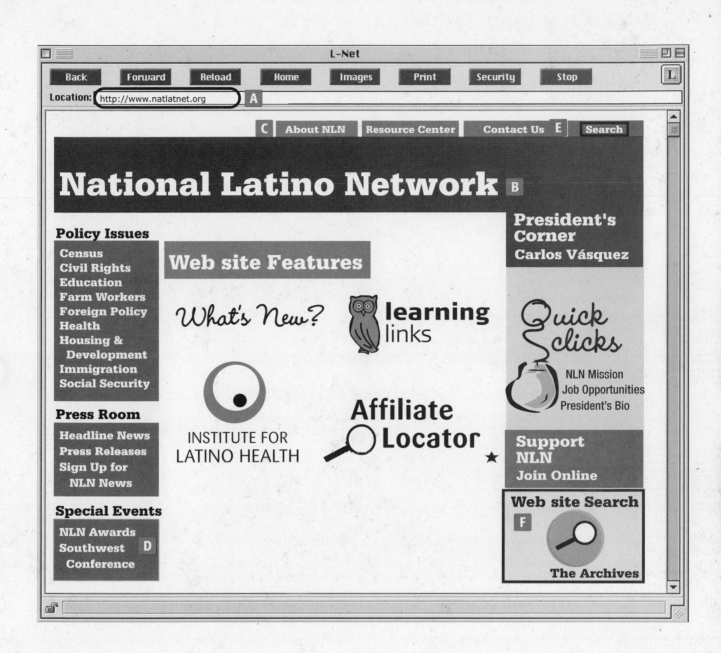

**L-Net**

Back | Forward | Reload | Home | Images | Print | Security | Stop

Location: http://www.natlatnet.org **A**

**C** About NLN | Resource Center | Contact Us **E** | Search

# National Latino Network **B**

**President's Corner**
**Carlos Vásquez**

**Policy Issues**

Census
Civil Rights
Education
Farm Workers
Foreign Policy
Health
Housing &
   Development
Immigration
Social Security

**Web site Features**

What's New?

learning
links

Quick
clicks

NLN Mission
Job Opportunities
President's Bio

INSTITUTE FOR
LATINO HEALTH

Affiliate
Locator

**Press Room**

Headline News
Press Releases
Sign Up for
   NLN News

**Support
NLN**
Join Online

**Special Events**

NLN Awards
Southwest **D**
   Conference

**Web site Search**
**F**

The Archives

# Reading Technical Directions

Reading technical directions will help you understand how to use the products you buy. Use the following tips to help you read a variety of technical directions.

**A** Look carefully at any **diagrams** or **other images** of the product.

**B** **Read all the directions** carefully at least once before using the product.

**C** Notice **headings** or **lines** that separate one section from another.

**D** Look for **numbers, letters,** or **bullets** that give the steps in sequence.

**E** Watch for **warnings** or **notes** with more information.

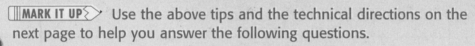 **MARK IT UP** Use the above tips and the technical directions on the next page to help you answer the following questions.

1. What kind of battery do you need for the clock?

   *a 1.5 volt battery*

2. How do you know if the time displayed is AM or PM? Circle the answer on the next page.

3. Underline the steps to follow in setting the alarm.

4. How long will the alarm sound if you don't turn it off?

   *60 seconds*

5. **ASSESSMENT PRACTICE** Circle the letter of the correct answer.
   Which of the following is NOT a safe place to set up the clock radio?
   **A.** on a stable, flat desk
   **B.** in the bathroom
   **C.** away from open windows
   **D.** on a bedside table

## Alarm Clock Radio
### INSTRUCTIONS FOR USE

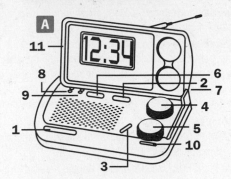

1. SNOOZE/LIGHT BUTTON
2. FUNCTION SWITCH
3. BAND SWITCH
4. TUNING CONTROL
5. VOLUME CONTROL
6. TIME/ALARM SET SWITCH
7. BATTERY DOOR (RADIO)
8. HOUR BUTTON
9. MINUTE BUTTON
10. EJECT BUTTON
11. BATTERY HOLDER (CLOCK)

### BATTERIES
### FOR RADIO:

To insert batteries, remove the BATTERY DOOR (7) and insert 2 AAA batteries, observing the correct position of the polarity.

### FOR CLOCK:

Pull out the BATTERY HOLDER (11). Use a 1.5 volt battery and place with positive electrode facing front. Reinsert battery holder.

### **C** HOW TO PLAY THE RADIO

- Press the EJECT BUTTON (10) to open lid.
- Turn the FUNCTION SWITCH (2) TO "ON" position.
- Use the BAND SWITCH (3) to select broadcasting band (AM or FM).
- Turn the TUNING CONTROL knob (4) to select the listening station.

### **D** TO SET THE TIME

- Slide the TIME/ALARM SET SWITCH (6) to the "T.SET" position.
- Depress the HOUR BUTTON (8) until the correct hour is displayed. Be careful to set time to AM or PM as required. When PM time is registered, a "P" will apppear on the display.
- Depress the MINUTE BUTTON (9) until the correct minute is reached.

### TO SET THE ALARM

- Slide the TIME/ALARM SET SWITCH (6) to the "AL.SET" position. "AL" indicator will appear on the display.
- Depress the HOUR BUTTON (8) until the desired alarm hour is displayed. Be careful to correctly set alarm to AM or PM as required. When PM time is registered, a "P" will appear on the display.
- Depress the MINUTE BUTTON (9) until the desired alarm time is reached.

### WAKE TO ALARM

- Set the FUNCTION SWITCH (2) TO "ALARM" position. When the desired alarm time is reached, you will hear a sequential "BEEP" alarm for 60 seconds.
- To shut the alarm off temporarily, press the SNOOZE/LIGHT BUTTON (1) once. The alarm will stop for 4 minutes, then come on again.
- To stop the alarm completely, set the FUNCTION SWITCH (2) to "OFF" position.

### WAKE TO MUSIC

- Set the FUNCTION SWITCH (2) TO "AUTO" position.
- The radio will turn on automatically at your desired alarm time.

### SAFETY PRECAUTIONS **E**

- Do not place the unit near a moisture environment, such as a bathtub, kitchen, sink, etc. The unit should be well protected from rain, dew, condensation, or any form of dampness.
- Do not place the unit on surfaces with strong vibration. Place the unit only on flat, stable, and level surfaces.

# Product Information: Directions for Use

Many of the products you buy come with instructions that tell you how to use them correctly. Directions for use may appear on the product itself, on its packaging, or on a separate insert. Learning to read and follow directions for use is important for your safety. As you read each strategy below, look at the sample.

**A** Read any **headings** to find out what kinds of information are given with the product.

**B** Read the directions, which usually tell you *why, how, when,* and *where* to use the product, *how much to use, how often,* and *when* to stop using it.

**C** Carefully read any **warnings** given with the product. The manufacturer will usually tell you what to do if you experience any problems.

**D** Look for any **contact information** that tells you where to call or write if you have a question about the product.

---

**Solution of Hydrogen Peroxide 3% U.S.P.**

**Active ingredient:** (Hydrogen peroxide 3%)  A

**Inactive ingredients:** 0.001% Phosphoric Acid as a stabilizer and purified water

**Indications**: For topical use to help prevent infection in minor cuts, burns, and abrasions, or to cleanse the mouth.

**Directions:** Apply locally to affected areas. To cleanse the mouth, dilute with an equal amount of water and use as a **B** gargle or rinse. Do not use in excess of ten consecutive days.

**Warnings:** **C**

- FOR EXTERNAL USE: Topically to the skin and mucous membranes. KEEP OUT OF EYES.

- If redness, irritation, swelling, or pain persists or increases or if infection occurs, discontinue use and consult a physician.

- KEEP THIS AND ALL DRUGS OUT OF THE REACH OF CHILDREN. **In case of accidental ingestion, seek professional assistance or contact a Poison Control Center immediately**.

**Storage:** Keep bottle tightly closed and at controlled room temperature 59°–86° F (15°–30° C). Do not shake bottle.

**Questions?** (888) 555-1234 **D**

---

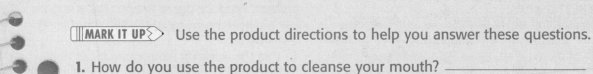

‖MARK IT UP‖▷ Use the product directions to help you answer these questions.

1. How do you use the product to cleanse your mouth? _____

   *mix it with an equal amount of water and use as a gargle or rinse*

2. Circle the active ingredient in this product.

3. What should you do if someone accidentally swallows this product? Underline the answer.

4. Draw a box around the number you should call if you have questions about the product.

5. **ASSESSMENT PRACTICE** Circle the letter of the correct answer.
   When should you stop using this product?
   A. when the temperature drops below 59° F
   B. if pain and swelling increase
   C. if you have a minor abrasion
   D. ten days after you buy it

# Reading a Bus Schedule

Knowing how to read a bus schedule accurately can help you get where you need to go–on time. Look at the sample bus schedule as you read the tips below.

**A** Look at the **title** to know what the schedule covers.

**B** Identify **labels** that show **dates** or **days of the week** to help you understand how the daily or weekly schedule works.

**C** Look at **place labels** to know what stops are listed on the schedule.

**D** Look for **expressions of time** to know what hours or minutes are listed on the schedule.

**E** Pay attention to the **organization** of the information. Read across the row to see when a bus will reach each location.

**A** Route 238  Quincy Center Station - Holbrook/Randolph Commuter Rail Station via Crawford Sq.

**WEEKDAY MORNINGS** **B**

| **C** Leave Quincy Station | Leave S. Shore Plaza | Leave Crawford Square | Arrive Holb./Rand. Commuter Rail Sta. | Leave Holb./Rand. Commuter Rail Sta. | Leave Crawford Square | Leave S. Shore Plaza | Arrive Quincy Station |
|---|---|---|---|---|---|---|---|
| **D** 5:25A | 5:43A | 5:58A | ... | 6:25A | 6:29A | 6:42A | 7:08A |
| 6:10 | 6:28 | 6:43 | 6:47A | 6:50 | 6:54 | 7:07 | 7:35 |
| 6:25 | 6:43 | 6:58 | 7:03 | 7:20 | 7:25 | 7:38 | 8:06 |
| 6:45 | 7:03 | 7:19 | 7:24 | 7:50 | 7:55 | 8:08 | 8:36 |
| 7:05 | 7:25 | 7:41 | 7:46 | 8:25 | 8:30 | 8:43 | 9:11 |
| 7:30 | 7:50 | 8:06 | 8:11 | 8:55 | 9:00 | 9:13 | 9:41 |
| 7:55 | 8:15 | 8:31 | 8:36 | 9:25 | 9:30 | 9:46 | 10:14 |
| 8:15 | 8:35 | 8:51 | 8:56 | 10:05 | 10:10 | 10:26 | 10:54 |
| 9:10 | 9:30 | 9:46 | 9:51 | 11:00 | 11:05 | 11:21 | 11:49 |
| 10:05 | 10:25 | 10:41 | 10:46 | | | | |
| 10:55 | 11:15 | 11:31 | 11:36 | | | | |

**E**

▍MARK IT UP⟩  Use the bus schedule and the strategies on this page to answer the following questions.

**1.** Circle the name of one stop on this route.

Students should circle Quincy Station, S. Shore Plaza, Crawford Square, or Holb./Rand.

Commuter Rail Station.

**2.** What time does the last bus leave Quincy Station for Holb./Rand. Commuter Rail Station on weekday mornings?

10:55 AM

**3.** If you took the 7:25 AM bus from Crawford Square, when would you arrive at Quincy Station?    8:06 AM

**4. ASSESSMENT PRACTICE** Circle the letter of the correct answer. If you have a 10:15 meeting at S. Shore Plaza on Tuesday, what's the latest bus you can take from Holb./Rand. Commuter Rail Station?

**A.** 8:25        **B.** 8:55        **C.** 9:25        **D.** 10:05

# Test Preparation Strategies

In this section you'll find strategies and practice to help you with many different kinds of standardized tests. The strategies apply to questions based on long and short readings, as well as questions about charts, graphs, and product labels. You'll also find examples and practice for revising-and-editing tests and writing tests. Applying the strategies to the practice materials and thinking through the answers will help you succeed in many formal testing situations.

# Test Preparation Strategies

You can prepare for tests in several ways. First, study and understand the content that will be on the test. Second, learn as many test-taking techniques as you can. These techniques will help you better understand the questions and how to answer them. Following are some general suggestions for preparing for and taking tests. Starting on page 206, you'll find more detailed suggestions and test-taking practice.

## Successful Test Taking

 **Study Content Throughout the Year**

1. **Master the content of your class.** The best way to study for tests is to read, understand, and review the content of your class. Read your daily assignments carefully. Study the notes that you have taken in class. Participate in class discussions. Work with classmates in small groups to help one another learn. You might trade writing assignments and comment on your classmates' work.

2. **Use your textbook for practice.** Your textbook includes many different types of questions. Some may ask you to talk about a story you just read. Others may ask you to figure out what's wrong with a sentence or how to make a paragraph sound better. Try answering these questions out loud and in writing. This type of practice can make taking a test much easier.

3. **Learn how to understand the information in charts, maps, and graphic organizers.** One type of test question may ask you to look at a graphic organizer, such as a spider map, and explain something about the information you see there. Another type of question may ask you to look at a map to find a particular place. You'll find charts, maps, and graphic organizers to study in your textbook. You'll also find charts, maps, and graphs in your science, mathematics, literature, and social studies textbooks. When you look at these, ask yourself, What information is being presented and why is it important?

4. **Practice taking tests.** Use copies of tests you have taken in the past or in other classes for practice. Every test has a time limit, so set a timer for 15 or 20 minutes and then begin your practice. Try to finish the test in the time you've given yourself.

**☑ Reading Check** In what practical way can your textbook help you prepare for a test?

**5. Talk about test-taking experiences.** After you've taken a classroom test or quiz, talk about it with your teacher and classmates. Which types of questions were the hardest to understand? What made them difficult? Which questions seemed easiest, and why? When you share test-taking techniques with your classmates, everyone can become a successful test taker.

## Use Strategies During the Test

**1. Read the directions carefully.** You can't be a successful test taker unless you know exactly what you are expected to do. Look for key words and phrases, such as *circle the best answer, write a paragraph,* or *choose the word that best completes each sentence.*

**2. Learn how to read test questions.** Test questions can sometimes be difficult to figure out. They may include unfamiliar language or be written in an unfamiliar way. Try rephrasing the question in a simpler way using words you understand. Always ask yourself, What type of information does this question want me to provide?

**3. Pay special attention when using a separate answer sheet.** If you accidentally skip a line on an answer sheet, all the rest of your answers may be wrong! Try one or more of the following techniques:

- Use a ruler on the answer sheet to make sure you are placing your answers on the correct line.

- After every five answers, check to make sure you're on the right line.

- Each time you turn a page of the test booklet, check to make sure the number of the question is the same as the number of the answer line on the answer sheet.

- If the answer sheet has circles, fill them in neatly. A stray pencil mark might cause the scoring machine to count the answer as incorrect.

**4. If you're not sure of the answer, make your best guess.** Unless you've been told that there is a penalty for guessing, choose the answer that you think is likeliest to be correct.

**5. Keep track of the time.** Answering all the questions on a test usually results in a better score. That's why finishing the test is important. Keep track of the time you have left. At the beginning of the test, figure out how many questions you will have to answer by the halfway point in order to finish in the time given.

☑ **Reading Check** What are at least two good ways to avoid skipping lines on an answer sheet?

## Understand Types of Test Questions

Most tests include two types of questions: multiple choice and open-ended. Specific strategies will help you understand and correctly answer each type of question.

A **multiple-choice question** has two parts. The first part is the question itself, called the stem. The second part is a series of possible answers. Usually four possible answers are provided, and only one of them is correct. Your task is to choose the correct answer. Here are some strategies to help you do just that.

1. Read and think about each question carefully before looking at the possible answers.

2. Pay close attention to key words in the question. For example, look for the word *not*, as in "Which of the following is not a cause of the conflict in this story?"

3. Read and think about all of the possible answers before making your choice.

4. Reduce the number of choices by eliminating any answers you know are incorrect. Then, think about why some of the remaining choices might also be incorrect.

   • If two of the choices are pretty much the same, both are probably wrong.

   • Answers that contain any of the following words are usually incorrect: *always, never, none, all,* and *only.*

5. If you're still unsure about an answer, see if any of the following applies:

   • When one choice is longer and more detailed than the others, it is often the correct answer.

   • When a choice repeats a word that is in the question, it may be the correct answer.

   • When two choices are direct opposites, one of them is likely the correct answer.

   • When one choice includes one or more of the other choices, it is often the correct answer.

   • When a choice includes the word *some* or *often*, it may be the correct answer.

   • If one of the choices is *All of the above*, make sure that at least two of the other choices seem correct.

   • If one of the choices is *None of the above*, make sure that none of the other choices seems correct.

☑ **Reading Check** What words in a multiple-choice question probably signal a wrong answer?

An **open-ended test item** can take many forms. It might ask you to write a word or phrase to complete a sentence. You might be asked to create a chart, draw a map, or fill in a graphic organizer. Sometimes, you will be asked to write one or more paragraphs in response to a writing prompt. Use the following strategies when reading and answering open-ended items:

1. If the item includes directions, read them carefully. Take note of any steps required.

2. Look for key words and phrases in the item as you plan how you will respond. Does the item ask you to identify a cause-and-effect relationship or to compare and contrast two or more things? Are you supposed to provide a sequence of events or make a generalization? Does the item ask you to write an essay in which you state your point of view and then try to persuade others that your view is correct?

3. If you're going to be writing a paragraph or more, plan your answer. Jot down notes and a brief outline of what you want to say before you begin writing.

4. Focus your answer. Don't include everything you can think of, but be sure to include everything the item asks for.

5. If you're creating a chart or drawing a map, make sure your work is as clear as possible.

☑ **Reading Check** What are at least three key strategies for answering an open-ended question?

# Reading Test Model
## LONG SELECTIONS

**DIRECTIONS** Following is an excerpt from an article entitled "The Empire of the Aztecs." Read the excerpt carefully. The notes in the side columns will help you prepare for the types of questions that are likely to follow a reading like this. You might want to preview the questions on pages 212–213 before you begin reading.

## from The Empire of the Aztecs

When the Spanish explorer Hernán Cortés marched into the Aztec capital of Tenochtitlán in 1519, he was amazed at what he found. Tenochtitlán, the site of present-day Mexico City, was built on two islands in the middle of Lake Texcoco. Tenochtitlán was connected to the mainland by causeways, or raised earthen roads. The city was much larger and more populous than any city in Spain. The people enjoyed a sophisticated lifestyle fueled by a prosperous economy. In fact, life in the Aztec empire five hundred years ago was remarkably similar to life in Mexico today.

**Family Life**  The family was at the center of Aztec society. An Aztec family usually consisted of a husband and wife, their unmarried children, and some of the husband's relatives. Everyone had a role to play that contributed to the family's well-being. The husband supported the family by farming or working at a craft. His wife tended to the home. She cooked and wove cloth, which she used to make the family's clothing. Each family belonged to a larger social group

**READING STRATEGIES FOR ASSESSMENT**

Find the author's main idea. Think about the focus of the article. What has the author set out to do?

called a *calpolli*. The *calpolli* was made up of closely related families who shared farmland. Its structure was similar to a small village.

Boys were taught by their fathers until around age 10. Then they attended schools established by their *calpolli*, where they received a general education and military training. Some children, especially the children of noble families, attended temple schools. There they received the religious training necessary to become priests or community leaders.

**Housing** The type of house an Aztec family occupied depended on where the family lived. At higher elevations, the climate required houses made of adobe, a mixture of sun-dried earth and straw. In the lowlands, where the climate was milder, houses were constructed with branches or reeds cemented together with clay. They were then topped with thatched roofs. Most homes consisted of several buildings: the main dwelling where the family lived and worked, a sweathouse for taking steam baths, and a storehouse.

**Clothing** In Aztec society, most people wore similar types of clothing. Men wore a piece of cloth that encircled their hips and a cape that was knotted over one shoulder. Women wore a wraparound skirt topped by a loose, sleeveless blouse.

Draw conclusions How are Aztec families similar to families today? How are they different?

Notice topic sentences. A topic sentence reveals the purpose of a paragraph by telling you what the paragraph is about.

As in many societies today, clothing was an indicator of social and economic status. The clothing most ordinary Aztecs wore was woven from the coarse fibers of the maguey plant. Nobles, however, enjoyed clothing made from soft cotton cloth. In addition, their clothing was often decorated with feathers and other ornaments to signal their status in society.

**Diet**  The Aztecs dined on meat and vegetables, and some of their dishes remain popular to this day. Hunters brought home ducks, geese, rabbits, and deer. The farms of the *calpolli* provided corn, avocados, squashes, papayas, sweet potatoes, beans, and tomatoes.

A staple of the Aztec diet was the *tlaxcalli*, a thin pancake made from corn. We know it today by its Spanish name—*tortilla*. *Tlaxcallis* often were used to scoop up other foods. When the Aztecs wrapped *tlaxcallis* around bits of meat or vegetables, they called the result *tacos*.

The favorite beverage of the Aztecs was a drink made from chocolate. Because chocolate was made from expensive cacao beans, only wealthy nobles could enjoy it regularly.

**Economy**  As in modern societies, the success of the Aztec empire was largely due to its economy. The Aztec economy was based on agriculture. In addition to fruits and

**Pay attention to foreign words and phrases.** Foreign words and phrases will appear in italic type. Each word or phrase will be defined the first time it is used.

**Observe comparisons.** How is the success of the Aztec society like the success of modern societies?

vegetables, the Aztecs grew cotton and cacao beans and harvested latex to make rubber.

Aztec agricultural methods were similar to methods still in use today. In heavily forested areas, farmers used a technique called "slash-and-burn." They would cut down the trees and burn them, making a clearing in which crops could be planted. Where the landscape was hilly, farmers cut terraces into the hills. These terraces greatly increased the acreage of level land that could be farmed. In wetland areas, farmers created islands, called *chinampas*, by scooping and piling up the fertile mud of the wetland.

The bounty from the Aztec farmlands, along with the works of artists and craftspeople, found its way to marketplaces throughout the empire. The largest market anywhere in the Americas was in the city of Tlatelolco. Cortés himself estimated that this market attracted over 60,000 traders each day. The Aztecs traded because they had no money in the modern sense of that word. Instead, they offered one type of good in exchange for another type—cacao beans for a richly decorated blouse, for example, or a jaguar pelt for brightly colored bird feathers.

**Language** The language the Aztec spoke, *Nahuatl*, belonged to a family of languages called Aztec-Tanoan. This language family included languages spoken by Native

**Notice supporting details.** What three types of farming methods did the Aztecs use? Where did they use each type?

Think about the author's purpose. Is this article meant to inform, persuade, entertain, or describe?

Americans, including the Comanche and the Shoshone.

The Aztecs had a written language, but it was based on pictures, not unlike the hieroglyphs of ancient Egypt. Each picture represented either an idea or the sound of a *Nahuatl* syllable. Because their written language was limited, the Aztecs used it mainly for government and religious purposes.

**The Arts**  Artistic expression was important to the Aztecs. They created monumental sculptures to decorate their temples and other important buildings. Craft workers produced beautiful metalware, pottery, wood carvings, and weavings.

The Aztecs valued music and literature as well. Flutes, rattles, and drums provided a musical background for religious ceremonies. Poetry and historical accounts were handed down orally through the generations.

**Religion**  The central focus of Aztec life was religion, and this is where Aztec society differed greatly from societies today. Hundreds of Aztec gods and goddesses presided over every aspect of human life: farming, the weather, war, fertility, the sun, the wind, and fire, to name just a few. In addition to a 365-day solar calendar, the Aztecs also had a 260-day religious calendar.

This calendar helped Aztec priests decide the best time of the year to plant crops, go to war, or build new temples.

The Aztec gods demanded a great deal of attention from their followers. To appease their gods, the Aztecs held many religious ceremonies. The centerpiece of these ceremonies was human sacrifice. The Aztecs believed that the gods drew strength and bravery from the blood of sacrificial victims. Most of the victims were slaves or prisoners of war. In fact, the Aztecs sometimes went to war just to get prisoners for their religious ceremonies.

Now answer questions 1–6. Base your answers on the excerpt from "The Empire of the Aztecs." Then check yourself by reading through the Answer Strategies in the side columns.

**1** Which of the following best describes the author's purpose?

   **A.** to entertain

   **B.** to inform

   **C.** to describe

   **D.** to persuade

**2** What is a *tlaxcalli*?

   **A.** a thin corn pancake

   **B.** a drink made from cacao

   **C.** a *tortilla* wrapped around meat or vegetables

   **D.** a social group

**3** Which of the following best expresses the author's main idea?

   **A.** Hernán Cortés was amazed when he first saw the Aztec city of Tenochtitlán.

   **B.** The Aztecs enjoyed a sophisticated lifestyle.

   **C.** Life in the Aztec empire was similar in many ways to life today.

   **D.** The family was at the center of Aztec society.

**4** Which of the following is NOT a conclusion you can draw about how Aztec and modern families are alike?

    **A.** Children went to school for their education.

    **B.** Parents provided for their families.

    **C.** Families are part of larger social groups.

    **D.** Relatives of the husband live with the husband's family.

> **Note key words.** Pay attention to the key word or words in the question. The key word here is *not*.

**5** Which method of farming involved clearing the forest?

    **A.** slash-and-burn

    **B.** crop rotation

    **C.** cutting terraces

    **D.** creating islands

> **Don't rely on memory.** Each of the responses to this question is a type of farming. One of them, however, is never mentioned in the excerpt. Before answering, look back at the excerpt and find the types that *are* mentioned.

**6** In what ways is the Aztec religion similar to and different from modern religions?

> **Plan your response.** Read the question carefully. This question asks you to compare and contrast. Look for similarities and differences and state them in your own words.

### Sample short response for question 6:

The Aztec religion shares many similarities with modern religions. The Aztecs recognized the existence of gods. They believed these gods would protect them if they respected and worshipped the gods. Also, the Aztecs held regular religious services and ceremonies. The most important difference between the Aztec religion and modern religions is human sacrifice. Today, people pray to their god or gods and make offerings, but no religions practice human sacrifice.

> **Study your response.** Notice how the writer follows the same organization as the question—similarities first and then differences.

# Reading Test Practice
## LONG SELECTIONS

**DIRECTIONS** Now it's time to practice what you've learned about reading test items and choosing the best answers. Read the following selection, "The Gauchos of the Pampa." Use the side columns to make notes about the important parts of this selection: the setting, important ideas, comparisons and contrasts, difficult vocabulary, interesting details, and so on.

## The Gauchos of the Pampa

In the mythology of Argentina, no one sits taller in the saddle than the gauchos. Part expert horsemen and part outlaws, these free spirits of the Pampas played a brief but crucial role in the development of cattle ranching and agriculture in Argentina. Although the gaucho era lasted barely a century, it remains an essential part of Argentina's culture, celebrated in literature and song.

**La Pampa** Stretching across central Argentina from the Atlantic coast to the foothills of the Andes, *la Pampa*, the Pampa, is a nearly flat plain. It is bordered to the north by the Gran Chaco and to the south by Patagonia. The Quechuas gave the Pampa its name. In their language it means "flat surface." Today, the region is commonly known as "the Pampas." It was onto this great plain that the Spanish introduced both cattle and horses. Soon, great herds of these animals were running wild throughout the eastern Pampas.

**The Rise of the Gauchos** Portuguese, Dutch, British, and French traders were eager to exploit the resources provided by the herds, namely hides and tallow, a waxy white fat used to make soap and candles. In turn, the horsemen of the Pampas were eager to help the traders because cattle and horse rustling was a profitable, if illegal, business. Thus were born the gauchos, who soon established their own culture on the plains of Argentina.

The gauchos lived simply, in mud huts with thatched roofs, sleeping on piles of hides. They formed families and had children, but their marriages were rarely officially recognized by the state or the church. Favorite pastimes of the gauchos included horseback riding and guitar playing.

**Tools of the Gaucho Trade** Everything about the gaucho lifestyle was geared to existence on the plains, including their clothing. Typically, a gaucho wore long, accordion-pleated trousers called *bombachas* that were tucked securely into high leather boots. A wide silver belt was cinched at the waist. A warm woolen poncho and a brightly colored scarf completed the costume.

The gaucho's weapons were simple and effective: a lasso, a sharp knife, and, most importantly, a *boleadora*, or *bola*. The bola consisted of three long leather cords attached at one end. At the other end of each cord was a stone or iron ball. Galloping after a stampeding herd of horses or cattle, the gaucho would twirl the bola in the air and then release it, parallel to the ground, at the legs of a fleeing animal. The bola would wrap itself around the animal's legs and send it crashing to the ground.

**The End of an Era**  Toward the end of the 18th century, many of the gauchos had become legitimate animal handlers. They were hired by businessmen who had acquired large herds of wild cattle and horses. Then, during the 19th century, large tracts of the Pampas were carved into vast ranches called *estancias* or estates. The wild animals of the Pampas were slowly replaced with purebred stock from Europe. Railroads were built across the Pampas to transport livestock and tractors replaced horses on the ranches. The gaucho lifestyle had come to an end, and the remaining gauchos were now *peones*, or farmhands.

**Celebrating the Gaucho**  Although the gaucho lifestyle ended, the gaucho legend lives on. During the heyday of the gaucho, a rich literary tradition had begun chronicling their exploits. In 1872, José Hernández wrote his epic poem *El gaucho Martín Fierro (The Gaucho Martin Fierro)*. Fifteen years later, the celebrated gaucho minstrel Santos Vega was the subject of three poems by Rafael Obligado. As late as 1926, Argentinian writer Ricardo Güiraldes added to the body of gaucho literature with *Don Segundo Sombra: Shadows in the Pampas.*

Like the age of the American cowboy, the gaucho era was a colorful time in the history of the Pampas. Even today, the legend and spirit

of the gaucho is kept alive through traveling
gaucho shows, reminders of a time when the
Pampas and the proud, independent people
who lived there shaped the future of Argentina.

Now answer questions 1–7. Base your answers on the selection "The Gauchos of the Pampa."

**1** Which of the following best describes the main idea of this selection?

**A.** The gauchos were free spirits.

**B.** The gauchos played a crucial role in the development of cattle ranching and agriculture.

**C.** The gaucho era lasted barely a century.

**D.** The gauchos were expert horsemen and outlaws.

**2** Patagonia lies in which direction from the Pampas?

**A.** north

**B.** west

**C.** east

**D.** south

**3** Why did the gauchos agree to help the European traders?

**A.** Cattle rustling was illegal.

**B.** Cattle rustling was profitable.

**C.** Cattle rustling was an outlaw's trade.

**D.** Cattle rustling was not profitable.

**4** Which of the following does NOT describe the gaucho lifestyle?

**A.** The gauchos lived on large ranches.

**B.** The gauchos lived in mud huts.

**C.** The gauchos enjoyed playing the guitar.

**D.** The gauchos slept on piles of hides.

**5** Why was the bola an effective weapon?

 **A.** It had long leather cords attached at one end.

 **B.** It was easy to twirl and throw.

 **C.** It had three heavy stone or iron balls.

 **D.** It tripped the animal being hunted so the animal could no longer run.

**6** Why does the author describe the gauchos as "proud, independent people"?

 **A.** because they were outlaws

 **B.** because they endured harsh conditions on the Pampas

 **C.** because they made a living successfully by their own rules

 **D.** because they agreed to work for others

**7** Explain why the era of the gauchos came to an end.

# THINKING IT THROUGH

The notes in the side columns will help you think through your answers. See the answer key at the bottom of the next page. How well did you do?

> Each answer lists a detail from the opening paragraph. However, since the main idea tells about the focus of the *entire* selection, you can easily eliminate three of the four choices.

**1** Which of the following best describes the main idea of this selection?

    **A.** The gauchos were free spirits.

    **B.** The gauchos played a crucial role in the development of cattle ranching and agriculture.

    **C.** The gaucho era lasted barely a century.

    **D.** The gauchos were expert horsemen and outlaws.

> Skim the reading looking for the key word *Patagonia.*

**2** Patagonia lies in which direction from the Pampas?

    **A.** north

    **B.** west

    **C.** east

    **D.** south

> Notice that answer choices A and C say the same thing. Answer choices B and D are opposites—a good clue that either B or D is the correct answer.

**3** Why did the gauchos agree to help the European traders?

    **A.** Cattle rustling was illegal.

    **B.** Cattle rustling was profitable.

    **C.** Cattle rustling was an outlaw's trade.

    **D.** Cattle rustling was not profitable.

> Read the question carefully. A word printed in capital letters is important to understanding the question correctly.

**4** Which of the following does NOT describe the gaucho lifestyle?

    **A.** The gauchos lived on large ranches.

    **B.** The gauchos lived in mud huts.

    **C.** The gauchos enjoyed playing the guitar.

    **D.** The gauchos slept on piles of hides.

**5** Why was the bola an effective weapon?

  **A.** It had long leather cords attached at one end.

  **B.** It was easy to twirl and throw.

  **C.** It had three heavy stone or iron balls.

  **D.** It tripped the animal being hunted so the animal could no longer run.

> Notice that the first three choices just describe properties of the bola. Only the last choice describes how the bola worked to bring down prey.

**6** Why does the author describe the gauchos as "proud, independent people"?

  **A.** because they were outlaws

  **B.** because they endured harsh conditions on the Pampas

  **C.** because they made a living successfully by their own rules

  **D.** because they agreed to work for others

> This question asks you to infer meaning. What do "proud" and "independent" mean? Which answer choice reflects the meaning of the two words?

**7** Explain why the era of the gauchos came to an end.

The gaucho era came to an end because Argentina was changing. First, the once wild herds were acquired by people who wanted to manage them and profit from them. The gauchos were hired by these people. Then, the Pampas was "carved into vast ranches." These ranches meant that the gauchos could no longer roam freely. Railroads were built to transport the cattle, making cattle drives unnecessary. Soon, the only way the gauchos could make a living was to work as farmhands.

> This is considered a strong response because it
> - directly addresses the question and stays focused on the topic.
> - uses supporting details from the selection, including a quotation, to make its point.
> - is written clearly, using correct spelling, grammar, and punctuation.

**Find the main idea and supporting details.** Circle the main idea of this article. Then underline the details that support the main idea.

**Use context clues.** To discover what a "pack animal" is, study the words and phrases around it. Which phrase helps define it?

**Notice important details.** Underline the details that explain why alpaca wool is so desirable.

# Reading Test Model
## SHORT SELECTIONS

**DIRECTIONS** "Warmth from the Andes" is a short informative article. The strategies you have just learned can also help you with this shorter selection. As you read the selection, respond to the notes in the side column.

When you've finished reading, answer the multiple-choice questions. Use the side-column notes to help you understand what each question is asking and why each answer is correct.

## Warmth from the Andes

Southeastern Peru and Western Bolivia make up a geographic region called the *Altiplano*, or High Plateau. This largely desolate mountainous area is home to one of the most economically important animals in South America—the alpaca.

The alpaca is related to the camel and looks somewhat like another well-known South American grazing animal, the llama. Alpacas live at elevations as high as 16,000 feet. At such altitudes, oxygen is scarce. Alpacas are able to survive because their blood contains an unusually high number of red blood corpuscles, the cells that carry oxygen throughout the body.

For several thousand years, the Native Americans of the region have raised alpacas both as pack animals for transporting goods and for their most important resource—wool. Alpaca wool ranges in color from black to tan to white. It is lightweight yet strong and resists moisture. Also, it is exceptionally warm. Alpaca wool is much finer than the wool from sheep. In fact, it is so luxurious that when the Inca civilization dominated the *Altiplano* region, garments made from Alpaca wool could be worn only by royalty.

Alpacas are usually sheared once each year by herders in Bolivia and Peru. Some of the wool is sold to manufacturers in the United States and Europe to be woven into cloth as soft and sought after as cashmere. The herders sell the rest to local weavers, who use it to produce beautiful shawls and other fine garments.

**1** Which of the following best describes the main idea of the article?

   **A.** Alpacas can survive at high altitudes.

   **B.** The *Altiplano* is a high plateau.

   **C.** The alpaca is related to the camel.

   **D.** The Alpaca is one of the most economically important animals of South America.

**Identify the focus.** Each answer choice offers information from the article, but only one choice explains what the entire article is about.

**2** Which of the following best describes what pack animals do?

   **A.** transport goods

   **B.** survive at high altitudes

   **C.** provide wool for clothing

   **D.** graze on the *Altiplano*

**Pay attention to the context of unfamiliar words.** Find the sentence in the article where *pack animals* is used. Notice that only one answer choice is a phrase found right next to *pack animals*.

**3** Why is alpaca wool highly prized?

   **A.** It resembles the fur of camels.

   **B.** It has been woven for thousands of years.

   **C.** It is lightweight, warm, strong, and resists moisture.

   **D.** It can be worn only by royalty.

**Evaluate details.** Something "highly prized" has important qualities. Which answer choice talks about the qualities of alpaca wool?

**Answers:**
1. D, 2. A, 3. C

Read the title. What does the title tell you the chart is about?

_____

_____

Read the labels What do the labels on the left side of the chart tell you? What about the labels at the top of the chart?

## ANSWER STRATEGIES

Read the question carefully. Notice that the questions asks for depth in feet, not meters.

Read the labels carefully. Be sure you understand which column represents square miles and which represents square kilometers.

Follow rows and columns carefully. If necessary, use your finger to trace across a row or down a column so that you don't accidentally wind up in the wrong place with the wrong information.

**DIRECTIONS** Some test questions ask you to analyze a visual rather than a reading selection. Study this chart carefully and answer the questions that follow.

### Largest Lakes of Central and South America

|  | Surface Area (sq. mi./sq. km.) | Depth (feet/meters) | Elevation (feet/meters) |
|---|---|---|---|
| Lake Maracaibo, Venezuela | 5,200/13,468 | 197/60 | sea level |
| Lake Titicaca, Bolivia and Peru | 3,200/8,288 | 990/302 | 12,500/3,810 |
| Lake Nicaragua, Nicaragua | 3,150/8,159 | 230/70 | 102/31 |

4 What is the depth, in feet, of the deepest lake?

A. 990

B. 12,500

C. 302

D. 13,468

5 What is the surface area of Lake Titicaca in square kilometers?

A. 3,200

B. 302

C. 8,288

D. 3,810

6 At what altitude is Lake Maracaibo?

A. 197 feet

B. sea level

C. 12,500 feet

D. 31 sq. km.

Answers:
4. A, 5. C, 6. B

# Reading Test Practice
## SHORT SELECTIONS

**DIRECTIONS** Use the following to practice your skills. Read the paragraphs carefully. Then answer the multiple-choice questions that follow.

During the 1990's, Spanish opera singer Placido Domingo teamed up with two other singers, Italy's Luciano Pavarotti and Portugal's José Carreras, to form a wildly popular singing group known as The Three Tenors. They enjoyed worldwide success, touring and appearing on television. Domingo's musical career, however, got its start much earlier—mid-century, in fact.

Born in Madrid in 1941, Domingo and his parents moved to Mexico City in 1950 where he began studying singing at the National Conservatory of Music. Ten years later, Domingo made his opera debut in a production of *La Traviata* in Monterrey, Mexico. After a three-year stint with the Israeli National Opera, Domingo joined the New York City Opera in 1966. Two years later, he made his debut with the Metropolitan Opera of New York.

Over the next three decades, Domingo dazzled audiences with his technical skill and virtuoso acting. Thirty-six years after his debut in Monterrey, Domingo became the artistic director of the Washington (D.C.) Opera. Then, in 2000, he assumed the same post at the Los Angeles Opera.

**1** What was the author's purpose in writing this selection?

**A.** to persuade readers that Placido Domingo is a great opera singer

**B.** to explain who The Three Tenors were

**C.** to inform readers about the career of Placido Domingo

**D.** to describe the roles Placido Domingo has sung during his career

**2** Which of the following is NOT a conclusion you can draw from the selection?

**A.** Domingo is the greatest opera singer of his generation.

**B.** Domingo has had a successful career as an opera singer.

**C.** Domingo, Pavarotti, and Carreras captivated audiences with their singing.

**D.** Domingo is widely respected in the opera world as a singer and an artist.

**DIRECTIONS** Use the graph below to answer the questions that follow.

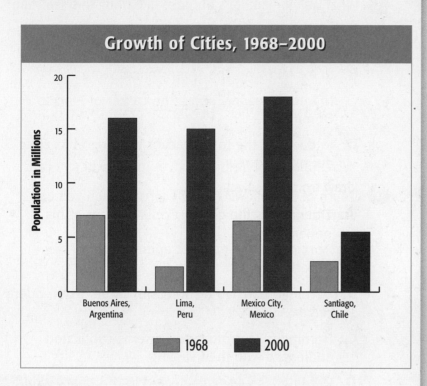

**Growth of Cities, 1968–2000**

Population in Millions

1968 ■ 2000

3 Which city had the SMALLEST population in 1968?

A. Lima

B. Buenos Aires

C. Santiago

D. Mexico City

4 Which city had the LARGEST population in 2000?

A. Lima

B. Buenos Aires

C. Santiago

D. Mexico City

5 Which city had the SMALLEST increase in population between 1968 and 2000?

A. Lima

B. Buenos Aires

C. Santiago

D. Mexico City

# THINKING IT THROUGH

First read all of the answer choices. Then think carefully about the kind of information the article does and does not contain. The author's purpose will become clear.

**1** What was the author's purpose in writing this selection?

    **A.** to persuade readers that Placido Domingo is a great opera singer

    **B.** to explain who The Three Tenors were

    **C.** to inform readers about the career of Placido Domingo

    **D.** to describe the roles Placido Domingo has sung during his career

Notice the word in capital letters in the question. Then ask yourself which of the answer choices is not supported by information in the selection.

**2** Which of the following is NOT a conclusion you can draw from the selection?

    **A.** Domingo is the greatest opera singer of his generation.

    **B.** Domingo has had a successful career as an opera singer.

    **C.** Domingo, Pavarotti, and Carreras captivated audiences with their singing.

    **D.** Domingo is widely respected in the opera world as a singer and an artist.

Look at the key to discover which color denotes 1968. Then look for that color in the graph.

**3** Which city had the SMALLEST population in 1968?

    **A.** Lima

    **B.** Buenos Aires

    **C.** Santiago

    **D.** Mexico City

The tallest bar on the graph will give you the correct answer.

**4** Which city had the LARGEST population in 2000?

    **A.** Lima

    **B.** Buenos Aires

    **C.** Santiago

    **D.** Mexico City

This question asks you to compare 1968 with 2000. Look for the smallest difference in the two bars for each city to find the correct answer.

**5** Which city had the SMALLEST increase in population between 1968 and 2000?

    **A.** Lima

    **B.** Buenos Aires

    **C.** Santiago

    **D.** Mexico City

**Answers:**
1.C, 2.A, 3.A, 4.D, 5.C

# Functional Reading Test Model

**DIRECTIONS** Study the following nutrition label from a jar of tomatillo salsa. Then answer the questions that follow.

| Nutrition Facts |  |
| --- | --- |
| Serving Size 2 TBSP (30 g) | |
| Servings Per Container 15 | |
| **Amount Per Serving** | |
| Calories 10 | |
| Calories from Fat 0 | |
| | **% Daily Value\*** |
| **Total Fat** 0 g | 0% |
| Saturated Fat 0 g | 0% |
| **Cholesterol** 0 mg | 0% |
| **Sodium** 230 mg | 10% |
| **Total Carbohydrate** 2 g | |
| Dietary Fiber 0 g | 0% |
| Sugars 1 g | |
| **Protein** 0 g | |
| Vitamin A 6% • Vitamin C 8% | |
| Calcium 4% • Iron 0% | |
| \* Percent Daily Values are based on a 2,000 calorie diet. | |

**1** How many calories does this whole bottle of salsa contain?

**A.** 10

**B.** 150

**C.** 15

**D.** 30

**2** If you ate two servings of salsa, how many mg. of sodium would you consume?

**A.** 460

**B.** 10

**C.** 230

**D.** 690

**3** Is salsa a smart food choice for people trying to limit their fat intake?

**A.** No, because it has 230 mg. of sodium per serving.

**B.** Yes, because the serving size is just 2 TBSP.

**C.** No, because it has ten calories per serving.

**D.** Yes, because each serving has 0 g. of fat.

**READING STRATEGIES FOR ASSESSMENT**

**Examine the structure of the label.** Notice the type of information included in each of the four parts of the label.

**Do the math.** Remember that the "% Daily Value" and vitamin and mineral numbers on the label are for just a single serving.

**ANSWER STRATEGIES**

To find the correct answer, multiply the number of calories per serving by the number of servings in the bottle.

Again, multiplication is the key to finding the correct answer.

To answer this question, just look at that part of the label that tells how much fat each serving contains.

**Answers:**
1.B, 2.A, 3.D

# Functional Reading Test Practice

**DIRECTIONS** Study the following travel advertisement for a vacation package to Puerto Rico. Circle the information that you think is the most important. Then answer the multiple-choice questions that follow.

---

### EXPERIENCE THE EXCITEMENT OF PUERTO RICO!

Snorkeling! Windsurfing! Sailing! Golf!
First-Class Entertainment!

4 days/3 nights at the
San Juan Adventure Resort

only **$479** per person
airfare included *

Adventure Resort Package also includes
continental breakfast, two beach passes,
two spa treatments

\* Price based on double occupancy. Airfare from
New York City only. From Chicago add $175. From
Los Angeles add $350. Single travelers add $200.

---

1. Which of the following is NOT included in the $479 price?

   A. beach passes

   B. windsurfing

   C. spa treatments

   D. continental breakfast

2. How much will this vacation package cost a single traveler from Los Angeles?

   A. $479

   B. $654

   C. $679

   D. $1,029

3. For which of the following is this vacation package the LEAST expensive per person?

   A. two sisters from New York

   B. a stockbroker from Los Angeles

   C. a single traveler from New York

   D. a college student from Chicago

## THINKING IT THROUGH

The notes in the side column will help you think through your answers. Check the answer key at the bottom of the page. How well did you do?

> Although the ad mentions windsurfing prominently, it does not indicate that this activity is included in the price.

**1** Which of the following is NOT included in the $479 price?

   **A.** beach passes

   **B.** windsurfing

   **C.** spa treatments

   **D.** continental breakfast

> To answer this question, read the small type at the bottom of the ad and add the extra charges to the advertised price.

**2** How much will this vacation package cost a single traveler from Los Angeles?

   **A.** $479

   **B.** $654

   **C.** $679

   **D.** $1,029

> Read each answer choice carefully. How many people are traveling? Where are they coming from? Then use the information in the ad to determine who will get the best deal.

**3** For which of the following travelers is this vacation package the LEAST expensive per person?

   **A.** two sisters from New York

   **B.** a stockbroker from Los Angeles

   **C.** a single traveler from New York

   **D.** a college student from Chicago

**Answers:**
1. B, 2. D, 3. A

# Revising-and-Editing Test Model

**DIRECTIONS** Read the following paragraph carefully. Then answer the multiple-choice questions that follow. After answering the questions, read the material in the side columns to check your answer strategies.

¹Madrid, the capital of Spain. ²It is home to one of that nations cultural treasures—the Prado museum. ³The building was constructed in the late eighteenth century as a museum of natural science. ⁴Then they decided to change it to an art museum in 1819 and it has more than 9,000 works of art. ⁵The museum is located on a street called the Paseo del Prado. ⁶Their are many famous paintings they're, including works by El Greco, Velázquez, and Goya.

1. Which sentence in the paragraph is actually a fragment, an incomplete thought?

   A. sentence 5
   B. sentence 3
   C. sentence 1
   D. sentence 4

2. In sentence 2, which of the following is the correct possessive form of *nation*?

   A. nation's
   B. nations's
   C. nations'
   D. nations

## READING STRATEGIES FOR ASSESSMENT

**Watch for common errors.** Highlight or underline errors such as incorrect spelling or punctuation; fragments or run-on sentences; and missing or misplaced information.

## ANSWER STRATEGIES

**Incomplete Sentences** A sentence is a group of words with a subject and a verb that expresses a complete thought. If either the subject or the verb is missing, the group of words is an incomplete sentence.

**Possessive Nouns** In sentence 2, the word *nation* is singular. So, it takes the singular possessive form.

**3** What is the best way to rewrite the first part of sentence 4?

    **A.** Then he decided to change it to an art museum

    **B.** Then the government decided to change it to an art museum

    **C.** Then the government decided to change the natural science museum to an art museum

    **D.** Then he decided to change the natural science museum to an art museum

**4** Which sentence in the paragraph is a run-on sentence?

    **A.** sentence 2

    **B.** sentence 5

    **C.** sentence 1

    **D.** sentence 4

**5** What is the best way to rewrite the first part of sentence 6?

    **A.** They're many famous paintings their

    **B.** There are many famous paintings they're

    **C.** There are many famous paintings there

    **D.** Their are many famous paintings there

**6** Sentence 5 is out of place. Where should sentence 5 occur?

    **A.** after sentence 2

    **B.** before sentence 2

    **C.** after sentence 5

    **D.** after sentence 3

**Answers:**
1. C, 2. A, 3. C, 4. D, 5. C, 6. A

# Revising-and-Editing Test Practice

**DIRECTIONS** Read the following paragraph carefully. As you read, circle each error that you find and identify the error in the side column—for example, *misspelled word* or *incorrect punctuation*. When you have finished, circle the letter of the correct choice for each question that follows.

¹On December, 17, 1830, one of the most greatest leaders in South American history died. ²He was born in Venezuela, which was ruled by Spain. ³As a young man, Simón Bolívar tours Europe, and he vows to free Venezuela from Spanish rule. ⁴After a series of setbacks. ⁵Bolívar began winning his fight to oust the Spanish from South America. ⁶By 1824, Spanish rule in South America was over and Bolívar is now known as *El Libertador* and the "George Washington of South America."

**1** Which sentence in the paragraph is a fragment?

  **A.** sentence 4

  **B.** sentence 2

  **C.** sentence 6

  **D.** sentence 7

**2** What is the correct way to write the date in sentence 1?

  **A.** Dec./17/1830

  **B.** December 17 1830

  **C.** December 17, 1830

  **D.** December, 17 1830

**3** In sentence 1, which of the following is the correct form of the superlative adjective?

A. greatest

B. greater

C. more great

D. more greatest

**4** Which of the following errors occurs in sentence 2?

A. unclear pronoun reference

B. incorrect capitalization

C. incorrect punctuation

D. incorrect verb tense

**5** Which of the following is the correct way to rewrite the first part of sentence 3?

A. As a young man, Simón Bolívar tours Europe, and he vowed

B. As a young man, Simón Bolívar toured Europe, and he vows

C. As a young man, Simón Bolívar is touring Europe, and he vows

D. As a young man, Simón Bolívar toured Europe, and he vowed

**6** Which of the following is the best way to punctuate the middle of sentence 6?

A. Spanish rule in South America was over: and Bolívar is now

B. Spanish rule in South America was over. Bolívar is now

C. Spanish rule in South America was over; and Bolívar is now

D. Spanish rule in South America was over—and Bolívar is now

# THINKING IT THROUGH

Use the notes in the side columns to help you understand why some answers are correct and others are not. Check the answer key on the next page. How well did you do?

**1** Which sentence in the paragraph is a fragment?

A. sentence 4

B. sentence 2

C. sentence 6

D. sentence 7

> Remember that a sentence has a subject and a verb and expresses a complete thought. Which sentence is lacking either a subject or a verb?

**2** What is the correct way to write the date in sentence 1?

A. Dec./17/1830

B. December 17 1830

C. December 17, 1830

D. December, 17 1830

> When writing a date, the name of the month should be spelled out, and the day and year should be separated by a comma.

**3** In sentence 1, which of the following is the correct form of the superlative adjective?

A. greatest

B. greater

C. more great

D. more greatest

> A superlative adjective is formed by adding –*est* to the adjective or placing the word *most* before the adjective. Never do both at the same time.

**4** Which of the following errors occurs in sentence 2?

**A.** unclear pronoun reference

**B.** incorrect capitalization

**C.** incorrect punctuation

**D.** incorrect verb tense

**5** Which of the following is the correct way to rewrite the first part of sentence 3?

**A.** As a young man, Simón Bolívar tours Europe, and he vowed

**B.** As a young man, Simón Bolívar toured Europe, and he vows

**C.** As a young man, Simón Bolívar is touring Europe, and he vows

**D.** As a young man, Simón Bolívar toured Europe, and he vowed

**6** Which of the following is the best way to punctuate the middle of sentence 6?

**A.** Spanish rule in South America was over: and Bolívar is now

**B.** Spanish rule in South America was over. Bolívar is now

**C.** Spanish rule in South America was over; and Bolívar is now

**D.** Spanish rule in South America was over—and Bolívar is now

**Answers:** 1.A, 2.C, 3.A, 4.A, 5.D, 6.B

# Writing Test Model

**DIRECTIONS** Many tests ask you to write an essay in response to a writing prompt. A writing prompt is a brief statement that describes a writing situation. Some writing prompts ask you to explain *what, why,* or *how.* Others ask you to convince someone of something.

As you analyze the following writing prompts, read and respond to the notes in the side columns. Then look at the response to each prompt. The notes in the side columns will help you understand why each response is considered strong.

## Prompt A

Some child-rearing experts believe that young people should be kept busy after school and on the weekends with a variety of structured activities, such as music lessons, sports, dance classes, and so on. Others say that young people today have been "overscheduled" and need more time to themselves—to read, think about the future, and even just to daydream.

Think about your experiences and the way your non-school time is structured. Do you think lots of structure, more personal time, or a combination of the two is most beneficial to young people? Remember to provide solid reasons and examples for the position you take.

## Strong Response

Today was a typical day for my little brother Jeff. He got up at five o'clock to go to the local ice rink for hockey practice. Then he was off to school. At the end of the school day, Jeff

**ANALYZING THE PROMPT**

**Identify the focus.** What issue will you be writing about? Circle the focus of your essay in the first sentence of the prompt.

**Understand what's expected of you.** First, circle what the prompt asks you to do. Then identify your audience. What kinds of details will appeal to this audience?

**ANSWER STRATEGIES**

**Capture the reader's interest.** The writer begins by describing a typical busy day in his younger brother's life.

had a piano lesson followed by a meeting of his Cub Scout troop. After a quick dinner, he did homework for two hours. He finally got to bed at ten o'clock. That's a lot to pack into a single day, especially since Jeff is just seven years old! I think that in addition to sports, music, and other activities, kids like Jeff need some time to themselves.

Many parents, mine included, think a busy kid is a safe kid. They believe that the less time a kid has on his hands, the less likely he'll wind up doing something he shouldn't be doing or being with people he shouldn't be with. That's probably true for many kids. After all, it's hard to get into trouble when you spend every day being carpooled from one activity to another.

But some busy kids do get into trouble anyway. Jeff's friend Mark got caught trying to shoplift a CD last weekend, and he's involved in just as many activities as Jeff is. So having a busy schedule is no guarantee that a kid won't get into trouble.

Plus, I think kids benefit from having free time to go to the movies, play video games, read, or even just be by themselves. Growing up isn't always easy, and kids need some time alone to figure things out, think about what's important to them, and decide what they really want to do.

Last Saturday afternoon, Jeff's soccer practice was canceled because of thunderstorms. We went to see a movie and later spent some time talking and listening to music in my room. It was the first time in months that we had time just to hang out together, and we really enjoyed it. Jeff said it was like having a day off. I think more kids like Jeff could use a day off too.

---

**State the position clearly.** The last sentence of the first paragraph makes the writer's position clear to the reader. Now the writer can spend the rest of the essay developing his argument.

**Address opposing views.** The writer brings up an opposing view—that busy kids are less likely to get into trouble—and admits that it might sometimes be true.

**Use good examples to support the position.** Here, the writer uses an example to make the point that not all busy kids stay out of trouble.

**Use logical reasoning to further develop the position.** The writer offers logical reasons why free time is important.

**Restate the position in the conclusion.** Using another concrete example, the writer restates his position that kids need some time to themselves.

## Prompt B

Depending on where you live, each season of the year can be very different than it is in other parts of the country. Which season do you enjoy the most—summer, autumn, winter, or spring? What is that season like in your part of the country? What makes it special to you?

## Strong Response

Here in the upper Midwest, the seasons seem as different from one another as night and day. Summer usually arrives suddenly. The temperatures soar, the humidity rises, and fierce thunderstorms add drama and sometimes destruction to the season. Autumn brings a crisp, cool, and colorful change as the leaves turn golden and the air turns chilly. Winter can be bitterly cold, and heavy snows often make the simple trip to school a real ordeal.

Then comes spring. Spring is a truly magical time of the year. I can sense spring long before it actually arrives. There's a certain scent in the air, and something is different about the way the sunlight looks. Soon the winter snows are reduced to muddy puddles. The tree branches swell with buds, and the first green shoots of crocus and tulip leaves struggle up out of the ground. Most magical of all, the early morning hours just after dawn are filled with the cries of migrating birds heading back north.

Because my family lives in a small community surrounded by farmland, I get to experience a different kind of spring than many people do. The fields behind our house fill up with wildflowers that season the air with perfume and color. A trip to Jefferson's Pond offers a chance to watch ducks and geese resting on their long

**Look for the main idea.** The first few sentences of the prompt present the subject you will write about. Try restating the subject in your own words.

**Understand what's expected of you.** What does the prompt ask you to do? Explain something? Persuade someone? State your personal feelings?

## ANSWER STRATEGIES

**Create an intriguing introduction.** The writer arouses the reader's curiosity by leaving out one of the four seasons.

**Include specific details.** The writer uses specific details about each season to make the description vivid.

**Include the kind of information the prompt asks for.** Notice how the writer follows the directions in the prompt by explaining what spring is like in her part of the country.

**Use sensory details.** Details that appeal to the reader's sense of sight, sound, and smell bring the description to life.

seasonal journeys. The apple and cherry trees at the McKlintock family orchards explode with blossoms until they look like giant balls of cotton candy.

Mostly, however, I love spring because it is a season of hope. The earth is coming back to life, filled with possibilities. I feel like I am, too.

Make comparisons. Comparing the blossoming trees to balls of cotton candy helps the reader experience the scene as the writer does.

Write a powerful conclusion. The writer ends the essay by comparing herself to her favorite season.

# Writing Test Practice

**DIRECTIONS** Read the following writing prompt. Using the strategies you've learned in this section, analyze the prompt, plan your response, and then write an essay explaining your position.

**Prompt C**

You have volunteered to participate in your community's semiannual blood drive. Your task is to write a letter to your community newspaper encouraging everyone in town to consider giving blood.

Think about all the ways your community benefits from having an adequate blood supply. Write a letter that explains what these benefits are. Include specific examples. End your letter by appealing to your fellow citizens' sense of civic pride and duty.

# Scoring Rubrics

**DIRECTIONS** Use the following checklist to see whether you have written a strong persuasive essay. You will have succeeded if you can check nearly all of the items.

### The Prompt

☐ My response meets all the requirements stated in the prompt.

☐ I have stated my position clearly and supported it with details.

☐ I have addressed the audience appropriately.

☐ My essay fits the type of writing suggested in the prompt (letter to the editor, article for the school paper, and so on).

### Reasons

☐ The reasons I offer really support my position.

☐ My audience will find the reasons convincing.

☐ I have stated my reasons clearly.

☐ I have given at least three reasons.

☐ I have supported my reasons with sufficient facts, examples, quotations, and other details.

☐ I have presented and responded to opposing arguments.

☐ My reasoning is sound. I have avoided faulty logic.

### Order and Arrangement

☐ I have included a strong introduction.

☐ I have included a strong conclusion.

☐ The reasons are arranged in a logical order.

### Word Choice

☐ The language of my essay is appropriate for my audience.

☐ I have used precise, vivid words and persuasive language.

### Fluency

☐ I have used sentences of varying lengths and structures.

☐ I have connected ideas with transitions and other devices.

☐ I have used correct spelling, punctuation, and grammar.

# Apuntes

# Apuntes

# Apuntes

# Apuntes

# Credits

## Illustration

**15–16** Nneke Bennett; **20–21** Ruben de Anda; **36–37, 41–42** Rick Powell; **56–57, 61–62** Enrique O. Sánchez; **77–78** Rubén de Anda; **82–83** Fabricio Vanden Broeck; **97–98** Fian Arroyo; **102–103** Rubén de Anda; **119–120** Eduardo Espada; **124–125** Susan M. Blumbaugh

## Photography

**T1, i, 3, 4, 5** Martha Granger/EDGE Productions; **9** Beryl Goldberg; **10** *top* Patricia A. Eynon, *bottom* Odyssey Productions; **11** Beryl Goldberg; **25** Martha Granger/EDGE Productions; **26** School Division/Houghton Mifflin Company; **31** John Boykin/PhotoEdit; **32** *top left* Martha Granger/EDGE Productions, *top center* Susan Kaye, *top right* J.P. Courau/DDB Stock Photo, *bottom left* Doug Bryant/DDB Stock Photo, *bottom center, bottom right* Martha Granger/EDGE Productions; **42** Robert Frerck/Woodfin Camp; **46** *top* Bob Daemmrich/Stock Boston, *inset* Robert Frerck/Odyssey; **47** *left* Bob Daemmrich, *bottom* Martha Granger/EDGE Productions; **51** *top* Raymond A. Mendez/Animals Animals, *bottom* Jaime Santiago/DDB Stock Photo; **52** *top* Thomas R. Fletcher/Stock Boston, *bottom* School Division/Houghton Mifflin Company; **66** Dave G. Houser; **67** *top* Martha Granger/EDGE Productions, *bottom* Patricia A. Eynon; **68** *top* Martha Granger/EDGE Productions, *center, bottom* Rogers/Monkmeyer Press; **72, 73, 87** Martha Granger/EDGE Productions; **88** *left* "Retrato de Jaime Sabartés" ("Portrait of Jaime Sabartés" ) (1899-1900), Pablo Picasso. Charcoal and watercolour on paper, 50.5 cm x 33 cm. Giraudon/Art Resource, New York. © 2003 Artists Rights Society, New York / Picasso Museum, Sabartés Collection, Barcelona, Spain, *right* "Maya con una muñeca" ("Maya with Doll") (1938), Pablo Picasso. Oil on canvas, 73 cm x 60 cm. Giraudon/Superstock. © 2003 Artists Rights Society, New York / Picasso Museum, Paris; **92, 107, 108, 109** Martha Granger/EDGE Productions; **113** Jeff Greenberg/PhotoEdit; **114** *top* School Division/Houghton Mifflin Company, *bottom* Eric A. Wessman/Viest Associates, Inc.; **115** Wolfgang Kaehler; **131** "Cumpleaños de Lala y Tudi" ("Lala and Tudi's Birthday Party") (1989), Carmen Lomas Garza. Oil on canvas, 36" x 48". Collection of Paula Maciel Benecke & Norbert Benecke, Aptos, California. Photograph by Wolgang Dietze. © 1989 Carmen Lomas Garza; **169** Lee Foster/Bruce Coleman, Inc.; **179** Timothy Fadek/Corbis; **181** *quinceañera* Martha Granger/EDGE Productions; *Sweet 16 party* Ryan McVay; **183** Dennis MacDonald/PhotoEdit; **185** © 1978 George Ballis/Take Stock; **189** Jacques Jangoux/Getty Images